DATE DUE

DEC 2 1 1989		
SEP 6 1984		
SEP 2 6 1995		
WITHDRAWN		

DEMCO 38-297

THE ORIGINS OF
CIVILIZATION

THE ORIGINS OF CIVILIZATION

WOLFSON COLLEGE LECTURES
1978

EDITED BY
P. R. S. MOOREY

CLARENDON PRESS · OXFORD
1979

Oxford University Press, Walton Street, Oxford OX2 6DP

OXFORD LONDON GLASGOW
NEW YORK TORONTO MELBOURNE WELLINGTON
KUALA LUMPUR SINGAPORE JAKARTA HONG KONG TOKYO
DELHI BOMBAY CALCUTTA MADRAS KARACHI
NAIROBI DAR ES SALAAM CAPE TOWN

Published in the United States by
Oxford University Press, New York

British Library Cataloguing in Publication Data

The origins of civilization.—(Wolfson College.
Lectures; 1978).
 1. Civilization—History
 I. Moorey, Peter Roger Stuart II. Series
 909   CB68   ~~79-40671~~
 ISBN 0–19–813198–4 *80- 479919*

Set, printed and bound in Great Britain by
Fakenham Press Limited, Fakenham, Norfolk

PREFACE

THE ANNUAL Wolfson Lectures have established themselves since 1970 as one of the major events of the academic year in Oxford. Speakers are asked to give a general survey of their topic, which is suggested to them, with particular reference to new discoveries or fresh lines of research. They are requested to address themselves to an audience which, though predominantly academic, is composed largely of people who are not specialists in the lecturer's own field of study. The college chose 'The Origins of Civilization' as the subject for 1978, and asked me to organize an appropriate series of lectures.

Paper plans were inevitably modified to adjust to the interests of available speakers, but only very slightly. We were most fortunate to secure at relatively short notice a very distinguished group of contributors. All of them graciously accepted the topics assigned to them even if, as was sometimes the case, it involved stepping outside their current research interests. I am most grateful to them all. I alone am to be held responsible for the choice of topics. A course of lectures on this enormous subject might be constructed in innumerable different ways. My basic plan was simple. Two introductory lectures were intended to sketch in the emergence of man and his development as hunter, farmer, and fisherman. As the first of these lectures, by Professor Michael Day, has been printed elsewhere it is not included here. Then, taking civilization in its most precise sense, there were to be reviews of the evolution of urban societies in four key areas: the Near East, Europe, China, and Mesoamerica. Two general lectures would bring the course to a close, one on the exceedingly complex, but often currently disregarded role of religion in early human societies; the other on the development of writing in the Old World.

One theme was deliberately avoided in planning the course. No speaker was asked to lecture specifically on current hypotheses about the causes of civilization, integrating in general terms selected archaeological data and sociological theories. It was hoped that listeners might assess for themselves as the course proceeded, what it was that 'civilized' some societies and not others, and why the process has varied so markedly. Was it a matter of man's response to particular environments, of irrigation, of levels of technology, of population pressures, of evolving social structures, of property concepts, of ideology or trade? Or was it a subtle interaction of a varied selection of such factors operating under different pressures in different regions? We now place the readers in the same position as the listeners.

I am most grateful to Mrs Gillian Moore and Mrs Beryl Schweder at Wolfson for valuable clerical support in organizing and preparing the lectures for publication, to Mr Paul Boddington and his assistants for help with their smooth running, and to Mr Robert Lush and his staff for managing the hospitality which followed.

P. R. S. MOOREY

CONTENTS

LIST OF PLATES

(at end)

ACKNOWLEDGEMENTS

We are most grateful to the following people and institutions for permission to reproduce certain figures in Mr Hawkin's lecture:

Professor E. L. Bennett (fig. 48, part); Dr J. Chadwick and the Cambridge University Press (figs. 49–50); Professor A. Morpurgo Davies (fig. 48, part); Professor I. J. Gelb (figs. 42, 43 and 47); the Management Committee of the Griffith Institute, Oxford (fig. 46); Professor C. F. A. Schaeffer (fig. 51a, b); and Professor D. Schmandt-Besserat and Undena Publications (fig. 44).

LIST OF FIGURES

I

PRIMITIVE MAN AS HUNTER, FISHER, FORAGER, AND FARMER

GRAHAME CLARK

SINCE MUCH of the primary data surviving from prehistory relates directly or indirectly to the quest for food, and since in any case the only communities to leave archaeological traces were those successful in securing food, it would be perverse to overlook or indeed to fail to concentrate very considerable attention on the early history of subsistence. But let there be no misunderstanding, this is emphatically not to argue for a reductionist view. The mere fact that man like other animals has to eat in order to survive does not mean that he need or should be judged primarily as an organism. Man is of supreme interest not so much because he is an animal that has to eat or even, I would submit (for I am no gastro-archaeologist), as one whose highest purpose is to eat, as for the aspirations he is able, having eaten, to entertain. The real reason why early subsistence is of interest is that the manner in which men secure their food to some extent conditions (and is, of course, conditioned by) the kind of cultural environment in which such aspirations can be entertained and realized.

You will hardly need to be reminded of the constraints traditionally held to have applied to societies that depend exclusively on hunting, fishing, and foraging, still less perhaps of the liberating effect widely supposed to have issued from the adoption of farming. All the same, it hardly seems appropriate to treat as a mere backdrop the period during which men survived entirely by what they were able to appropriate from wild species of animals and plants, considering that this encompasses all but a small part of human history anywhere and until modern times the entire history of quite extensive areas of the world. It is surely essential if we are correctly to assess our existing situation to appreciate and fully digest the fact that by and large the experience of mankind has been that of an omnivorous predator. Less than ten generations have experienced the heavy constraints of industrial society, and then only in confined territories, and hardly more than a few hundred the less burdensome, though still considerable, ones of farming. If the object of history is to widen perspectives and in this way to deepen understanding, it is strange to find this subject increasingly equated in the schools with the history of industrial society and hardly less so, if a visitor may be pardoned the comment, to find the Oxford Chair of European Archaeology restricted to so narrow a slice of time as that since men first engaged in farming.

Our knowledge of the economy practised by the earliest men (*Homo erectus*) has been won to a substantial extent from the exploration of Lower Pleistocene deposits in East Africa carried out by the late Louis Leakey, his wife Mary, and their associates. The key information comes from occupation levels in beds I and II in Olduvai Gorge, northern Tanzania, dating from between *c*. 2·0 and 0·7 million years ago.[1] The animal bones from bed I show that meat was already providing a significant component of diet. Although, as we know from recent observation of chimpanzees and baboons in the wild, these animals were not by any means averse to meat, it remains a fact that this was invariably obtained from animals smaller than themselves and remained an extra rather than a basic component of diet. The regular eating of meat, including that of prey as large or larger than the hominids themselves, is widely recognized to define 'a highly significant adaptive shift' in diet.

The notion that Lower Pleistocene man confined his predation to small species and concentrated on young individuals can no longer be sustained. Although remains of medium-sized antelopes predominated in the food refuse investigated from the East African sites, it appears certain that much larger species were also represented.[2] This is shown by the bones scattered in general refuse and most strikingly at kill sites featuring the partly broken-up carcasses of individual animals. These included such large forms as hippopotamus from the KSB tuff at East Rudolph and the elephant and dinothere from Olduvai locus FLK N. The frequent presence of stone artefacts both on kill sites and among refuse scatter emphasizes the adaptive advantages these things conferred on man as distinct from other primates. This was so despite the extreme simplicity of the earliest stone industries. The artefacts fell into two main categories, sharp flakes and the crude core-tools

[1] L. S. B. and M. D. Leakey, *Olduvai Gorge, 1951–1961. Excavations in Beds I and II* (Cambridge, 1971); G. Isaac and E. R. McCown (eds), *Human Origins: Louis Leakey and the East African Evidence* (Benjamin, California, 1976).

[2] G. Isaac and E. R. McCown (eds), op. cit. 497 ff.

and discoids from which these had been struck. Even with such equipment it would have been possible to shape wooden weapons including spears and at the same time to cut and dismember slaughtered animals whether for meat or as sources of raw materials. When fire first came into use as an aid in making artefacts, for rendering dwellings more habitable, in hunting and in cooking, remains an open question. Although present in the earliest deposits to be examined in any volume both in western Europe and north China,[3] it is absent from Middle Pleistocene as well as Lower Pleistocene deposits in the African continent. On the other hand, Desmond Clark may well be correct in attributing this to the greater speed at which charcoal is broken down in tropical soils.[4]

The hunting of large mammals depended on social as well as technological factors. It involved among other things an organized system of co-operation among hunters who, to judge from ethnographic observation, would have been exclusively men. The reason for this is not far to seek. Hunting involved movements that might be extensive and of long duration. In this respect the role of women was complementary, that of staying close to the home base, nourishing, tending, and bringing up the young during the increasingly long period of dependence during which they had to acquire learned behaviour of ever-increasing intricacy and scope. Guarding the home base and looking after the family by no means excluded women from the food quest. As we know from observation of people like the recent Australian aborigines (Pl. 1)[5] or the Bushmen of South Africa,[6] domestic duties could readily be combined with foraging for plant food and small animal products, activities, it may be added, through which young children could most readily be initiated into the food quest by their mothers. The partnership of the sexes was from the beginning quite as much economic as sexual and in each regard focused on the home base. It is a matter of some moment that what may have been the stone footings of the kind of artificial shelter that might have served as the focus of a primary biological family were observed at the very base of the Olduvai sequence[7] along with bone refuse and stone artefacts. The earliest human economies are likely to have been based on a subdivision of functions

[3] K. P. Oakley, *Frameworks for Dating Fossil Man* (3rd. edn, London, 1969), 237, 239.

[4] J. D. Clark in Isaac and McCown, op. cit. 43.

[5] D. F. Thomson, 'The Seasonal Factor in Human Culture illustrated from the life of a contemporary nomadic group', *Proc. Prehist. Soc.* V (1939), 209–21; M. J. Meggitt, *The Desert People* (Sydney, 1962).

[6] R. B. Lee, 'Kung Bushman Subsistence: an input–output analysis', *Environment and Cultural Behaviour*, ed. A. P. Vayda (New York, 1969).

[7] Mary D. Leakey in Isaac and McCown, op. cit. 437 f.

between the men who concerned themselves with hunting, and had to be prepared to operate at a distance from the home base, and the women who watched over the young, cooked, maintained the home base and engaged in foraging in the near neighbourhood. Hunting large animals with primitive equipment must for its part have involved active co-operation between the males. The basis of this rested if we may judge from ethnographic parallels on institutionalized sharing of the meat (Pl. 2), a social bond that held together complete bands, just as the division between hunting and foraging cemented individual family units. The system by which the earliest communities lived was thus based throughout on co-operation and sharing rather than struggle. Once established it was self-regulating and, until replaced by competitively more effective ones, long enduring. This may well help to explain why it was that the earliest cultural patterns were so slow to change.

The archaeological evidence recovered from the Middle Pleistocene (c.0·7 to 0·1 million years ago) continues to reflect a way of life resembling that of the phase just reviewed. The importance of hunting as a component of the food quest and the prowess of those who pursued it are particularly manifest in the material preserved in the limestone fissure of Choukoutien near Peking.[8] The fact that men equipped with stone tools no more elaborate than those from the lower beds at Olduvai were able to master animals as large as the elephant and the rhinoceros and as fierce as the sabre-toothed tiger and other carnivores, as well as herbivores of widely varying habit, testified to their adaptability and the effectiveness of their social co-operation. Large animals like the elephants at Torralba, Spain,[9] continued to be butchered where they finally succumbed, and their meat distributed among those sharing the same hunting territory. On the other hand, to judge from the proportions in which different parts of their skeletons were represented on human settlements, it appears that smaller animals were as a rule dismembered and carried to the home base in convenient joints. Analysis of stones from settlement sites suggests that most were obtained within a radius of 5 km, with occasional exceptions extending to 65 km, which argues that home base territories were comparatively restricted. The fine stratigraphy at Kalambo Falls, Zambia,[10] extending in time well into the earlier part of the Upper Pleistocene in

[8] D. Black, P. Teilhard de Chardin, C. C. Young and W. C. Pei, 'The Choukoutien Cave Deposits ...', *Mem. Geol. Surv. China*, Ser. A, no. II (Peking, 1933).

[9] F. C. Howell, 'Observations on the earlier phases of the European Lower Palaeolithic', *American Anthrop.* 68 (1966), 88–201.

[10] J. D. Clark, *Kalambo Falls Prehistoric Site*, I, II (Cambridge, 1969, 1974).

Sub-Saharan Africa, suggests that the site was frequently revisited. This in turn argues that dense accumulations of artefacts are at least as likely to indicate frequent returns to the same location as its use by large numbers of people at once.

The use of fire is now for the first time positively documented at sites as widely distributed as Hoxne and Torralba in England and Spain and Choukoutien in north China, all in the northern part of the zone occupied by man during the Middle Pleistocene. Indeed the evidence of fossil pollen pointing to forest clearance and the expansion of open vegetation when the site at Hoxne[11] was occupied by Acheulian man argues that fire may well have been as useful to the Middle Pleistocene hunters of England as it was to the recent aborigines of Australia. A noteworthy innovation at this time in respect of flint and stone technology was the emergence of cleavers and bifacial hand-axes. On the other hand, it needs to be stressed that these forms were confined to Africa and proximate parts of Asia and Europe, and supplemented rather than replaced earlier forms. Butchery probably continued to be carried out by the flake component, but the precise roles of bifaces and cleavers remain enigmatic. It was nevertheless the latter which provided the dynamic element. Broadly speaking the direction of evolution was towards the production of forms with more regular working edges while reducing the quantity of raw flint or stone used. On the other hand the new Acheulian forms displayed a uniformity over immense territories so great that the origins of individual specimens could often only be guessed at by identifying the material from which they were flaked.

It was only with the emergence of different variants of the large-brained *Homo sapiens* during the Upper Pleistocene that the first noteworthy advances in conceptual life, technology, and economy can be detected in the archaeological record. Indeed these first became really marked with the appearance not much more than 35,000 years ago of men of modern type (*Homo sapiens sapiens*). Even so, certain notable advances may be attributed to the archaic form represented in Europe from Iberia to south Russia, in north Africa and from south-west to central Asia by Neanderthal man (*Homo sapiens neanderthalensis*). The most notable development in the conceptual field was unquestionably the practice of careful burial with the implication this carries of a personal awareness of death. The contrast with the situation at Choukoutien is particularly marked. There not one of the forty or so individuals of the

[11] R. G. West and C. B. M. McBurney, 'The Quaternary Deposits at Hoxne, Suffolk and their Archaeology', *Proc. Prehist. Soc.* XX (1954), 131–54; see p. 135.

species *Homo erectus pekinensis* was accorded burial. On the contrary the bones showed clear signs of the practice of cannibalism: the long bones were split as if for the extraction of marrow and the foramen magnum, the aperture at the base of the skull, was in some cases enlarged to allow the removal of the brain. In certain instances, as witnessed by discoveries in the cave of Krapina in Croatia or again at Monte Circeo in Italy, Neanderthal man continued to practise cannibalism.[12] On the other hand, he generally buried his dead as we are forcibly reminded by the cemetery of ten graves in front of the Mugharet-es-Skhūl, Mount Carmel.[13] Often the lower limbs were drawn up, sometimes so closely as to suggest that the corpse was bound tightly before it stiffened. One of the Mount Carmel burials, that of a man of forty-five, clasped the two lower mandibles of a large boar, and a child burial from Teshik-Tash, Uzbekistan[14] (Pl. 3), was ringed by goat skulls held in position by ramming their horns into the sub-soil.

One of the most noteworthy achievements of Neanderthal man was to break out of the frost-free zone to which previous hominid populations had been confined[15] and initiate the process by which during the later Upper Pleistocene and recent ages man extended his domain over the rest of the world (Fig. 1). The northward expansion into the territories of the USSR was all the more striking in that it seems mostly to have occurred during the earlier part of the Würm glaciation. Although the main weight of settlement was concentrated between the Don and the Bug in south Russia, smaller numbers of settlers equipped with Mousterian artefacts are now known to have advanced along the corridor between the eastern margin of the Scandinavian ice-sheet, which then extended over much of the north part of European Russia, and the northern Urals reaching as far as Krutaya Gora well beyond latitude 65° N.[16] In keeping with this we now have evidence, notably from Molodova in the Dnestr Valley,[17] for more elaborate dwellings, which takes the form of oval settings of animal bones and teeth. These enclosed fireplaces and cultural debris and are generally considered to have served to weight the

[12] F. M. Bergounioux in G. H. R. von Koenigswald (ed.), *Hundert Jahre Neanderthaler* (Cologne, 1958), 152 f.

[13] D. A. E. Garrod and D. M. Bate, *The Stone Age of Mount Carmel*, I (Oxford, 1937), 97–107.

[14] H. L. Movius, 'The Mousterian Cave of Teshik-Tash, South-eastern Uzbekistan, Central Asia', *Am. School of Prehistoric Research Bull.* XVII (1953), 11–71.

[15] G. Clark and A. Piggott, *Prehistoric Societies* (New York, 1965), 59 f.

[16] C. B. M. McBurney, *Early Man in the Soviet Union. The Implications of Some Recent Discoveries*, Reckitt Archaeological Lecture, British Academy, 1976.

[17] O. P. Chernish, *The Palaeolithic Site Molodova V* (Kiev, 1961).

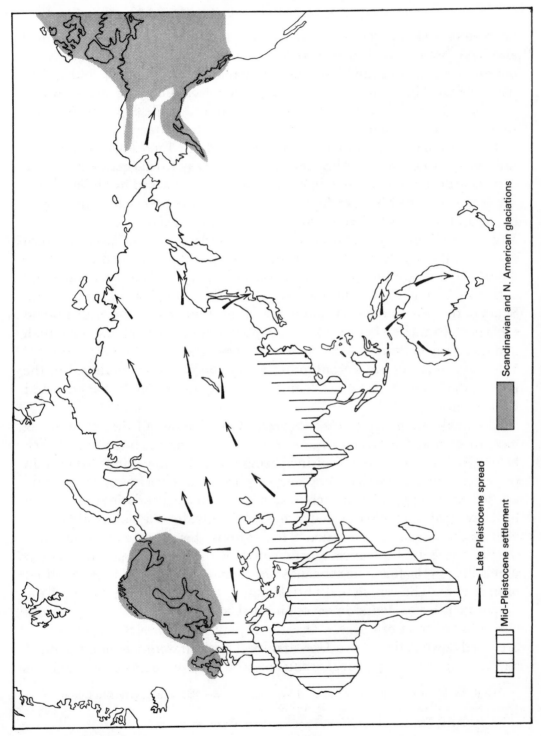

Fig. 1. Late Pleistocene expansion of human settlement.

→ Late Pleistocene spread

→ Mid-Pleistocene settlement

Scandinavian and N. American glaciations

perimeters of skin coverings stretched over timber supports. Clothing must also have been needed in such relatively cold conditions at least for wear out-of-doors, and this can hardly have been made of anything else at that time than animal skins. The preparation of these for clothing and shelter would have been a heavy task and it is suggestive that well-made flint scraping tools were a leading component of most Mousterian industries.

There are many signs that artefacts were adapted more sensitively than previously to local needs. Although it would be easy to exaggerate the trend, there is little doubt that the Upper Pleistocene was marked by an increasing acceleration in the rate of technological change and conversely in the degree of cultural diversity.[18] Every advance in our knowledge of the Levalloiso-Mousterian industries associated with Neanderthal man from western Europe and north Africa to south-west Asia and the inhabited zone of the USSR helps to define more accurately their diversity, both as regards size and still more as regards the techniques and forms of implement represented. South of the Sahara the stone industries of this time reflect above all a broad ecological distinction between those adapted to the grasslands and savannah and those encountered when colonization began to extend into the forest.[19] Whereas industries in the continuing Acheulian tradition continued in the former, the latter elicited quite distinctive configurations in the Sangoan and Lupemban.

The final emergence of *Homo sapiens sapiens*, having all the attributes of modern man and to which without exception all the existing races of men belong, ushered in a period of increasingly rapid change and diversity in respect of culture. Archaeology suggests that the decisive threshold was crossed around 35,000 years ago in terms of radiocarbon dating. Since men have diverged from other primates most strikingly, from a biological point of view, in the size and organization of their brains, it is appropriate to emphasize the conceptual advances documented in the artefacts surviving from prehistory. In the first place one may note a marked elaboration in the ritual of interment. The ceremonial burials dating from the closing stages of the Upper Pleistocene, found in caves and rock shelters as well as at open sites over a broad tract of Eurasia, already displayed many of the features that prevailed down to the onset of Christianity. The dead were commonly clothed and accompanied by personal ornaments and accoutrements. The provision

[18] C. B. M. McBurney, 'The Geographical Study of the older Palaeolithic stages in Europe', *Proc. Prehist. Soc.* XVI (1950), 163–83; esp. pp. 173 ff.
[19] J. D. Clark, *The Prehistory of Africa* (London, 1970), Chap. IV.

of ornaments was in itself a notable innovation. Despite the number of Neanderthal burials excavated, many of them under scientific conditions, not one has yielded so much as a single bead. By contrast the Upper Palaeolithic burials investigated in Europe were normally enriched by ornaments. Sometimes these were extremely numerous. The burials at Sungir (Pl. 4) in central Russia,[20] for example, were smothered under some 8,000 perforated ivory beads, some of which were found to delineate outlines of the garments, presumably of skin, in which they had been laid to rest. Taken together also the ornaments placed with the dead at this time reveal a rich diversity in respect of materials, forms, and workmanship.

An even richer insight into the aesthetic awareness of the early representatives of modern man is provided by the works of art displayed on the walls and ceilings of caves and rock shelters and incorporated in archaeological deposits over a territory extending from Spain to the Urals.[21] Whatever motives inspired the Quaternary artists and whatever may have been their role in social life, it is evident that some of the earliest representatives of modern man created works of art capable of holding their own against the products of later ages and more sophisticated cultures. In addition to the exact observation, manual dexterity, and aesthetic sensibility which they exhibit, detailed study under magnification indicates that some of the engravings incorporate evidence of a system of notation that may well have served some of the functions performed by writing and mathematical symbols in more complex societies.

Several of the trends already established by Neanderthal man and his relatives were carried further by their immediate successors. Modern man still sought the shelter of caves and rock shelters. Similarly in territories like the Ukraine or the loess areas of central Europe (Pl. 5), where natural shelters were absent or scarce, he continued to construct dwellings sufficiently robust to make warm home bases. Whether due to an accident of survival or to a genuine advance it is too early to say, but the more numerous structures dating from the closing phases of the Upper Pleistocene in Europe include examples more elaborate than anything surviving from earlier periods. Good instances are provided by the dome-shaped houses from Mezhirich near Kiev,[22] the walls of which were built of interlocking mammoth jaws supporting skulls and the roofs of which were presumably formed of animal skins weighed down by mammoth tusks. From this time also eyed needles and

---

[20] O. N. Bader, *Quartär* bd. 18,191 and 21,103; C. B. M. McBurney, op. cit. (1976), Pls VI–VIII.
[21] A. Leroi-Gourhan, *Préhistoire de l'art occidental* (Paris, 1965).
[22] I. G. Pidoplichko, *Late Palaeolithic Dwellings of Mammoth Bones in the Ukraine* (Kiev, 1969).

representations like the mammoth ivory figurine of a fur-clad man from Buret, Siberia,[23] provide reliable evidence for the first time of skin clothing.

Expansion of the geographical territories settled by man which had already been begun by Neanderthal man was notably advanced. New lands were colonized in northern Europe as the Scandinavian ice-sheet contracted,[24] but expansions of much greater significance were carried forward from the Far East and south-east Asia. The Japanese islands were certainly occupied at this time, if not before.[25] There is evidence that the Yukon on the Asian side of the North American glaciated zone was already occupied by around 30,000 years ago.[26] When this barrier was breached towards the close of the Ice Age by the parting of the Laurentide and Cordilleran ice-sheets, the Paleo-indians spread south to inherit game reserves of immense wealth. Within a remarkably short time they had reached the Atlantic and had moved southwards, through Middle America, to the southern tip of South America. Another territory hardly less vast in extent was colonized from south-east Asia. The relatively low sea-level prevailing during the last glaciation meant on the one hand that Borneo and most of Indonesia were joined to south-east Asia and on the other that New Guinea and Tasmania formed part of the continent of greater Australia. This meant that at this time the continent could be approached mainly over dry land leaving only a few sea breaks, none of them very formidable, to be crossed by boat or float. Precisely when the first entry was made has yet to be decided, but though this certainly occurred more than 20,000 years ago it is suggestive that all the human remains so far identified in Australia are of *Homo sapiens sapiens* character.

A basic role in the quest for food continued to be played by hunting. Indeed in more than one respect this activity seems to have been carried on in a more sophisticated and specialized manner. Attention seems frequently to have been focused on particular species of animal as with mammoth in south Russia and parts of central Europe. A highly gregarious species like the reindeer seems to have invited a particularly close relationship in western and northern Europe during the late-glacial period,[27] involving a certain degree of seasonal movement on the part of its human predators. Many new types of weapon were introduced, including spears, darts, and harpoons with detach-

[23] A. P. Okladnikov, *Yakutia* (Montreal, 1970), 30 f.

[24] G. Clark, *The Earlier Stone Age Settlement of Scandinavia* (Cambridge, 1975), Chap. I.

[25] G. Clark, *World Prehistory in New Perspective* (3rd edn, Cambridge, 1977), 321 ff.

[26] C. R. Harington, R. Bonnichsen, and R. E. Morlan, 'Bones say man lived in Yukon 27,000 years ago', *Canadian Geogr. J.* 91 (1975), 428.

[27] G. Clark, op. cit. (1975), Chap. I.

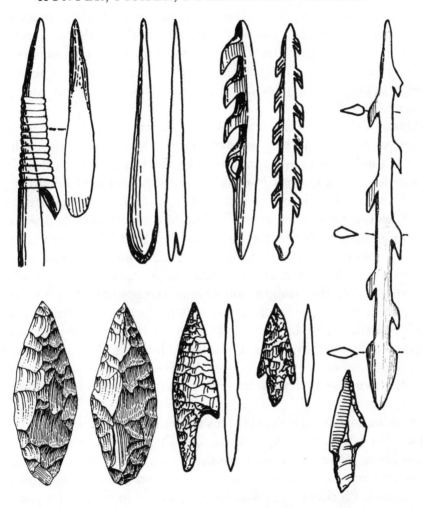

FIG. 2. Some of the many varieties of projectile head of flint, antler, and bone made by Upper Palaeolithic man in western Europe.

able head, as well as in some contexts bows and arrows. The manufacture of hunting equipment as well as of the implements used in preparing skins and making clothes and ornaments was associated with the use of a wider range of materials and a more sophisticated technology, including in particular the fabrication of many composite artefacts. The flint worker for instance had to produce a wide range of specialized tools for gutting, grooving, piercing, sawing and scraping, as well as the armatures, points, barbs and cutting edges, of a variety of weapons (Fig. 2). A far more varied and sophisticated use was made of antler, bone, and ivory, materials that for most purposes could only be used in the form of blanks detached by ringing or grooving by means of burins and other flint tools.[28] The wider range of materials employed and the greater degree of specialization in respect both of function and technique of production made far more rapid change and a greater diversity both in space and time.

Analysis of the materials used for ornaments, tools, and weapons shows that these were sometimes obtained from a considerable distance. The amber and shells used for personal adornment by the inhabitants of the Mezhirich dwellings for example must have come from distances of between 350 and 500 km.[29] Again, the chocolate-coloured flint mined from a district c.80 km south of Warsaw was used over a radius of some 180 km by the makers of Swiderian industries during the Late-glacial period,[30] just as the Zarzians of the Zagros mountains flaked obsidian derived from the region of Lake Van in eastern Anatolia.[31] Whatever the mechanism, whether seasonal movement, exogamy, or the straight exchange of exotic substances, or some combination of these, it is plain that desirable materials were being distributed over wide territories by late Upper Pleistocene hunters. Like the Australian aborigines of recent times the Pleistocene hunters thus benefited from a redistributive process that wrought the same kind of purpose as trade was to do among settled societies with a relatively advanced subdivision of labour.

Despite his success in expanding his settlement, diversifying and elaborating more effective material equipment, and ultimately developing and exploring new areas of self-awareness, modern man was held back in his social development for at least twenty-five millennia and in some cases down even to modern times. Precisely what was limiting the realization of his potential? It was surely not, as has so often been suggested, that hunting and foraging were so demanding that they left neither time nor energy for progress. On the contrary, systematic study of hunter-gatherers as these could recently be observed in action has shown repeatedly that they manage to supply their needs at the cost of a surprisingly low input of energy. Richard Lee's model

[28] J. G. D. Clark and M. W. Thompson, 'The Groove and Splinter Technique of working antler in Upper Palaeolithic and Mesolithic Europe', *Proc. Prehist. Soc.* XIX (1953), 148–60.

[29] I. G. Pidoplichko, op. cit., Fig. 56.

[30] S. K. Kozlowski, 'The System of Providing Flint Raw Materials in the Late Palaeolithic in Poland', *Second International Flint Symposium, Maastricht 1976*, 66–9.

[31] C. Renfrew, J. E. Dixon, and J. R. Cann, 'Obsidian and Early Cultural Contact in the Near East', *Proc. Prehist. Soc.* XXXII (1966), 30–72.

study has shown for instance that the Kung Bushmen of South Africa[32] make do on the equivalent of a two-and-a-half day week. This helps among other things to account for the fact that people like the Australian aborigines, while depending entirely on what they could grub, catch, or forage, nevertheless maintained decorative arts, ritual observances, mythology, and a web of social obligations whose intricacy and richness continues to fascinate modern anthropologists. Similarly it helps to explain how it was that as early as the Middle Pleistocene Palaeolithic man was already fabricating artefacts, notably bifacial hand-axes, to standards of perfection far beyond what was required from a merely functional standpoint. Even more it allows us to account for the cave art of the late Upper Pleistocene, including such things as the rock-paintings of Altamira, Lascaux, or Le Portel, the relief carvings of Cap Blanc or Le Roc, the modelled or sculptured female figurines extending from France to the USSR or the designs engraved on small objects from innumerable cave deposits (Fig. 3). The archaeological data from this time

FIG. 3. Spiral designs carved on bone objects of Upper Magdalenian age from Isturitz, Basses Pyrénées, France.

already reflects an amplitude of leisure. It was this and the pleasurable way of life that went with it, rather than penury and a day long grind, that explains why social life remained so static. Is it really so surprising that a self-regulating mode of life returning rich satisfactions for little work should have perpetuated itself for so long?

What then were the factors that held back hunter foragers and conversely made possible the dynamic progress that followed on the adoption of farming? Before attempting to answer this it is important to look more closely at what

[32] R. B. Lee, op. cit.

we mean by farming. As the work of Eric Higgs and Mike Jarman and their team at Cambridge has emphasized in recent years,[33] the distinction between hunter–forager and farmer is much less clear-cut than might be imagined from the dialogue of cultural evolutionists. In part this is a question of semantics. As I indicated in my contribution to the symposium on early agriculture held jointly by the Royal Society and the British Academy in 1976:

Words like crop, harvest or husbandry are so closely linked in our minds with the agricultural basis of our own society that we are only too prone to overlook the fact that human societies of whatever kind depend for their subsistence, directly or indirectly, on cropping, harvesting and husbanding animals and plants ... The convention by which economies based on such activities as foraging and hunting are considered to be merely predatory, whereas those based on farming are held to be productive, in a sense begs the question. Both systematically exploit natural resources.[34]

Although it is vital to an understanding both of the origins of the new economy and of the complexity of subsistence systems operating at any particular time that the dichotomy between hunter–foragers and farmers should not be overdrawn, it remains an inescapable fact that, however gratifying a life they were capable of affording, no society depending exclusively on hunting and foraging has ever entered upon the wider experience of civilization. And the converse is no less true. All those who share in the consciousness of civilized existence have up to the present depended in the last resort on the cultivation of crops and/or the maintenance of animal herds. Since those who follow me in this series will be speaking on the archaeology of civilized societies, it is necessary, therefore, to consider what was really involved in the transition from hunting and foraging to farming. The more so in that it helps to explain the rich diversity of the several civilizations of mankind as this is encountered in the archaeological record.

The essential change in the transition to farming lay in the greater degree of control over the animals and plants contributing to sustenance. It is important from the outset to emphasize the dynamic element in the new relation-

---

[33] E. S. Higgs (ed.), *Papers in Economic Prehistory* (Cambridge, 1972); *Palaeoleconomy* (Cambridge, 1975).

[34] G. Clark, 'Domestication and Social Evolution' in *The Early History of Agriculture*, 5–11, ed. Sir J. Hutchinson, British Academy, 1977.

ships. Control by its very nature invites intensification, since the more effec-
tively it is exercised the more productive and, therefore, the more adaptive it
becomes. The key to farming was domestication and the essence of domestication is that the animals and plants subject to it were attached to the home
bases of those who controlled them. The relationship was mutually advantageous. Livestock were protected from all but one of their natural predators,
had their food supplemented when necessary by fodder, and were afforded
shelter when conditions were too inclement in the open. Plants were advan-
taged by removing or at least reducing competition from weeds or grazing
animals, and positively through cultivation of the soil, drainage or irrigation
as the case may be, and sometimes also enrichment through the addition of
manure. The farmer for his part gained by having reasonably assured supplies of preferred foods virtually on his doorstep. Naturally there was a price
to pay for greater security and convenience. The practice of farming involved
the domestication of the farmer himself as well as of his crops and his herds.
Quite apart from the need to adjust to the social requirements of larger and
more complex communities, the new economy was in itself more demanding.
Looking after livestock, not least milking them, involved a rigid daily time-
table and meant that in effect the farmer became a servant of his animals. The
practice of agriculture was even more onerous, more particularly when this
involved the clearance (Pl. 6) and taking into cultivation of virgin lands (Pl. 7)
terracing or irrigation. The adoption of agriculture, though a decisive step,
was only one on the lofty and seemingly endless ladder of progress, the
attainment of each rung of which imposed an extra burden. Why then did not
our forebears rest content on the lower rungs? If progress exacted such a price,
why did men embark on it? The short answer is that this was the price of
survival. Economic, technological, and intellectual, not to mention social
advances were by nature adaptive, favouring those who adopted them,
penalizing those who failed to do so. Only in the remote backwaters that once
gave scope for anthropologists was it possible to stay for a time unregenerate.
Today almost the last refuge has been engulfed. On the highlands of New
Guinea[35] men who hardly more than a generation back were happily polish-
ing their stone axes are busy putting crosses on ballot papers and qualifying
for income tax.

    The practice of farming certainly involved risks. So long as men lived in

---

[35] L. J. Brass, 'Stone Age agriculture in New Guinea', *Geogr. Rev.* XXXI (1941), 555–69; G. Lerche
and A. Steensberg, 'Observations on spade-cultivation in the New Guinea Highlands', *Tools and Tillage*
II (1973), 87–104.

bands of hardly more than twenty persons and had the freedom of extensive territories they were able to select from a large number of seasonal resources and stood in little danger of starvation. The greater density of population made possible by farming on the other hand presented hazards all the more serious when we remember the low yields of crops in antiquity and the liability of herds to pestilence. Yet to some degree the risks of farming were counterbalanced by the relative ease with which crops could be stored and by the fact that livestock herds constituted in themselves living reserves from which dairy products, meat, and such products as hides, horn, and wool could be obtained at will. A further resource was open to early farmers. Foraging and hunting, not to mention fishing, continued to provide ancillary sources of foodstuffs, though ones that ceased to be quantitatively significant with each increase in the density of population. Another consideration, particularly relevant to prehistory, is that fully sedentary settlement and a marked increase in the density of population were neither of them achieved suddenly. The distinction between nomadic and fully sedentary settlement was not clear-cut. The home base was peripatetic before it became permanently static and there were many gradations between the two. In particular it need not invariably follow that hunter–foragers were nomadic or farmers fully seden-tary. Under certain conditions the opposite might have obtained in the past as it certainly has done in the ethnographic present. Above all, whatever their main source of food, the same people might be sedentary at one time and nomadic at another time of the year.

Yet there is no question that for a number of reasons the practice of farming conferred advantages. For one thing, in so far as it made it possible to obtain all that was needed within a narrow radius of a permanent home base, it freed men from the need to range over extensive territories and made it possible to occupy the same settlement not merely throughout the year but over a period of years. This in turn made possible a marked increase in both the density of population and in the potential size of groups able to live together, giving them marked advantages in the competition for land and resources. Indirectly also the enlarged size of settlements for long restricted in most territories to villages permitted an increase in the subdivision of labour which in turn favoured advances in technology. Another dynamic out-come and accompaniment of domestication was the way it increased productivity through its impact on the genetic composition of favoured animals and plants.

This can be documented rather neatly from the sample of 1,248 maize cobs recovered from successive levels of the San Marcos cave in the valley of Tehuacan, Mexico:[36]

	Strata	Average length mm	Average number of spikelets	Settlement phase
AD 800 ——	B	55	163	Cities served by irrigation
BC 200 ——	C¹	47	134	
900 ——	C	45	120	Villages and ceremonial centre
1500 ——				
2300 ——	D	43	113	Semi-permanent villages
3500 ——				
c.5000 ——				

It is because such genetic changes ensured higher yields from the same input of energy and in this way provided the economic base for the emergence of peasant societies and ultimately of imposing civilizations that they are of such diagnostic significance. In principle they can only have come into existence as an outcome of human selection working on biological mutations. This could in large measure have been exercised unwittingly. The mere act of growing preferred plants close to the home base in soil enriched by organic waste would alone have exerted some influence and this could only have been increased by assisting such plants by removing or reducing competitors. Again, once the notion of growing preferred plants in concentrations, as distinct from foraging, took root, the convenience of harvesting crops at one time would have operated selectively in the case of such cereals as wheat, barley, or maize. Whereas in wild species those specimens with a brittle rachis gained an advantage by achieving a wider dispersal of seed, in the case of cereals harvested at one time variants with a relatively tough rachia were more likely to feature in the seed corn. Again, the process of threshing would certainly have favoured mutant maize with relatively soft glumes. None of this in the least detracts from the likelihood that when farming had attained a certain importance in subsistence its practitioners would have begun to influence the character of herds and crops in a directly purposeful though, of course, empirical fashion by favouring the breeding of more productive strains.

The process of establishing closer relations between human societies and preferred species of animal and plant must by its very nature have been

[36] P. C. Mangelsdorf, R. E. MacNeish, and W. C. Galinat, 'Prehistoric Wild and Cultivated Maize' in *The Prehistory of the Tehuacan Valley*, I, ed. D. S. Byers (Univ. Texas Press, 1967).

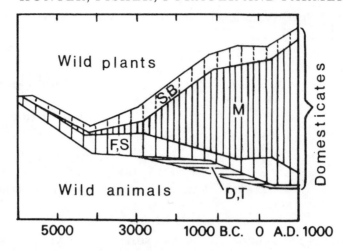

FIG. 4. The transition from wild to predominantly domesticated sources of plant and animal food in the valley of Tehuacan, Mexico, between 6000 BC and AD 1000. M=maize; S,B=squash and beans; F,S=fruit and seeds; D,T=dog and turkey.

gradual, worked out in the context of prevailing ecological systems. To think of farming as if it was an abrupt invention capable of being diffused like some new gadget is hardly possible today when so much is known about its development in different territories. Systematic investigations in the Tehuacan Valley (Fig. 4) and the district of Oaxaca, Mexico,[37] backed up by radiocarbon dating shows that for several thousand years domesticated species like avocado, beans, maize, and squash remained quantitatively inconspicuous by contrast with a multitude of foraged plants.

The decisive turning-point is usually marked in the archaeological record by a number of closely linked changes, notably a sharp upturn in the proportion of domesticated animals and plants accompanied by a reduction in the number of species, together reflecting a more intense concentration and a heavier investment in the form of cultivation and maintenance. With this is associated a greater degree of sedentarism, a markedly greater overall density of population and the possibility of larger numbers of people living together in single settlements. In technology a common, though by no means invariable innovation is the appearance of pottery containers and cooking vessels[38] to supplement and in part replace those made of organic materials.

[37] For a useful summary, see N. Hammond, 'The Early History of American Agriculture: recent research and current controversy' in Sir J. Hutchinson, op. cit., 120–8.
[38] G. Clark, op. cit. (1977), 61 f.

Cultivated plants and domestic animals might be introduced in territories beyond the range of their original prototypes, as we know happened in temperate Europe and North America or again in the Pacific. Their diffusion was subject only to ecological constraints which imposed limits and involved genetic adaptations that slowed it down. On the other hand, it is certain that domesticated species can only have been developed in territories where their wild prototypes were available.[39]

Given the advantages that accrued to communities that succeeded in developing closer relations with animals and plants to the point of domestication, it is hardly to be wondered at that the process should have unfolded in so many parts of the world. Whether this occurred completely independently or whether in some instances it was stimulated from outside is of no great moment. What is important is that the process unfolded in territories with widely different ecologies. One of the clues to the astonishing diversity of human civilizations is that they rest on the cultivation and raising of such a wide variety of species. The raising, harvesting, and preparation of plants as various as rice, beans, maize, manioc, potato, wheat, barley, rye, or yams, would alone have served to promote diversity not merely in subsistence and technology, but also in settlement and social organization. Even within the cereal zone of Europe widely differing regimes adjusted to regional ecosystems are reflected in the archaeological record of early peasant communities. One has only for example to compare the dry farming regime of the Mediterranean zone, complemented by the cultivation of almonds, figs, olives, and vines, with the mixed farming of the deciduous zone based on year-round rainfall or again with the regime of the marginal economies of much of Scandinavia and north Russia, where the growing season was too short for cereals to play more than a subsidiary role, to appreciate the importance of the ecological factor.

In view of the lectures which follow I would only conclude by emphasizing that if farming provided the economic base for civilization it hardly accounts for it. For this we must look to social dynamics. Prehistoric farmers, no less than hunter–fishers, were severely limited by their egalitarian nature as evinced for example by the plans and contents of their houses (Fig. 5). Such social structure as they did display was strictly segmental. There were distinctions of age and sex, but hardly yet of hierarchy. By contrast, the high cultures or civilizations considered by later lecturers in this series were invariably the product of vertically or hierarchically structured societies. Hierarchy and

[39] J. R. Harlan and D. Zohary, 'Distribution of Wild Wheats and Barley', *Science* 153 (1966), 1074–8.

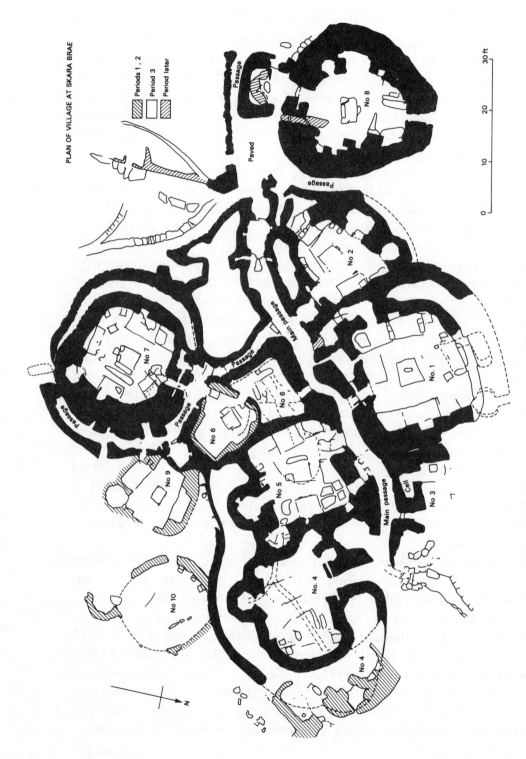

PLAN OF VILLAGE AT SKARA BRAE

Periods 1, 2
Period 3
Period later

Fɪɢ. 5. Cluster of Neolithic dwellings at Skara Brae, Orkney, Scotland. The equal status of the inhabitants is suggested by the similarity both in the character and scale of the dwellings and in the regular pattern of their furnishings.

social inequality were not merely the invariable accompaniment but the formative factor in the emergence of high cultures. And by high cultures I mean those whose upper classes observed, or failed to observe, canons of behaviour furthest removed from those of the lower animals. In terms of archaeology high cultures are those whose noblest artefacts diverge most notably from the sticks and stones of *Homo erectus* and in so far as they relate to the higher levels in the hierarchy transcend most clearly the homely products of prehistoric societies in respect of complexity, diversity, and sophistication. It is a matter of fact based on stratigraphy that the material embodiments of high culture invariably appear in the context of hierarchically organized societies. Again, the archaeology of the lower levels in hierarchical societies normally approximates more closely to that of earlier phases in the history of the same tradition. Whereas the peaks of cultural achievements, the finest products of human craft, were exclusively associated with and indeed helped to define and signal the highest levels in hierarchical societies, the objects and structures used by the mass of the population, including the very craftsmen who made the noblest insignia and built the grandest monuments, were often comparable with those of their prehistoric forebears. The conclusion is surely inescapable that without a hierarchical structure, without a marked degree of inequality in consumption, the astonishing diversity and perfection of Chinese, Egyptian, Anglo-Saxon, or indeed any other civilization could hardly have been achieved. When the organizers of the recent Chinese exhibition denounced the luxury and depravity of the feudal classes they never stopped to ask themselves whether the superlative jades, silks, porcelains, and paintings would ever have been fabricated unless to exhibit and proclaim a status superior to that of the artificers. Archaeology tells us what the cultures of China, Egypt, or Britain were like before class societies developed in these lands. The prehistoric peasants were egalitarian. They were illiterate. Their products were more vital, but in many respects as dull as those used by the lower levels in say Shang China, Pharaonic Egypt, or Anglo-Saxon England. Archaeology tells that the finest artefacts made by man, the most superb and diverse embodiments of his humanity, were made to celebrate social systems founded on hierarchy and inequality.[40]

[40] The implications of this are spelt out in an essay entitled 'Archaeology and Human Diversity' due to appear in the *Annual Review of Anthropology* (Palo Alto, California) 8 (1979).

II

EARLY URBAN COMMUNITIES IN THE NEAR EAST, *c*.9000–3400 BC

James Mellaart

ARCHAEOLOGICAL DISCOVERIES over the last thirty years have greatly expanded the geographical distribution of early urban cultures in the Near and Middle East. As a result it is highly doubtful if we can still maintain that civilizations only arose in the riverine valleys of the Nile, Lower Mesopotamia, or the Indus, at dates which fall some time in the third millennium BC. Stimulated by pre-war discoveries, the great prehistorian, V. Gordon Childe, formulated the theory of two great innovations: the Neolithic revolution, i.e. the change of early man from hunter to farmer, followed by a second Urban revolution, i.e. the change from villager to literate town dweller. The former was supposed to have taken place *c*.5000 BC, the change to civilization *c*.3000 BC or soon afterwards, but only in Lower Mesopotamia, Egypt, and the Indus valley, in the latter two areas perhaps under Mesopotamian influence. These ideas greatly intrigued culture historians and the bulk of the archaeological profession. H. Frankfort went further and suggested that Lower Mesopotamia was the only home of civilization in the Near East, all other regions forming a barbarous periphery, except Egypt which owed its civilization to Mesopotamian stimulus. Likewise, Sir Mortimer Wheeler suggested that the Indus civilization was a latecomer and owed its origins to Mesopotamian trading contacts, 'ideas have wings', after 2400 BC. Syria and Palestine, Anatolia and Iran were barbarous hinterlands in this theory, suppliers of raw materials, sources of potential danger to the established civilizations, and only partly civilized through Mesopotamian contacts in the second millennium BC. The centre of the civilized world was and remained Lower Mesopotamia—Sumer and Akkad, later Babylonia.

Post-war excavations, in which archaeologists became increasingly aware of the need to co-operate with botanists and zoologists in elucidating the problems involved in plant and animal domestication, soon proved some of the old theories wrong. Wild wheat and barley did not grow in the valleys of the Nile, Tigris, Euphrates, or Indus which ruled out an autochthonous Neolithic development in these valleys. Sheep and goat were not native to Egypt, sheep not native to Palestine, or Iraq; hence the presence of such creatures demanded an explanation, as to how and when man had introduced them.

The scientific contribution showed that a much larger territory had to be surveyed and investigated in order to solve the problems of the origins of the new Neolithic economy. Research now shifted to the despised periphery, 'the hilly flanks of the Fertile Crescent'. Braidwood's astronomically expensive expedition turned to Iraqi Kurdistan and discovered a number of sites which he claimed illustrated man's development from cave to village. The village was Jarmo—the material, twenty years after the end of the excavations, is still largely unpublished. His findings seemed to support Childe's theoretical sequence: from cave site, via semi-permanent open-air settlement to fully agricultural permanent village, first without pottery, then with. At this stage the scene was set for the conquest of the fertile alluvial soils of the Mesopotamian plain, where previous excavators had discovered the now classic sequence Hassuna–Samarra–Halaf–Ubaid–Uruk, followed by the rise of civilization either during Jemdet Nasr, c. 3100, or at its end, c. 2900 BC, in the immediately following Early Dynastic period. Braidwood's finds were humble enough not to upset previous beliefs and theories; things had progressed in a simple, orderly and predictable way, or so it seemed, to what he called an efficient village farming economy, largely self-sufficient, with only a modicum of barter to produce a few luxury goods, not available in the village itself.

The challenge to this picture of rural self-sufficiency came almost at once, and from a most unexpected quarter; in fact from K. Kenyon's excavation at Jericho. Its location—200 m below sea-level—at the deep end of the Jordan valley, did not fit very well with the hilly flanks theory. Wheat and barley did not grow there wild, yet they were found fully domesticated in the pre-pottery Neolithic (PPN) settlements of the site, an earlier (A), radiocarbon dated between c. 8350 and 7350, and a later (B) which covered the seventh millennium BC—the later period being roughly contemporary with Jarmo. But what really caused consternation was the size of the two Jericho settlements, eight acres for the earlier site and an even larger site in the later period, with estimated populations of 2,000–3,000 people. A city wall, twice rebuilt, a rock-cut ditch, a huge stone tower surrounded by storage rooms (Pl. 8), perhaps communal to the numerous round houses of the PPNA settlement, hardly fitted into Braidwood's scheme which showed for this period the semi-permanent site of Karim-Shahir, with no evidence for agriculture, no architecture, and only a random pattern of pebbles perhaps the base of one or more flimsy huts. The PPNB site at Jericho with its rectangular architecture, red plastered floors and door jambs, two possible shrines and the well-known modelled and painted skulls introduced another feature hitherto judged absent in the Neolithic period—art. As for self-sufficiency, the earlier settlement already imported Anatolian obsidian, and in the later there is turquoise matrix from Sinai as well, together with Red Sea cowries, evidence for long-distance trade. Moreover, subsequent discoveries have shown that Jericho was served by subsidiary settlements throughout the Jordan valley and the Wadi Arabah and Sinai, the best known of which is undoubtedly Beidha, which in the PPNB shows craft specialization in workshops, groups of which surround various large houses, themselves served by what looks like a quarter of shrines away from the main settlement. Beidha was of course fully agricultural, but appears to have been more than a satellite village, and is more like a small trading and manufacturing emporium. Jericho, in comparison, must be regarded as urban.

Recent years have seen an essentially similar development on the middle Euphrates, east of Aleppo at the two now submerged sites of Mureybet and Tell Abu Hureyra. Here, as at Jericho and Beidha, essentially Mesolithic (Natufian) settlements develop into large agricultural settlements in the pre-pottery Neolithic periods: among these Tell Abu Hureyra might have claimed urban status. Again, smaller settlements probably were satellite villages like Bouqras and Sheikh Hasan. The setting for these sites is important; they are remote from the postulated oak and pistachio woodland zone of the hilly flanks. They are *in* the Fertile Crescent and in the great river valley of the Euphrates, since the ninth millennium BC. This shows only too clearly that there may have been earlier settlement in Mesopotamia and early settlement was not confined to the hill zones. In fact an Aceramic Neolithic site has recently been tested by a Russian expedition at Tell Magsaliya near the Jebel Sinjar in North Iraq—but details are not yet available. At the southern end of the Fertile Crescent, in Iranian Khuzistan, the earliest levels of Alikosh, the so-called Bus Mordeh phase, again show agricultural colonization of the alluvium, albeit by seasonal occupation from a higher base like Ganjdareh in the Zagros mountains, at a time contemporary with Karim Shahir and Jericho. Preceramic A was followed by a permanent village in

Preceramic B, contemporary with Jarmo. Hence we must now envisage a descent of agriculturalists into Mesopotamian lowlands well before the sixth millennium BC. Urban sites, however, are still confined to the Levant and to a newcomer, southern Anatolia with the key site of Çatal Hüyük, radiocarbon dated between 6300 and 5400 BC, hence overlapping the end of PPNB and the beginning of the next, the pottery Neolithic period. Çatal Hüyük is not our earliest Neolithic site in Anatolia; we have others the earliest of which is Aşikli Hüyük, not yet excavated, which may go back into Pre-pottery Neolithic A of the Levant. Then follow in sequence Aceramic Hacilar, Suberde, and Can Hasan III and no doubt the lower unexcavated levels of Çatal Hüyük itself, contemporary with Pre-pottery Neolithic B in the seventh millennium. Engaged in the obsidian trade with the Levant, it comes as no surprise to find features similar to Syria and Palestine: red plastered floors, rectangular architecture, paintings on floors and walls of geometric designs, similarities in crops, stone industries, figurines, etc.

Yet the great economic innovation is the rise of simple irrigation agriculture, with new hybrid crops, first attested at Can Hasan III and then at Çatal Hüyük, at the latter site accompanied by domestication of cattle, and possibly sheep for wool.

Economically more than self-sufficient, Çatal Hüyük (Pls 9–10) soon grew into a vast site covering thirteen hectares, or four times the size of Jericho c.6000 BC, with a population conservatively estimated at between 5,000 and 7,000 people, quite possibly more. It enjoyed an uninterrupted flourish of culture of at least eight hundred years in some fourteen successive building levels, which were dug on a scale larger than that of any previously mentioned site, yet uncovered only 3 to 4 per cent of the entire settlement. As a result, the picture we have of Neolithic life is considerably richer than that for any earlier settlement, but it is still not complete; we know nothing about a bazaar quarter with workshops, the quarters of the poor, or any cattle enclosures or mortuary arrangements, such as must have existed.

The quantity, quality, variety, and technological perfection of much of the material found at this site strongly suggests specialization of craftsmen, probably full-time; builders, carpenters, plasterers, painters, mat and basket makers, weavers (Pl. 16), makers of wooden vessels, stone vessels, beads in bone, stone, shell, etc. metalworkers of trinkets, beads, rings in copper both native and smelted from ores, and lead, bone carvers, potters, carvers of stone statuettes, armourers who fashioned the exquisitely chipped obsidian, flint and chert weapons (Pls 17–18) and tools as well as obsidian mirrors. Add to

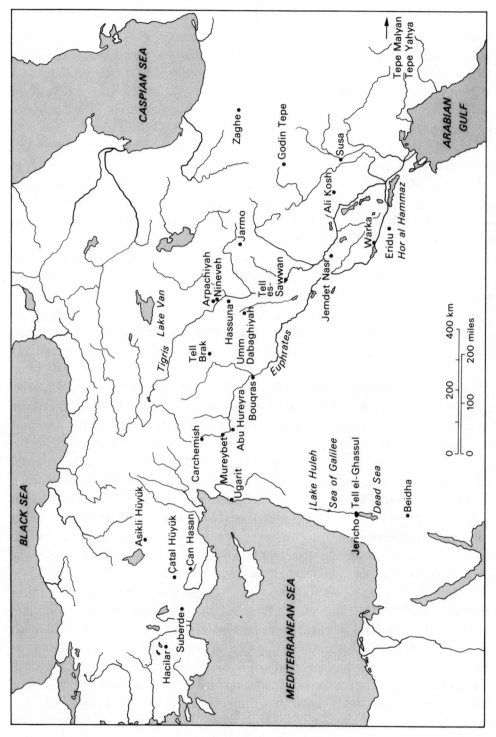

FIG. 6. Map of the Near East.

that the traders and prospectors, the undertakers—at Çatal Hüyük the dead
were excarnated before burial—hardly a job to be done *en famille*—priests
and priestesses, possibly a ruling class and the farmers who produced the
food, and we can be fairly sure that we have reached a stratified society at a
date some three thousand years before the third millennium, previously
regarded as the period in which such developments had reached a similar
level of sophistication.

Naturally, some of the features typical of the civilizations of the third
millennium are still absent—the people had not yet developed a script; they
recorded things in wall paintings or reliefs in plaster, often in monumental
compositions which might be up to 3·5 m high. Some of the wall paintings,
2 m high, were carried around the four sides of a shrine with a length of 18 m
(Pls 11–12). The subject-matter, again not surprisingly, is strongly religious:
the baiting and capture of animals, perhaps a glorification of domestication,
goddesses giving birth to animal heads; scenes of vultures with headless
corpses; textiles, matting, and symbols and, most surprising of all, a landscape with a settlement and behind it an erupting volcano. There are no
strictly historical events depicted; such scenes are rare enough also in the
historical period, the Narmer palette from Egypt being a good exception.

About the type of society of the people of Çatal Hüyük we are still ignorant;
signs of authority abound—standard-size bricks, measurements, hierarchical adherence to traditional patterns of building, decoration, representation,
symbolism, etc. High-ranking burials are not uncommon, but whether these
represent priests, clan chiefs, war leaders, or kings is anybody's guess, and
one should beware of anachronistic interpretations.

Irrigation agriculture, cattle breeding, obsidian and textile trade, early
metallurgy and a very strong religious element characterize Çatal Hüyük's
society as much as all the later civilizations, and as far as I am concerned,
Çatal Hüyük represents an ancestral civilization, probably one of many still
to be discovered.

The cultural impact of the developed Aceramic and the early Ceramic
Neolithic cultures like Çatal Hüyük was extraordinarily wide-reaching—out
to Crete in the west; to northern Iran (Zaghe, Tell Sang-i-Cakmakh) and the
edge of the Karakum desert of Turkestan in the east. Umm Dabaghiyah in the
Iraqi Jezireh, with its plaster floors and wall paintings of onager hunts, Syrian
pottery and armament, marks its extension into the Assyrian plain.

Out of this complex of flourishing cultures, new ones were to develop,
characterized by a widespread use of painted pottery, during the second half

of the sixth millennium BC, from Hacilar in the west of Turkey through the Halaf culture of Syria and Iraq (Pls 14–15) to Djeitun in Turkestan (Pls 22–5).

Unfortunately, most of the excavated sites of this 'Early Chalcolithic period' were small ones without an overburden of later material and most of the urban sites of this period lay deeply buried below great mounds like Niniveh, Brak, Carchemish, Diyarbakir, Ugarit, to mention but a few, inaccessible to archaeologists without astronomical budgets. This is a period with an extraordinarily lively variety of cultures in contact with each other, stimulating development of all kinds through trade and takeover, conquest and influence, embracing larger than ever areas of the Near and Middle East, developing maritime trade in the Persian Gulf, the Mediterranean, and the Aegean.

Tell es-Sawwan is a rare example of a possible urban site of this period, and the type site of the Samarra culture (Pls 20–1). Situated on the banks of the Euphrates, in an area unsuitable to dry farming, it practised irrigation agriculture; the earliest site known to have done so in Mesopotamia. The earliest building level was surrounded by a ditch and contained some large buildings interpreted as temples, one containing up to seventeen rooms. Associated with level I was a cemetery which yielded an amazing collection of alabaster vessels and female figurines, jewellery, including copper and probably Iranian turquoise beads. There was still little pottery at this period, none painted, but by level III the classical Samarra painted pottery had developed which, rare in Mesopotamia, was painted often with naturalistic designs. Large T-shaped houses, neatly arranged, were now contained within a fortification wall which had replaced the earlier ditch. For temples and graves we have no evidence, the latter may have been grouped in a cemetery outside the settlement. The site is still being excavated and no final report is yet available. Compared to the richness of Çatal Hüyük, the amount of information is however limited.

This applies even more strongly to our next period, the Ubaid period of Mesopotamia, one of the most neglected periods in archaeological investigation of that country. Ubaid remains lay at the base of many of the great Bronze Age tells and temples have been found to underlie Uruk period ones at Eridu, Uruk, and especially Tepe Gawra near Niniveh. Other important remains lay buried below Susa, the capital of Elam, but nowhere have excavations been conducted on a large enough scale to provide us with a clear example of an Ubaid urban centre, Tepe Gawra qualifying only as a citadel.

Yet no one doubts that urban centres must have been common by now not only in Mesopotamia, but also in the west, where Tell el-Ghassul in Palestine covers a square km in size with temple structures, wall paintings, blocks of houses, industrial quarters and the like. Excavations have not progressed far enough to illustrate a Palestinian urban community of this period, though Palestine has yielded the most phenomenal hoard of arsenical copper objects yet known from the Near East, that of Nahal Mishmar. The Ubaid period seems to have developed into the Uruk one, *c.*4000 BC, a relatively short phase ending by 3400 BC, yet one of the most significant in the history of the Near East. It was a period of great changes, which saw the development not just of city states, but of authoritarian control of trade routes through the founding of merchant colonies in foreign territories—the thing we used to call imperialism. Its originators were the Sumerians of southern Mesopotamia under, we may assume, the lords of Uruk, its most important site.

The formative stages of the new developments during the Uruk period probably lay in the preceding Ubaid period of which we know uncomfortably little. The same can be said of the Early Uruk period, and not until its middle phase, when the so-called bevelled rim bowls, a mass-produced item, appears, do we find a vast expansion of Uruk people, not only in southern Mesopotamia, ancient Sumer, but also in the North of Mesopotamia, and all along the Euphrates in Syria and South Turkey. The same pottery also appears in Elam and late in the period in merchant colonies in Iran (Godin Tepe in the Zagros, Tepe Malyan, ancient Anshan, and Tepe Yahya far to the east in Kerman province) in each case associated with Elamite numerical or early written Proto-elamite tablets and cylinder seals, a novelty. Numerical tablets also occur at Tell Habuba Kabira South and Jebel Aruda east of Aleppo, which are probably Sumerian colonies in foreign territory of the Amuq F culture (Fig. 7). At Habuba Kabira South, the first of three settlements was unfortified, but the later settlements were provided with a solid many-towered mud-brick wall, facing west. The town plan could be partially established before the site was drowned by the Euphrates dam and contains houses of a type known from Uruk itself in level IV B. Temples of Uruk type were found at Tell Qannas, part of the Habuba site (Fig. 7), and on a hill top site of Jebel Aruda to the north, and some of these were decorated with cone mosaics. The Habuba site is thought to be somewhat earlier than Uruk IV, and lacks written records, but it contains bullae with imprints of Uruk style cylinder seals, pottery and bricks (Riemchen) identical to those of Uruk and small finds of amulets in alabaster in the form of animals, in

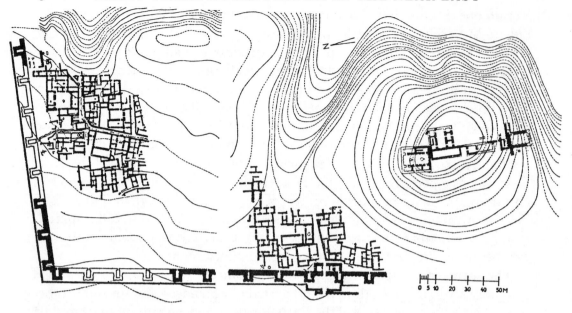

FIG. 7. Tell Habuba Kabira (South) in Syria: plan of town with inset of temples on Tell Qannas.

period of Uruk III. A number of cylinder seals of Jemdet Nasr style, but datable to the Uruk period, are important as they have frequently been used to date the last predynastic phase in Egypt to the Jemdet Nasr period, which should now be corrected to Uruk. Jemdet Nasr is contemporary with the First Dynasty in Egypt; on the dendochronologically calibrated radiocarbon scale the beginning of both the First Dynasty and the Jemdet Nasr phase should be *c.*3400 BC and not *c.*3100 BC. The discovery of these Sumerian colonies in North Syria has a further important result; contacts with Egypt, which was already obtaining timber from the Syrian–Lebanese coast are now easier to understand and we may conveniently drop the fantastic idea that Sumerians sailed around Arabia to Egyptian ports on the Red Sea. The presence of Uruk pottery, silver, obsidian, and lapis lazuli during the Gerzeaen period (*c.*4000–3400 BC) points to wider Egyptian contacts with its neighbours than has hitherto been recognized. The widespread trading connections of the Uruk period are only now coming to light; they reach from Eastern Afghanistan (lapis lazuli, gold) to Anatolia (timber, olive oil, silver) to Palestine and Egypt. The wealth that flowed into Uruk led to the invention of the cylinder seal and the keeping of records (i.e. writing); it also produced a great ceremonial centre at Uruk itself, with the first ziggurats in the temple precinct of Anu

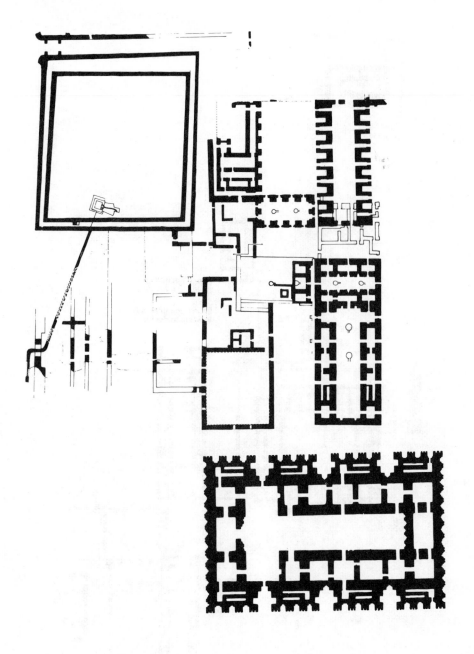

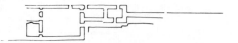

FɪG. 8. Warka in Iraq: Plan of level IVA in the Eanna complex.

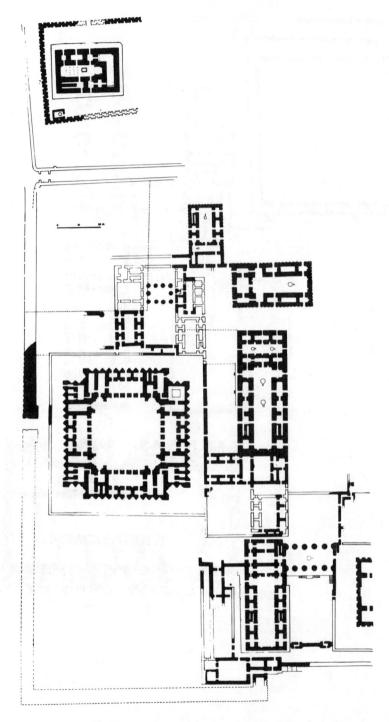

FIG. 9. Warka in Iraq: Plan of level IVB in the Eanna complex.

Mesopotamia more often associated with the final Uruk (the Jemdet Nasr) at Kullaba and a vast complex measuring already 300×200 m still under excavation in the Eanna precinct, which may be twice as large again (Figs 8–9).

There was a sudden upsurge in the arts; besides architecture, cone mosaics and glyptic, accomplished carving in stone appears as well as decorative metalwork, and scenes of daily life or religious ceremonies with the first picture of a king. By the late Uruk period, *c.* 3750–3400 BC, civilization seemed fully established.

BIBLIOGRAPHY

MELLAART, J.: *The Neolithic of the Near East* (London, 1975).
OATES, D. AND J.: *The Rise of Civilization* (Elsevier/Phaidon, 1976).

III

EARLY TOWNS IN EUROPE?

Stuart Piggott

IN OFFERING my contribution to this series I must make it clear what I am *not* going to include under what may sound an impossibly ambitious title. I shall not deal with the Aegean and its palace-centred civilizations of the Minoan and Mycenaean periods of the second millennium BC, nor the later (though still of course 'early') townships and cities of the Greek, Etruscan, or Roman world. What I propose to look at initially are the circumstances in continental Europe in which settlements of the type of the earliest agricultural communities of west Asia came into being, and to see in what degree the subsequent developments of the European settlement type was parallel with, or divergent from, what can be observed farther east, both areas starting from virtually identical prototypes around, let us say, the sixth or even seventh millennium BC. What we have to look for in the archaeological evidence (which alone is available to us in the wholly non-literate context of ancient Europe) is something we can agree on calling a 'town', and we must later return to the definition of such a social unit. East and east-central Europe will concern us at this stage of the enquiry, over a time-span of something over four thousand years, from about 6000 to 1500 BC. And then, as a separate phenomenon, we will look for towns among trans-alpine European communities in the last few centuries BC, at a time when fully urban civilizations had come into being in the Mediterranean and Aegean coasts and islands.

One more general point. At the risk of stressing the obvious I would like to remind you that a 'town', like any other form of human settlement, is the expression of a social concept, which archaeologically will be represented by such material remains as resist decay. If these do not include written records, our identification of the excavated remains as indicative of a 'town', rather than any other unit of settlement, is based on inferences from them fitted into a taxonomy of our own construction. With documentary evidence we might know what status the settlement had in the eyes of its inhabitants and their neighbours; in prehistory this knowledge is unattainable. Despite Sir Mortimer Wheeler's adjurations that 'the archaeologist is digging up, not *things*, but *people*', I recognize with Professor Atkinson that 'the raw material of prehistory is not men, but things',[1] and that our inferences from this raw material may supply the men, but must strictly respect the evidence, however disappointing some may find the outcome. I do not attempt to disguise my distrust of over-ambitious social reconstruction in the non-literate contexts of prehistory. As an anthropologist Sir Edmund Leach has voiced his opinion forcibly here: 'In archaeology the accumulation of more and more evidence increases our information about historical artefacts; it does not increase the probability of our social guesswork.'[2]

To turn now to this archaeological evidence itself. I would suggest that our thinking about the beginnings of agriculture in, say, Thessaly, Macedonia and the Balkans (where the earliest dated settlements occur), has been unconsciously confused by that concept of political geography going back to Herodotus, whereby Europe was separated antithetically from Asia: the ancient Near East as one thing, ancient East Europe another. If we forget this (and it is surely irrelevant here), and look rather at an Aegean-centred area of common, if locally variant, traditions, united and not separated by the sea, we may perhaps better understand the circumstances of the sixth millennium BC. We must look at an area of common traditions curiously coincident in boundaries with that of the Ottoman Empire at the dawn of early modern times. More than one heroic figure has swum across the Hellespont, and the distribution of obsidian from the island of Melos attests sea traffic even among pre-agricultural communities in Greece. If one takes the site of Troy as a convenient geographical, not archaeological, centre, an arc with a radius of 500 km will touch Hacilar in the south-east, and easily comprise, to west and north, the earliest settlements of stone-using agriculturalists in Greece, Yugoslavia and Bulgaria: Crete with Neolithic Knossos lies rather farther away to the south. All the European sites share with their more easterly counterparts the basic components of mixed farming in varying local proportions: domesticated sheep and goats throughout, cattle and pigs frequent, dogs occasional. Cultivated plant crops include predominantly wheat and barley as cereals, as well as legumes such as peas, lentils, and vetch.

---

[1] *Archaeology from the Earth* (Oxford, 1954) v; *Archaeology, History and Science*, Inaugural Lecture (Cardiff, 1960), 8; cf. M. A. Smith, 'The limitations of inference in archaeology', *Arch. News Letter* VI, i (1955), 3–7.

[2] *Cambridge Review* (Feb. 1974), 73.

Some hunting and fishing and the gathering of edible fruits and seeds augmented the diet. Of the domesticates and cultivars, the cereals and the ovicaprids must have their origin farther east; cattle and pig could be local domesticates but probably in the initial stages were also introductions across the Aegean. At first (as in west Asia), without pottery and with edge-tools of stone (including imported obsidian), ceramic techniques soon develop on individual lines, but in their inception the first north Greek settlements have a material culture which includes characteristic forms of figurines and the so-called 'stamp-seals', which like the domesticates point to more easterly origins, and some sort of model of culture diffusion must be adopted, as within the area traditionally thought of as the Near East itself. As Mellaart has recently said they 'clearly bear the stamp of the Anatolian tradition, and they are not, for example, Syrian, Lebanese or Cypriot'.[3]

In our search for towns, our essential basis must be these modest villages of settled, stone-using, mixed farmers, from Thessaly to the Thracian Plain, dating from before 6000 BC in Greece and not much later in Yugoslavia and Bulgaria in radiocarbon years (Fig. 10). Although we know that these are not coincident with dates in calendar years, I shall use such dates throughout, but in absolute terms these would indicate a much higher antiquity, perhaps by a millennium or so. With the establishment of such settlements, however small and scattered, the economic basis of pre-industrial Europe was assured, as it had been in Asia. From such population units could follow the further technological, economic, and social developments having as their tangible expression the use of bronze and iron, and towns and cities in ascending order of magnitude and complexity. By processes we very imperfectly understand, but which must have included both acculturation and actual population movements, agricultural economies were established across Europe to the Rhineland by the fifth, and the British Isles by the fourth millennium; by Mediterranean seaways to Italy by the sixth, and southern Iberia by the fifth.[4] Everywhere populations must have been tiny by recent European standards, but with the actual adoption of a sedentary, rather than an itinerant and mobile life, necessitated by an agricultural economy, biological

[3] J. Mellaart, *The Neolithic of the Near East* (London, 1975), 244–62, with refs.; R. Tringham, *Hunters, fishers and farmers of eastern Europe* (London, 1971).

[4] For general surveys, S. Piggott, *Ancient Europe* (Edinburgh, 1965); Tringham, op. cit.; P. Phillips, *Early Farming Communities of West Mediterranean Europe* (London, 1975); R. Whitehouse, 'Early Farming Communities in Europe', in D. Collins (ed.), *The Origins of Europe* (London, 1975), 143–68; B. Bender, *Farming in Prehistory* (London, 1975).

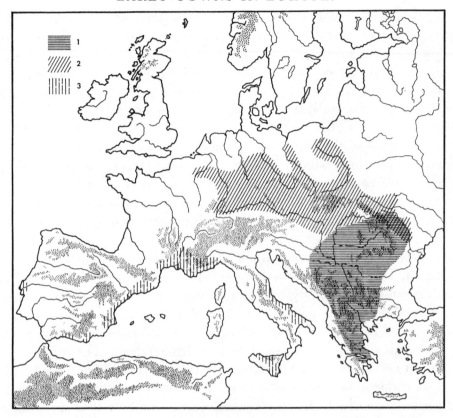

FIG. 10. Generalized distribution of agricultural communities in Europe, fifth millennium BC; 1. Starčevo and allied cultures; 2. Linear pottery cultures; 3. Impressed pottery cultures.

factors are likely to have operated in favour of a rise in population, no less than an increased and assured food supply to support it.[5]

Small populations in extensive territories of potential agricultural exploitation, employing unsophisticated farming techniques, may form no more than transient village communities which may shift their location in response to the exhaustion of their immediately available resources (often reckoned for convenience those within an hour's walk from the settlement). Such over-use may be particularly apparent in growing cereals, where continuous cropping leads to the exhaustion of the nitrogen in the soil, with consequent steeply falling yields after a few years: the ancient 'slash-and-burn' method of

[5] Cf. R. V. Short, 'The evolution of human reproduction', in *Contraceptives of the Future* (*Proc. Royal Soc. Lond.*), 1976, 3–24.

clearing forest for arable by fire, surviving in parts of Europe into the last century, provides well-documented examples, without going further afield for this widespread technique. Throughout most of early agricultural Europe such an impermanent settlement-pattern is reasonably to be inferred from the archaeological evidence, even if in some areas such as central Europe and the Rhineland in the Linear Pottery culture of the fifth millennium, some sort of a 'cyclical' pattern may perhaps be demonstrated, with a sequence of desertion and subsequent reoccupation of the sites of settlements of timber-built houses, at their largest with populations guessed at as around 300–400 persons.[6] It is hardly in such contexts that one would look for the emergence of a settlement capable of definition as a town, in which a certain permanence of duration seems one necessary pre-requisite, as we shall see.

But, as is well known, the problem of maintaining permanent settlements on the same site was early solved in west Asia, by whatever means. So far as obviating soil exhaustion by cereal cropping is concerned, this may involve varying modes of regeneration by means of long or short systems of fallow; manuring; soil replacement by flooding; or the alternation of crops, particularly of cereals with legumes, which fix the nitrogen level. These factors, with the ubiquitous use in a dry hot climate of mud and mud-brick for building, which on collapse or destruction forms a three-dimensional accumulation, produce as an archaeological phenomenon a mound or 'tell' of superimposed and stratified deposits, representing in tangible form the chronological duration of occupation on the site. It is therefore significant that in Europe it is in precisely that area which we have seen as the most westerly extent of the oriental tradition—north Greece and the Balkans—that superimposed settlements of 'tell' type, originating in villages of primary agricultural communities, appear from the sixth millennium onwards. The archaeological content of their sequential settlements, now reinforced by a large series of radiocarbon dates, shows us in more than one instance continuous, or virtually continuous, occupation over at least three thousand years, from the sixth to the late third millennium BC. These are radiocarbon dates, and calibration would extend the span still longer (Fig. 11).

It must be admitted that we still do not understand in detail the circumstances of soil aggradation at any tell site: co-operation between archaeologists and soil-scientists is overdue in determining the proportions of decayed

[6] Piggott, op. cit. 52.

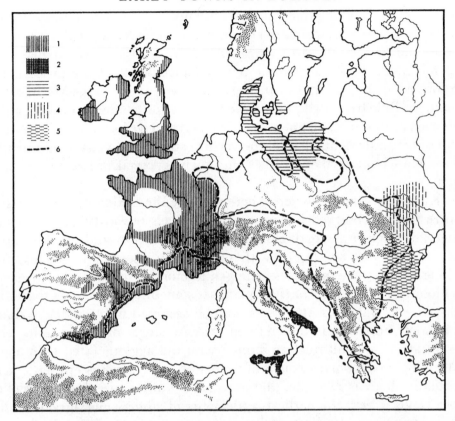

FIG. 11. Generalized distribution of agricultural communities in Europe, late fourth–early third millennium BC: 1. 'Western' cultures; 2. South Italian and Sicilian cultures; 3. TRB cultures; 4. Tripolye culture; 5. Boian, etc. cultures; 6. Area of settlement from fifth millennium BC.

house-ruins to other factors such as aeolian deposits, and the breakdown leading to true soil layers during temporary abandonment. But unequivocally the determining factor is the use of mud in greater or less degree as a building material, whether or not on a low stone base. Such building construction is a function of climate, and just as with the spread into temperate Europe of the first agriculturalists, wheat and barley, sheep and goats, were being humanly shifted out of their original ecological niches as domesticates, so the hot-weather house, flat-roofed and mud-walled, was being transferred to regions with lower temperatures, higher precipitation, and a more forested environment. In the process it was modified in two important respects, with its clay walls now increasingly framed on woodwork, and the flat roof replaced by a ridged or gable type, as contemporary models show us. Wholly mud walling and mud-brick is known from the early agricultural sites in Greece, and as far inland as Anzabegovo in Yugoslav Macedonia in the sixth millennium.[7] Whatever the detailed mechanics of the process, tells were formed up to 12 m or more in height, as at Karanovo in the Maritsa Plain of southern Bulgaria (a good example for us with its long radiocarbon date series even if, alas, it is still not fully published) and we know far less about the layout of the settlements than of the vertical stratigraphy, as in all the other and still more imperfectly published sites such as Azmak or Ezero in the same region.

At Karanovo (and elsewhere where we have the evidence) two consistent features can be observed from the earliest levels onwards: the houses are individual structures, with thin mud walls on a light post-and-wattle framing; small, rectangular or square with only rarely internal partitions, free-standing and in some instances arranged in more or less orderly streets (Pl. 26). Flooring of split poles or riven planks is sometimes present, in the houses or the streets. Gabled thatch roofs may be assumed from models. What is immediately apparent is the contrast of these single detached units, each appropriate to a small nuclear family, with the agglomerated planning of small contiguous rooms or courts of contemporary Near Eastern settlements in virtually all areas save one, that of Russian Turkmenia northwards of the Kopet Dagh, where the earliest settlements of stone-using agriculturalists such as Jeitun, of the sixth millennium, are similarly formed of square single-roomed mud-walled houses.[8] Connection is of course impossible, and we have a parallel creation of a social unit by bringing together family living-units, originally separate, into close proximity. In the later (fourth millennium) and by now copper-using phase at Karanovo, the oblong houses have taken on the so-called 'megaron' plan with porch, and a standard arrangement of hearth with adjacent corn-grinding slab at the far end, and seem to lie end-on to the access street (Fig. 12). A contemporary site at Polyanitsa in northern Bulgaria, though very small with only about twenty houses (the Karanovo settlement as we shall see was three times this size), has an extraordinarily ordered plan, as regular as a Roman camp, within its complicated square palisaded enclosure set with four entrances at the cardinal points. At Căscioarele in Romania another and smaller village of sixteen

[7] M. Gimbutas, 'Anza c.6500–5000 BC ...', *Journ. Field Arch.* I (1974), 26–66.

[8] Mellaart, op. cit. 212 and Fig. 130; V. M. Masson and V. I. Sarianidi, *Central Asia* (London, 1972), 33 and Fig. 9.

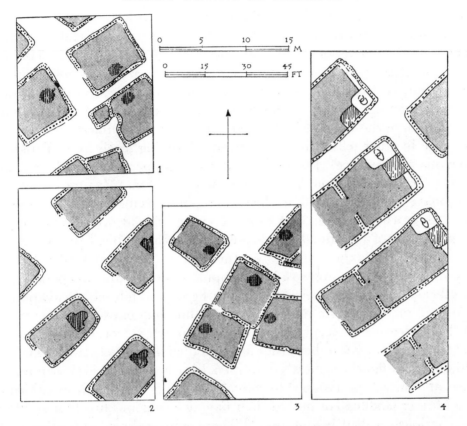

F IG. 12. Wattled and mud-walled houses at Karanovo, Bulgaria, from sixth–third millennium BC: 1.
Period I; 2. Period II; 3. Period V; 4. Period VI.

or so houses on an island, and again of the fourth millennium, shows no
planning whatever.[9]

The Karanovo stratification begins on virgin soil, as we saw, with a
settlement of 5000 BC or earlier of stone-using agriculturalists, with good
pottery, and three building levels totalling about a metre in thickness can be
traced. A break in stratification and a change of pottery styles around 4500
marks renewed occupation up to the end of the excavators' Phase IV, and
there follow sixteen building levels of V and VI forming an accumulation of
up to 6 m thick, in which evidence of copper-working now appears, spanning
a period from soon after 4000 to around 3000 BC in radiocarbon years—at all

[9] Polyanitsa, information and unpublished plan from Mrs Barbara Ottaway; Căscioarele, V. Dumitrescu, 'Principal results . . . of the excavations . . . at Căscioarele', *Studii si cercetari de istorie veche*, XVI
(1965), 215–37.

events a clear millennium. There follows a break, with the clear formation of an old land surface over an abandoned site, but occupation is taken up again in Phase VII, contemporary with nine building levels at Ezero dated between 2600 and 2300, with houses of the same general size and construction as before, but, as elsewhere in this phase, apsidal ends. The zenith of Karanovo had been reached in Phase VI: the metallurgy in copper and gold of the fourth millennium in the Balkans is attested not only in the numerous horizons of this date in other tells (with up to twenty building levels as at Tangiru in Romania for instance), but by the extensive copper mines at for instance Rudna Glava in Yugoslavia and Ai Bunar near Stara Zagora, and by the inordinate display of wealth in the contemporary cemetery at Varna on the Black Sea, where one deposit totalled 1·5 kg of gold ornaments, and the inference here of a stratified social system seems inevitable.[10] But throughout its long occupation the total of any settlement has been reckoned as between fifty and sixty houses, and so a likely population of around 300 persons, and no other site suggests noticeably larger figures. While no excavation has recovered total plans, no indication of any building of exceptional function has been identified, except perhaps for the timber structure with plastered and painted columns in the earlier fourth millennium levels at Căscioarele.[11] Although clay figurines, mostly of women, have been found in large numbers, they can nowhere be assigned to convincing shrines, and their identification as a Mother Goddess, or indeed their having a religious function at all, has been seriously called in question.[12] There is no evidence at any stage of literacy, and nowhere have defensive walls been recorded. What we should also remember is that throughout the stratified sequences of the Balkan tells of which Karanovo is typical, the only real change or innovation in material culture we can detect is the adoption of non-ferrous metallurgy about the middle of the fourth millennium. It is salutary to recall that in Mesopotamia, the Karanovo sequence would span the period between the Stone-Age villages of Hassuna and the literate city states of Sargon of Akkad.

It is at this point that we must pose the question: how do we define a town, and where in any definition would we put for instance the settlement of

---

[10] Ai Bunar, E. N. Chernykh, 'Aibunar, a copper mine of the fourth millennium BC', *Proc. Prehist. Soc.* XLIV (1978), 203–217. Rudna Glava, B. Jovanović, *Metallurgy of the eneolithic period in Yugoslavia* (Belgrade, 1971); Varna cemetery, *Thracian Treasures* ... (BM Exhibition Cat., London, 1976), nos 20–72; M. Gimbutas, 'Gold treasure at Varna', *Archaeology* XXX (1977), 44–51.

[11] V. Dumitrescu, 'Édifice destiné au culte ... de Căscioarele', *Dacia* XIV (1970), 5–24.

[12] M. Gimbutas, *The Gods and Goddesses of Old Europe* (London, 1974); P. Ucko, *Anthropomorphic Figurines* ... (London, 1968).

Karanovo VI? When Gordon Childe was trying to define his concept of an 'urban revolution', and was thinking of the ancient Near East, he listed his criteria for 'cities'.[13] They would be larger than earlier settlements; they would house specialized non-productive classes and a deity or divine king to whom tribute was paid; enshrined within monumental temple or palace buildings and organized by a ruling class of priests, officials, military commanders and so forth. Here too the invention of writing and recording systems could make possible the beginnings of mathematical and calendrical science, and patronage ensure the status of artist and fine craftsmen, and various forms of 'trade' would be carried out. The community as a whole would hold its allegiance to the city by virtue of residence within its walls.

Now this is the fully developed ancient city, far too grand for our humble enquiry for towns, and that Childe's definition demands an element of subjectivity and an appeal to factors not perceptible in purely archaeological evidence, is clear. This is a recurrent problem in any such enquiry. The modern geographer's concept of a town would be, as John Collis recently saw for Iron Age Europe, a settlement of population size and density above the normal of its surrounding territory, an administrative social and religious centre with nucleated industrial production of goods, and a system of distributing these locally and regionally. And Daphne Nash economically sums up when she points out in the same context that the 'principal standard definition' of a town is its 'social character', and goes on 'The critical difference between a village and a town is that in the former agriculture is a predominant occupation, while in a town a significant minority at least should be occupied in non-agricultural pursuits, such as administration, trade or manufacturing'.[14]

I have spent some time on definitions, but I believe not irrelevantly. The early European sites I have been describing, between the sixth and third millennia, have to be judged according to some such criteria, like their counterparts in western Asia. But unlike these, what goes for the earliest settlement in a stratified east European tell, goes for the latest. Continuity of settlement is maintained by a competent system of agriculture, but apart from metallurgy, no development can be traced in the sequence of material culture which would lead us to infer any changes within the social order whereby, in

---

[13] Childe was using the concept from the 1930s, but set out the criteria in detail in 'The Urban Revolution', *Town Planning Rev.* XXI, i (1950), 3–17; *Social Evolution* (London, 1951), 161.

[14] J. Collis, 'Town and market in Iron Age Europe', in B. Cunliffe and T. Rowley (eds), *Oppida in Barbarian Europe* (Oxford, 1976), 3–23; D. Nash, 'The growth of urban society in France', ibid. 95–133.

Mesopotamia for instance, we can with justice talk of the evolution of village to town, of town to city. Sheer size of course ought not to mislead: Sir Denys Page a few years ago brought home to us the smallness of Troy, and the Karanovo mound is about the same diameter as the walls of Troy VI.[15] We might think on a reduced scale for early east Europe, with the main population units not exceeding fifty or sixty households, and the lack of literacy could be paralleled in much larger sites, in early Anatolia or Turkmenia for instance, or again in the Levant. The signs inscribed on the curious tablets from Tartaria in Romania, and on a large number of clay objects of contemporary or even earlier date cannot be regarded as 'writing', and their alleged connection with the script of Uruk III can hardly be seriously maintained.[16] What does remain an outstanding phenomenon is the technological stagnation of the European sequence when compared with for instance Sumer or Elam, although in both areas the prototype village economy is on precisely the same level of achievement. The European tell sequences present us with the Sherlock Holmes' paradox of the curious incident of the dog in the night that so puzzled poor Watson—the dog did nothing in the night, and that was the curious incident. There is no development from village to unambiguous town, let alone city, only continuity in a rather low key.

That great historian Marc Bloch in the early 1940s read a paper to a congress of psychologists on 'Technical change as a problem of collective psychology',[17] for in history, he said 'we have a very clear impression that some societies are in themselves more "routine-minded" and others "more accustomed to change"; and we feel the need for discovering deeper reasons for attitudes which mere considerations of utility seem insufficient to explain.' 'Let us suppose', he went on, 'that there has been some new technique, either invented within a given society or introduced from outside. It will sometimes be accepted by that society, and sometimes rejected. If it is accepted, this will only take place more or less slowly and sporadically ... The invention will be accepted if it is, or appears to be, useful, and rejected if apparently useless or dangerous.' In 1952 an American anthropologist, Margaret Hodgen, explored the same theme of acceptance or rejection in the context of the history of technology in pre-industrial England.[18] Unaware of either of these

[15] D. L. Page, *History and the Homeric Iliad* (Berkeley, 1959).

[16] M. S. F. Hood, 'The Tataria tablets', *Antiquity* XLI (1967), 99–113; D. Berciu, *Romania* (London, 1967), 161.

[17] Reprinted in translation by J. E. Anderson, *Land and Work in Medieval Europe: papers by Marc Bloch* (London, 1967).

[18] M. T. Hodgen, *Change and History* (Viking Fund Pubs. XVIII) (New York, 1952).

studies, in 1965 I thought the same problem seemed to be posed in prehistoric Europe, and suggested that were two types of society, that of innovators and that of conservers. 'In one group, technological developments in the arts of war and peace must have been socially acceptable and therefore encouraged; in the other, once a satisfying *modus vivendi* for the community within its natural surroundings had been achieved, there seems to have been no urgent need felt to alter the situation.' And I quoted the anthropologist Ruth Benedict, who wrote 'Every human society everywhere has made a selection in its cultural institutions. Each from the point of view of the other ignores fundamentals and exploits irrelevancies.'[19] Anthony Snodgrass has recently taken up my original concept,[20] pointing out that its usefulness does not depend on adopting diffusionist models of culture change, now so unfashionable, and their abandonment in any given context 'will not to any serious degree affect the validity of the original antithesis between these two kinds of society': in conserving contexts 'even a society which achieves major technological advances unaided may nevertheless belong securely to the conserving type ... the decisive criterion for an innovating culture is not the mere independent *invention* of new techniques and types; it is the ability to *sustain* technological progress, together with social and economic advance.' Here I think we may see a way of looking at the European phenomena we have been considering, the failure to sustain the technological, social, and economic development Snodgrass calls for, from the original basis of the agriculturally competent village communities, with subsequent metalworking skills, that mark the foundation of the peasant economy of ancient Europe. The innovating and conserving model has been criticized for not in itself constituting an explanation, but it did not pretend to. Like Bloch I see it as a problem—'Why history offers a spectacle of two kinds of society, the stable and the inventive', to quote him again—and to recognize that a problem exists is surely better than seeing no problem at all.

Over much of Europe beyond the Mediterranean the later third millennium seems to have been a period of change. In the Balkans the occupation of tell sites ends at this time, and the precocious copper metallurgy established in the fourth millennium comes to a close and is replaced by different and less inventive metalworking traditions. In this context another technological increment appears, that of transport with ox-drawn, block-wheeled vehicles,

---

[19] *Ancient Europe*, 17 ff.

[20] A. M. Snodgrass, 'Conserving societies and independent development', in J. V. S. Megaw (ed.), *To Illustrate the Monuments* (London, 1976), 58–62.

contemporary with their appearance in south Russia, and the first sporadic
appearance of the horse, domesticated initially for meat and milk but soon for
transport, again in south Russia from the fourth millennium. These links
between the north Pontic coasts and east-central Europe have been magnified
by some into an invasion of Indo-Europeans from east to west: these are
Maria Gimbutas's Kurgan People, less clearly defined in archaeological
terms than devoutly believed in, and assiduously championed by their inven-
tor.[21] In central Europe one of the very few totally excavated settlements of
this time is set on a little hill within defences at Homolka in Bohemia, with a
radiocarbon date of about 2400 BC. It was a one-period site of about fifty or
sixty houses, and would fit neatly into Tom Quad in Christ Church, Oxford.[22]
Fortified settlements now become common, and by the beginning of the
second millennium the copper–tin alloy for edge tools that gives its name to
the Bronze Age of the nineteenth-century taxonomy was almost everywhere
in use.

Over most of Europe at this time we see a pattern of no more than exiguous
villages, or settlements inferred from cemeteries; by the middle second millennium in some areas—Wessex, Brittany, the Saale valley—social
stratification is suggested by a few exceptionally rich burials. But in the
Hungarian Plain and immediately adjacent regions, settlements of bronze-
using communities once again repeat the process of continuous occupation of
one site with clay-plastered, timber-framed houses leading to the formation of
tells up to 10 m or so high. Precise dating is difficult to establish in the absence
of radiocarbon determinations, but the sites must start early in the second
millennium, reach a peak about 1500 BC, and have an end marked by the
cessation or destruction of the final settlements on the tells which has been
equated with the arrival of newcomers from the north-west around the middle
of the thirteenth century BC. It looks then as if the continuity of use of these
sites could have spanned four or five centuries. We know lamentably little of
the houses or their layout, but they seem to have been oblong, timber-framed
and clay-daubed, set in a loose agglomeration: the immemorial pattern of
ancient Europe. One settlement (not a tell) at Barca in Slovakia has some two
dozen houses, up to 12 m long, in an ordered plan, but it is only 30 m or so
across.[23] Although permanence of settlement is demonstrable on the tell sites,

[21] e.g. M. Gimbutas, 'Proto-Indo-European culture . . .', in G. Cardona et al. (eds), Indo-European and
Indo-Europeans (Philadelphia, 1970), 155–97.
[22] R. W. Ehrich and E. Pleslová-Stiková, Homolka: an eneolithic site in Bohemia (Prague, 1968).
[23] M. Gimbutas, Bronze Age Cultures in Central and East Europe (The Hague, 1965), 200 ff.

it would be difficult to infer any other criteria which could justify us in seeing them as towns, save in a drastically diminished scale. They form interesting archaeological phenomena rather than demonstrations of incipient urbanization, and once again we seem to sense stagnation, even if other technological innovations, such as the harnessing of the domesticated horse for light fast traction, were being developed in circumstances which need owe nothing to stimuli from outside, such as from the Aegean, as has sometimes been suggested.

The achievement of what has been called High Barbarian Europe was not inconsiderable, but its archaeology does not permit us to infer any social structure in which centres of population reasonably to be considered towns formed a part. The new bronze technology demanded participation in a complex interchange system for its raw materials, copper, and tin. But how this redistributive system or 'trade' was effected we have no knowledge, nor indeed of the status of the metal-smith as a whole-time or part-time craftsman. Childe thought that temperate Europe in the mid-second millennium had 'an international commercial system' in which the bronze-working craftsman 'could escape the necessity of growing his own food and shake off the bonds of allegiance to an overlord or the more rigid fetters of tribal custom'. This 'Bronze Age system foreshadowed the peculiarities of European polity in Antiquity, the Middle Ages and Modern Times', so that 'the metics of Athens, the wayfaring journeymen of the Middle Ages and the migrant craft unionist of the nineteenth century are the lineal descendants' of the itinerant bronze-smiths of European prehistory.[24] In such a context, there would indeed have been a place for towns with their craftsmen and merchants, but it must be confessed that Childe's attempt to provide the trade unions with a prehistory was based on an over-optimistic series of inferences from the archaeological evidence.

But we must turn now and look beyond continental Europe to the Mediterranean world, as the backcloth against which the barbarian events of later prehistory beyond the Alps were played. In the Near East the Assyrian empire had developed; by the early eighth century Urartian power extended to north Syria and the Levantine coast, to be replaced by that of Assyria about 743–724 BC; Cyprus came under Assyrian domination in 709. The west coast of Asia Minor was colonized by the Ionian Greeks from the beginning of the first millennium. Further west, Phoenician trade and colonization took oriental urban traditions as far as Malta, Sardinia, and southern Spain certainly by

[24] *The Prehistory of European Society* (Harmondsworth, 1958), 172–3.

the eighth, perhaps in the late ninth century BC. After the eclipse of
Mycenaean civilization and the Greek Dark Ages the ninth century begins to
show a new order, emerging from the harsh rural simplicities of the world of
Hesiod and the *basileis*, which was to become the classic city state. We know
pitifully little about the archaeological realities of the first Greek towns, but at
Old Smyrna in Ionia a settlement of ordered rows of rectangular houses was
built over an earlier village in the mid-ninth century within a defensive wall
with ashlar bastions: it has been estimated that this could have been a town of
400–500 of these 'family cottages', with a consequent population of 2,000 or
so persons.[25] In Greece itself tradition saw a humble origin for the city not far
beyond memory—'a straggling village like the ancient towns of Hellas' said
Thucydides of Sparta. The early *poleis* have been thought to be 'nothing more
than large agricultural villages below a fortress-refuge' and the city state to
'have differed from the earlier tribal states principally in its citizens' conscious
awareness' of what it was, and what it stood for emotionally and politically.[26]
Greek exploration and settlement in the middle Mediterranean begins, as
Ridgway puts it, with 'trade' before the 'flag', and early eighth-century
Pithekoussai on Ischia to be followed by the colonies from the later eighth
century onwards, and the establishment of the Greek beach-head in Celtic
Europe at Massalia about 600 BC.[27] The early stages transitional between
Villanovan and the squalid huts on the Palatine, and the first towns and cities
in Etruria and Latium are unknown, but urban civilization with an orientalizing flavour was early developed. In the east, one must also remember not only
the Greek colonies on the Black Sea coasts from the seventh century at least,
but the 'almost continuous Persian presence in European Thrace and
Macedonia from about 513 till the end of the Greco-Persian wars in 479, with
an aftermath that lasted down to 450'.[28] When we look for the emergence of
towns in continental Europe from the middle first millennium BC onwards, we
are looking at peoples peripheral to the coastal urban communities from
Cadiz to the Crimea, with which they were in demonstrable trading contact:
to the Greeks barbarians, but hardly to be thought impervious to outside
stimuli or incapable of emulation.

In general, where we have the evidence, the settlement pattern from the

[25] A. M. Snodgrass, *The Dark Age of Greece* (Edinburgh, 1971), 369, 413; J. M. Cook, *The Greeks in the
East* (London, 1965), 31–3.
[26] C. G. Starr, *The Origins of Greek Civilization* (New York, 1961), 338.
[27] D. Ridgway, 'The first Western Greeks ...' in C. and S. Hawkes (eds), *Greeks, Celts and Romans*
(London, 1973), 5–38; M. Pallottino, *The Etruscans* (London, 1975).
[28] N. K. Sandars, 'Orient and orientalizing in Early Celtic art', *Antiquity* XLV (1971), 103, 112.

end of the second millennium BC onwards is that of villages, hamlets, or farmsteads. In north-west Europe, in what was to become the Germanic world, the sequence is well demonstrated. At Elp in the Netherlands a timber-built farmstead consisting of a long-house with living-quarters and cow-byre under one roof, with ancillary barn and sheds, was rebuilt four times over as many centuries between 1250 and 850 BC on much the same site, the prototype of a whole series of later long-house settlements growing from farms to villages of from twelve to twenty such houses, each sheltering by inference extended families and from one to two dozen head of cattle.[29] Here are the clear ancestors of the *tun* and *ham* of early historical Saxon settlement, going back to the last century BC: in Britain from the mid-second millennium BC the pattern of farmsteads rather than larger units seems similarly to have come through into history in the Celtic world. Tantalizing individual exceptions hint at the incompleteness of our knowledge however, in more than one region, such as Biskupin in Poland in the sixth century BC with its hundred or so identical one-roomed houses in ordered rows within a great timber-framed wall[30] (Pl. 27), or at the other end of Europe the contemporary mud-brick walled settlement at Cortes de Navarra on the Ebro north of Saragossa, which could have comprised fifty or more identical contiguous houses in streets.[31]

It is to the Celtic world of continental Europe, from the seventh century or so BC, that we must finally turn. The traditional peasant economies at which we have glanced adopted and exploited the last major pre-industrial technology of the ancient world, that of working in iron, in the first half of the last millennium BC. From the seventh, and increasingly in the sixth and fifth centuries BC, in what are archaeologically the phases of Hallstatt C and D, and Early La Tène, they were demonstrably linked to the urban Mediterranean world by trade exchanges, however organized and maintained. Archaeology presents us with a picture of a luxury trade operating from Massalia up the Rhône or from the Etruscan world across the Alps, into Burgundy and beyond to the Marne and northwards along what Fernand Braudel[32] characterized as the 'German Isthmus' of multiple land-routes linking the Mediterranean to the northern seas across the Alpine passes, of

[29] M. Todd, *The Northern Barbarians 100 BC–AD 300* (London, 1975), 95 ff.

[30] Piggott, *Ancient Europe*, 202.

[31] J. Maluquer de Motes, *El Yaciemento Hallstattico de Cortes de Navarra* (Pamplona, I, 1954; II, 1958); H. N. Savory, *Spain and Portugal* (London, 1968), 229.

[32] F. Braudel, *The Mediterranean and the Mediterranean World in the Age of Philip III* (London, 1976), 202 ff.

which there were after all some twenty-one, great and small, used in historical times. The main commodity of trade was wine—Greek wine shipped in amphorae to western ports—and with it fine bronze-work or painted vases for its display and consumption; Mediterranean coral; oriental goods such as ivory and silk are attested archaeologically and one suspects others yet undetected such as pepper and spices, while further less tangible contacts with the east have been seen in wheelwrights' techniques and perhaps in iron-working. Ivory, apes, and peacocks: at least one Barbary ape reached prehistoric Emain Macha, traditional seat of the Kings of Ulster, and if not peacocks, domesticated Indian jungle-fowl, the modern poultry, were eaten in south Germany and Bohemia in the sixth century BC.[33] Reciprocally, the products of the mines of the 'Salt Lords' of Hallstatt or Hallein must have been involved; northern amber, and on later classical analogies, probably furs, hides, salt meat, and of course slaves.

In this northern world between the sixth and first centuries BC we see the culmination of building fortified hill settlements that had its beginning in the second or third millennium BC, and even in remote Britain, in the earlier first. Frequently but not invariably on commanding eminences, the generic name of hillfort has become traditional usage for such sites, and it is with them that, in the penumbra of history, we come nearest to grasping the concept of a town in barbarian Europe, the more particularly as in the latest days of native independence they receive mention from, or were attacked by, the Romans, notably Julius Caesar in Gaul and Britain.[34] Searching in the Latin vocabulary for a word expressive of a stronghold recognized by Celts and Romans alike as embodying political power, Caesar and others employ the word *oppidum*, a town in fact, a word containing (as Varro thought) the senses of power, wealth, and strength. Of pre-Roman Verulamium, *oppidum Cassivellauni*, Caesar wrote 'The Britons call it an *oppidum* when they have fortified with a rampart and ditch dense woods where they are accustomed to gather to avoid an enemy attack', which has rather a rustic and impermanent implication, hardly fitting, for instance, contemporary Camulodunum; and far other were the Gaulish *oppida* such as Avaricum, a tribal centre of the Bituriges, who themselves, Caesar reports, regarded it as 'about the fairest town of all Gaul, the defence and pride of their nation', or Alesia, Bibracte, or Uxellodunum, the High Fort or indeed High Town (the Celtic *dunum* element may well be the

[33] Piggott, *Ancient Europe*, Chap. 5.

[34] Cunliffe and Rowley, op. cit.; A. L. F. Rivet, 'Hill-forts in action', in D. Hill and M. Jesson, *The Iron Age and its Hill-Forts* (Southampton, 1971), 189–202.

equivalent of Latin *oppidum*: it has a wide distribution, from Britain to the Balkans, in the Celtic world from the fourth to third century BC).[35] And a Czech archaeologist has recently pointed out that Cæsar 'quite clearly set down the hierarchy of settlements' in Celtic Europe when he described the Helvetii in 61 BC leaving their twelve *oppida*, 400 *vici* or villages, and *reliqua privata aedificata*, the farmsteads.[36] The good fortune of historical evidence makes us fairly confident that at least in the last few centuries BC, and by reasonable implication for some time before that, there were social units in continental Europe fulfilling the criterion I asked for at the beginning, status as a town 'in the eyes of its inhabitants and their neighbours'.

The literature of hillforts in Europe and Britain is enormous, and growing in significance as large-scale excavation at last reveals more of their internal planning: here Barry Cunliffe's ten years at Danebury in Hampshire is of course a shining record. An early and classic example from the sixth century BC is the Heuneburg in south Germany, a triangular promontory above the Danube, 300 m long and 200 m across its base with an extraordinary defensive wall of unbaked clay bricks on a stone base with a row of bastions along its landward face (Fig. 13). Both bastions and building techniques are Greek, and reinforce the evidence of Mediterranean contacts implicit in the imports from the site: Massaliote wine amphorae and Attic black-figure pottery of *c*.520–470 BC. The defences make one think of Celtic mercenaries returning from Greek service, rather than of wine-merchants: in contemporary burials in a barrow near by were silk embroideries and a quiver of Scythian-type arrows, just at the time, around 530–510, when Scythian archers were in Greek service.[37] One should not underrate the soldier of fortune who like Odysseus had seen the cities of many men.

The evidence of the later Celtic *oppida* of Europe (and probably too the hillforts of Thrace or Dacia) would appear to show the development of indigenous fortification techniques of long standing, and to provide the criteria demanded for ancient towns. Superficial areas may be very large, in part perhaps reflecting an economy where herds of cattle may need temporary protection within walls or ramparts; if Danebury is about the size of Troy, the walls of Manching in Bavaria, elaborately laced with iron-nailed timberwork

[35] H. Rix, 'Zur Verbreitung und Chronologie einiger keltischer Ortsnamentypen', in *Festschrift für Peter Goessler* (Stuttgart, 1954) 99–107; cf. Piggott, *Ancient Europe*, Fig. 96.

[36] Caesar, *BG* I.5; J. Bren, 'Earliest settlements with urban character in Central Europe', in Cunliffe and Rowley, op. cit. 81–94.

[37] Piggott, *Ancient Europe*, 183.

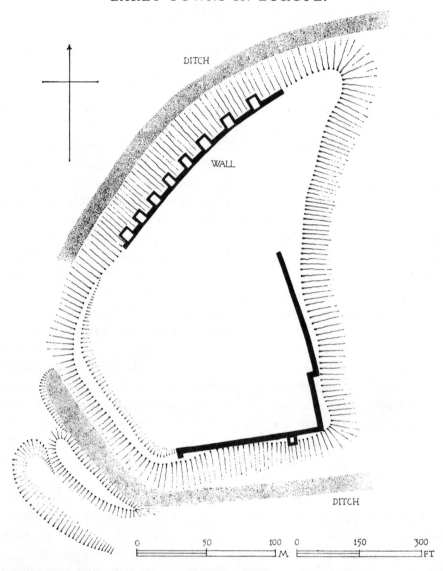

DITCH

WALL

DITCH

0   50   100   0   150   300

M   FT

FIG. 13. The Heuneburg hillfort, South Germany, with bastioned stone and clay-brick wall, Hallstatt
D culture, sixth century BC.

of a widespread Celtic type, would measure over 6 km in circuit. Fortification
bespeaks authority and command of communal labour and specialist skills,
and Manching in the first century BC consumed some 300 tonnes of iron spikes
in addition to unlimited timber, and to the Hallstatt Salt Lords we may add
the ironmasters of La Tène Germany. Temporal power under a ruler who

might eventually, as in Britain, call himself *rex* on his coinage, or have a kingly name himself, as Vercingetorix, is implicit in such strongholds, and increasingly excavations are revealing within hillforts sanctuaries and temple precincts indicative of spiritual and numinous prestige. And again as larger areas are excavated within the defences, evidence for orderly planning of usually timber buildings multiplies.[38] Trade is everywhere apparent archaeologically and confirmed by the texts—Caesar's account of the Venetic and British trade is only one example—and even if the long-distance trade in tin from the Cassiterides to Massalia, and that to Britain in Italian wine and Spanish oil and fish-sauce were respectively organized in late antiquity by Greek or Roman entrepreneurs,[39] their conduct must have employed native middlemen and used existing routes and transport facilities. The emergence of a merchant class in Celtic society centred on the *oppida* is surely not impossible, and perhaps the use of papyrus and stylus in the making of coins in south-east Britain from the early first century BC, better suggests literate merchants, accounts and bills of lading, than deathless verse and prose. Coinage, primarily likely not to have served in trade but 'to buy services or supplies or otherwise to meet inescapable obligations' such as for bribery or dowries, was certainly minted in some *oppida* in Britain and the Continent, but coin flan moulds, like the coinage, were not confined to them, and its circumstances of issue are still obscure.[40]

We have reached the end of our search for towns in prehistoric barbarian Europe, and surely found them in the *oppida* with more likelihood than in any of the earlier sites over which we have ranged. If Romanization had not overtaken them (and taken over their status and prestige as cantonal capitals) they might have approximated to the classical model, but only in so far as inchoate Celtic polity permitted. How far this very model brought about their emergence, and how far they grew from wholly indigenous social and economic circumstances, how much of innovation or conserving traditions may be implied, is perhaps something archaeology can never tell us.

[38] Piggott, op. cit. 216; Cunliffe and Rowley, *passim*.

[39] Caesar *BG*, III.8; cf. Strabo IV.194. Amphorae and their contents, D. P. S. Peacock, 'Roman amphorae in pre-Roman Britain', in Hill and Jesson, op. cit. 161–88.

[40] D. F. Allen, 'British potin coins: a review', in Hill and Jesson op. cit. 127–54; ibid., 'Wealth, money and coinage in a Celtic society', in J. V. S. Megaw (ed.), *To Illustrate the Monuments* (London, 1976), 200–8.

IV

THE CITY IN ANCIENT CHINA

WILLIAM WATSON

THE WALLED city on a rectangular plan has existed in China since the seventeenth century BC, first as the natural concomitant, in eastern no less than in western Asia, of Bronze-Age economy and polity, the creation of the lords of the plain in the age of 'anxiety, sacrifice and aggression';[1] and subsequently, until recent times, as a well-defined urban unit in which walls, gateways and guard houses, reticulated streets and centrally placed offices, all retained their function in administration. In China little survives besides fragments of boundary walls and a few foundation platforms to mark the place of ancient cities. In general the investigation of these remains has not yet been taken very far, even where the sites are quite abandoned and do not, as mostly appears to be the case, coincide with the location of modern towns. For the earliest period we are however fairly well informed on the broad design and to some extent on the function of two important foundations of the Shang dynasts, whose rule centred on the region of Honan during the second half of the second millennium BC. Here, on the middle course of the Yellow River, was the inventive nucleus of the bronze-based civilization, a place where two Neolithic traditions had met and mingled, where the primary, super-fertile loess of the west merged into the redeposited loess and river gravels of the wide deltaic region of the eastern plain. From Honan to the east the rural population was bound to the soil as much by the threat of flood and by the labour of containing the river (by late Neolithic times the middle course of the river must already have raised itself at places above the general level of the plain) as by the cultivation of the land. In both the western and the eastern parts of the Neolithic growth facilitated by the Yellow River, settled communities of unusual size had formed during the millennium which preceded the introduction of bronze metallurgy in the seventeenth or the sixteenth century BC.

[1] Lewis Mumford, *The Culture of Cities* (London, 1938).

In Kansu, Shensi, and Shansi the loessic terrain is sufficiently broken by ravines and hill spurs to provide a measure of isolation and protection for the settlements, which tended to retreat away from the mainstream along tributary valleys extending from the second terrace, and no traces of defensive walls or any rectangular arrangement of the village houses have been reported. The well-excavated type-site of the Yang-shao culture at Pan-p'o in Shensi, an area of 30,000 square metres measuring some 300 metres across, is far from being the largest of the settlements, if others may be judged from the surface indications. At Pan-p'o a part of the site is surrounded by a 6-metre deep trench, the purpose of which is not clear: it would have been poor defence that presented so great an obstacle to exit from the village, and the intention that it should serve to drain off rain water from the dusty (and so only slowly penetrable) surface of the loess is at least equally plausible. All the houses are said to have been contained within the curve of the deep trench, but there was much else beyond it: potting area, structures interpreted as cattle sheds, and the burial ground. The last, in Chinese tradition, deserved protection no less than the living quarters. If the run of trench has been correctly determined (a part remains unexcavated so this is not certain), one would surmise that the area which it enclosed would not give refuge for many more people than actually inhabited the houses, that is for some two or three hundred, so that the purpose was not to mark out and defend a ruler's demesne, in the Bronze-Age manner which is described below. We may guess at communal land-holding and perhaps agree with the excavators that the largest house was a general gathering-place and not a chief's residence. This house faced west—there was no regular orientation or pattern in the location of houses—and adhered to an old method of construction, far spread in East Asia, whereby the floor is sunk a little and the need for large timbers in the walls is avoided, only the central pillars being of any size. We know from the pollen count that high-growing timber was not to be had anywhere near.[2]

Archaeological data suggest that communities of this manifestly pre-city character continued unchanged in the western region until the use of bronze was introduced, at some time in the last two or three centuries of the second millennium, under the aegis of the Chou rulers. The latters' acquaintance with the polity and the arts of the city indeed seems strangely complete when they enter history as the conquerors of the Shang in the eleventh century BC. Thus far however no remains of pre-dynastic Chou date have been identified

[2] *An-yang Pan-p'o* (Archaeological Institute of the Academy of Sciences, Peking, 1963); W. Watson, 'Neolithic Settlement in East Asia', in P. Ucko *et al.* (eds), *Man Settlement and Urbanism* (London, 1972).

in the Chou *heimat* which might indicate an initial stage in progress towards the walled city and the organization of a city state. Farther east however, features typical of the first Bronze-Age urban culture are more clearly anticipated in a Neolithic context. At Ch'eng-tžu-yai near Dragon Mountain, Lung-shan, in Shantung, we see the eastern Neolithic at the point it had reached on the eve of bronze economy and of the establishment of Shang control throughout north China[3] (Fig. 14). The site is walled, and on a quite different scale from Pan-p'o, some 160,000 square metres being enclosed within the rectangle of its ramparts, these being raised on a platform of land strongly defensible on two sides where an escarpment falls steeply to the river. The soil is no longer pure loess, but gravelly, and could not be expected to retain the trace of habitations as clearly as they appear at Pan-p'o; but in the lack of any clear sign of house foundations it seems safe to assume that these were not sunk below the general surface in the Yangshao manner. The rectangle is aligned roughly north and south. The choice of an eminence for habitation follows the Neolithic custom of east China, as imposed by the conditions of the deltaic terrain, but the rampart and particularly the method of its construction introduce something new: layers of compacted soil, *pisé* (*hang-t'u*), each layer only a few centimetres thick and pounded hard with a tool-head equally small. The rampart measured about 8 m at the base, rising to about 6 m, with battered sides. At Ch'eng-tžu-yai the shapes of pottery vessels anticipate the shapes of some bronze vessels subsequently made in the Bronze Age, the practice of divination by cracking bone with heat is similar, and a number of potter's signs certainly resemble signs later identified as script characters in the oracular inscriptions of Shang. In view of these resemblances, are we to infer that the social processes which made possible the establishment of the city state, apart from the metal supply and the opportunity this gave for monopoly, were already well advanced in east China during the Neolithic period? The orthodox answer to this problem in present-day China is that the free communes of Neolithic farmers were at the beginning of the Bronze Age replaced by a uniform class of slave-owners established widely through the country; and the old Confucian view is maintained, that at this time began the age of emperors, whose writ ran through the whole of what became the territory of historical China. It is clear at least that the social order of the east-China Neolithic had changed in comparison with that of the more westerly Neolithic population. The size of the enclosure

[3] *Ch'eng-tzuu-yai* ..., ed. Li Chi *et al.* (translated in *Yale Publications in Anthropology*, no. 52, Yale Univ. Press, 1956).

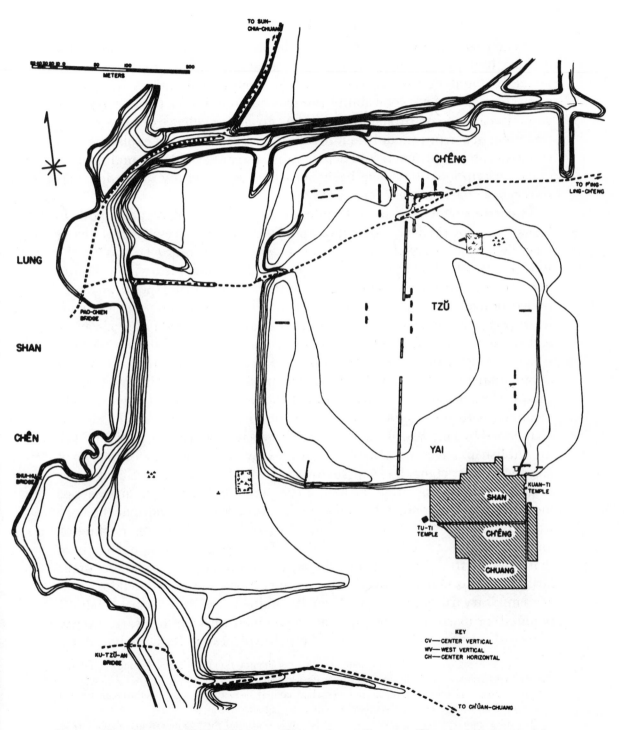

FIG. 14. The contours of the Neolithic site at Ch'eng-tžu-yai, Shantung. The raised earth around the western edge of the higher level appears to mark the line of a rampart of rammed earth. *c*.2000 BC.

at Ch'eng-tžu-yai and its rectangular shape, besides their implication for defence, hint also at changes of land tenure, and if the enclosure is seen as a refuge for population as well as the location of certain habitations, there is the suggestion of a new responsibility towards communities settled beyond the gates. Excavation on Bronze-Age sites has given no evidence of a chattel-like treatment of persons (mainly in funeral sacrifice) which is not explicable as a ritual dispatch of prisoners and dependants, and not even in the multifarious oracle inscriptions that have been unearthed is there any indication that slavery was basic to the economy.[4]

Two city sites of the second millennium have been excavated, both in Honan and both believed to be the capitals, occupied successively, of Shang kings, whose dynasty dates from the seventeenth century BC.[5] With the suddenness which characterizes much of East Asian history, the Shang dynasty introduces bronze-casting, chariot warfare, writing, politically controlled oracle-taking, and kingship and nobility, great tombs replete with treasure and human victims, all reflecting a totally changed order of society and a remarkably rapid advance of technique. The site of the earlier city, which has been the scene of successive excavations since 1956, coincides approximately with the perimeter of the modern town of Cheng-chou, in central Honan a short distance south of the Yellow River.[6] It is tentatively identified with the city of Ao named in the historical tradition, the capital abandoned by king P'an-keng in c. 1400 BC, when he moved north of the river to establish his government at the site now excavated near the modern town of Anyang. The rectangular wall surrounding the Shang city at Cheng-chou (Fig. 15), built by the same pisé method as that employed at Ch'eng-tžu-yai, measures 2 km from north to south and 1·7 km across. Its width at the base was about 20 m, so that it is thought to have risen to 10 m or more, the three or four metres' rise of a section which still stands suggesting an original height of that order. In straightness of the sides, north–south orientation and rectangularity of the corners the survey trace is tolerably accurate (its relation to a contemporary true north has not been determined) and the estimate of labour required for its construction—put at 10,000 men working for nearly twenty years—throws impressive light on the political power. Radiocarbon dates

---

[4] By far the best survey of the oracle sentences in an occidental language is Tsung-tung Chang, *Der Kult der Shang-Dynastie im Spiegel der Orakelinschriften* (Wiesbaden, 1970).

[5] The orthodox tradition puts the beginning of the Shang dynasty at 1765 BC. From the reconstructed text of the Bamboo Books Wang Kuo-wei calculated 1523 BC.

[6] The latest of a series of reports on excavations in and around the precinct of the Shang city at Cheng-chou appears in *Wen Wu*, 1977, no. 1. It gives the first results of radiocarbon dating for the wall.

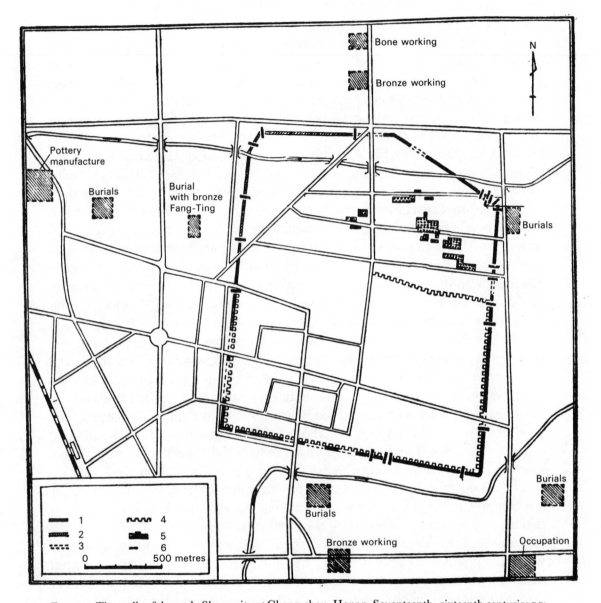

FIG. 15. The walls of the early Shang city at Cheng-chou, Honan. Seventeenth–sixteenth centuries BC:
1. Parts of the wall standing above ground; 2. Parts of the wall traced below the present ground surface;
3. Inferred continuation of the wall where nothing of it survives; 4. The line of the medieval wall; 5.
Building foundations of rammed earth; 6. Excavation cuttings.

from low-placed layers at one point of the wall give 1620 BC±135 and 1595 BC±135; it is found to be later than the initial-Shang site of Lo-ta-miao situated outside the wall, and contemporary with the lower level at the site of Erh-li-kang, whose deposits lie along the inner face of the wall. It thus appears certain that the Cheng-chou wall belongs to the first fully developed phase of Shang culture, and we may consequently attribute the political implications of its construction to the original political order of the Shang state itself. The rectangular plan probably accompanied a division of the land within the perimeter into regular rectangular insulae, an arrangement which is borne out by the alignment of the few *pisé* building foundations which it has been possible to identify within the walls. No gateways have yet been located, but it is a likely conjecture that the ceremonial direction was south, as it was in other, pre-Han cities where the internal features are better preserved. The ruler's palace would face south, as he would himself at audience. Some essential activities were carried on outside the walls: to the north a bronze-foundry and a workshop where bone objects were carved, these including cups made from human skulls; to the west a group of kilns, whose position recalls the like exclusion of the Pan-p'o kilns from the sector of the site occupied by houses; to the south another foundry. Apart from these industrial locations, a number of ordinary villages, dated by their pottery to the earliest years of the Shang period, are situated in some instances outside the wall but hard against it, and in other cases at distances of two or three kilometres. The chief of these, at Ehr-li-kang, lies about half a kilometre from the south-east corner of the city. The burials, both large and richly furnished and poorer graves, are located in defined areas some distance from the walls.

The romance of discovery attaches however not to the city of Ao, but to the site explored earlier by Academia Sinica near the village of Hsiao-t'un, a short distance to the north-west from the prefectural town of Anyang in north Honan (Fig. 16). Between 1928 and 1936 (that is, until the outbreak of war with the Japanese) excavation at this and some nearby places produced material which in the most literal sense laid the foundation for a new study of ancient China.[7] The *pisé* foundations of large buildings and the great shaft tombs (where two or four sloped approaches lead down to timber-built burial chambers) had been liberally furnished with sacrificial vessels, weapons and ornaments of bronze and other precious materials, and accompanied by no less liberal holocausts of human victims. The moralized and jejune picture of

[7] Li Chi, *Anyang* (Washington, 1977). This book gives the fullest account available in an occidental language of the course and results of the excavations undertaken by the Academia Sinica.

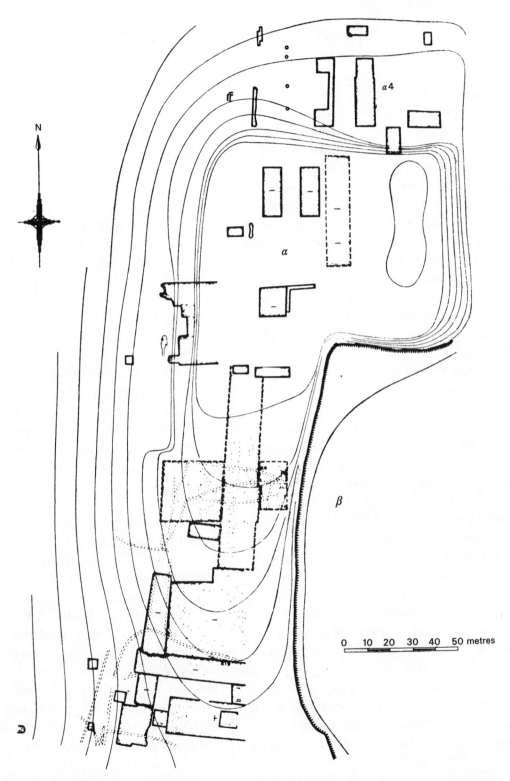

N

α4

α

β

0 10 20 30 40 50 metres

Fig. 16. The main excavation sectors at Hsiao-t'un.

the early state preserved in literary tradition faded in the dazzle of the revelation. Eventually the decipherment of sentences which were engraved on the fire-cracked scapulae and carapaces used for oracular response, supplied contemporary evidence for Shang government, religion and agriculture. The earliest bronze-using civilization of east Asia then appeared in much the same light as the comparable cultures of Mesopotamia and the Mediterranean, a despotism raised over tillers of the plain, formally a kind of theocracy, powerful and rich through the possession of abundant metal. Knowledge of the western Asiatic city state—established like the Shang state at the centre of a vast arable region and engaged in intermittent warfare with barbarian enemies on more or less distant frontiers—inevitably influenced the conclusion that was reached on the function of the city at Hsiao-y'un. But the view of this city as a political 'capital', apparently demonstrated by elaborately consecrated buildings and such items as the priceless archive of oracle texts located in store-pit H127, is still open to question and certainly must be qualified in the light of what is now known of the earlier Shang foundation at Cheng-chou.

When it is considered as a seat of government the most striking thing about Great Shang (as the Hsiao-t'un city seems to be designated in the oracle sentences) is the absence of a surrounding wall. Unlike the streams which passed through the Cheng-chou precinct, the Huan River which curves around Hsia-t'un on the north and east is wide enough to improve the defensiveness of the settlement had it been regarded in this way. But it seems not to have been so considered. Among all the *pisé* features located in excavation both before and after the Second World War, none lends itself to interpretation as a defensive rampart. Overbuilding during the Shang occupation and the disturbance caused by the lucrative probings of the local farmers in recent times hampered excavation, in particular obscuring the relation to the building foundations of a number of long ditches whose side had been reinforced with timber. The attention paid to drainage appears to be as elaborate and mysterious as the like feature at Mohenjodaro in the Indus valley. Rectangular *pisé* foundations were encountered in all sectors of the excavation. Those in the north, sector A, were well separated from each other and their outlines well defined, but a closer group of larger edifices existed in the southern sector C. The overlapping of the extremities of some of these podia appears to signify the connection of one edifice with another rather than casual rebuilding, and the interpretation of the whole as an integrated complex is supported by the siting of sacrificial pits along the sides of the podia, and within the space which the series of buildings enclosed. On the east the modern left bank of the Huan River is so close that it may be plausibly argued that buildings originally stood on this side too, so that the central space was wholly enclosed in a symmetrical scheme (Fig. 17). The ritual extravagance seen in the burials of chariots with their drivers, soldiers with weapons, servitors seated with fine bronze vessels, etc. (one might conclude that an entire contingent of Shang soldiery was consigned to the Yellow Springs), vouches well enough for the character of the buildings as palaces and temples, designed on a single rational plan of civic grandeur. The northern block of the complex (β_5) shows a uniquely elaborate trace along its western end (the eastern end having been destroyed by the river) and towards its centre a further elevation in the form of a rectangular platform built entirely of yellow earth. This last suggests the construction of a higher edifice using the principle of stepped podia which is described below from the ruins of a later city, and the existence of which is implied by the form of the Shang ideograph 高 *kao* (high), modified in modern script only by the substitution of a dot and horizontal for the original two-slope roof.

Other script characters reflect the use of timber in Shang architecture. On most of the *pisé* platforms largish flat boulders occurred sporadically, and on a podium α_4 of the northern Sector A a sufficient number of these pillar footings were preserved *in situ* to permit an interesting conjecture on the framing and roofing of the building (Fig. 18). The length of the foundation is 28 m, and its width 8 m narrowing at the north end to 7·3 m. It is doubtful whether timbers 8 m long could be got on the comparatively treeless plain. If the suggestion of a single ridged roof is correct we should perhaps assume that the longer pieces (required at points where no footing stone appears on the centre line) were imported from farther west: if the Egyptians could go to the Levant for their pillars, the Chinese could fetch theirs from the Shensi uplands. The roof can have been covered only with vegetable material, for no trace of clay or baked tiles was found. On α_4 the regularity of the bays and the sophistication of the pillar footings (elsewhere in one instance a dished bronze disc took the place of a boulder) show a system of trabeate architecture advanced from its Neolithic rudiments to a stage which is the start of the surviving tradition of East Asian architecture. In the northern sectors of the excavation there were many traces of industrial activity, in the manufacture of pottery, the carving of bone, ivory and jade; and not least in the casting of the ritual bronze vessels to which the art of Shang owes its fame more than to anything else. While fine bronze was produced at other places in the Shang territory, carved ivory,

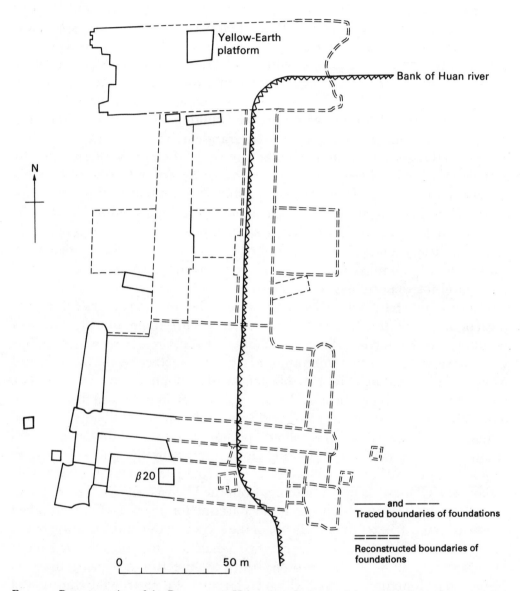

Yellow-Earth
platform

Bank of Huan river

N

β20

0   50 m

——— and — — —
Traced boundaries of foundations

====
Reconstructed boundaries of
foundations

FIG. 17. Reconstruction of the Beta area at Hsiao-t'un. Some surviving suggestions of symmetrical
arrangement are taken to indicate the symmetry of the whole plan, extending beyond the bank of the
Huan river whose westward erosion has been responsible for destroying much of the site.

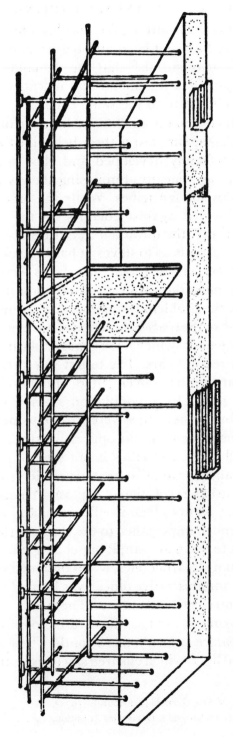

FIG. 18. Reconstruction of the building Alpha 4 at Hsiao-t'un, the position of pillar footings suggesting the bays and the framing of the roof.

ornate carved pottery made of pure kaolin and high-fired ceramic covered with thin felspathic glaze have not been attested beyond Hsiao-t'un and its immediate vicinity. We may surmise that the demands of ceremony and funeral paraphernalia provided a demand and incentive at the Shang city such as hardly existed elsewhere to the same extent.

Three views are expressed on the advent and function of the city under the rule of the Shang dynasts, the simplest of these being the theory now adopted in China: that as the economy developed and class contradictions grew sharper, cities were built as a means of imposing slavery on the population and repelling invasion by foreign tribes. While the oracle sentences often speak of expeditions directed against enemies 'of the directions', i.e. in remoter parts of the territory, the unwalled city at Hsiao-t'un does not itself suggest a clear military purpose; as to slaves, it has been observed above that Shang epigraphy gives no certain proof that slaves were recognized as a distinct group of the population on which production depended. Another conceptual approach to the problem is found in the recent attempt to bring China into the discussion of the *symbolic* function of ancient cities, in the terms of the theories of 'urban genesis' which have engaged the interest especially of American historians in recent years. The fullest interpretation along these lines sees the city built at a centre convenient for ritual assemblage, responding to a centripetal urge felt by a population sharing similar social and spiritual aspirations.[8] On this view cities were created to meet a popular need, and not at all as the instruments of an oppressive oligarchy or as a mere market-place. Above all the rise of cities is not seen to mark a revolution, social or technological, and a gradualist or static model is substituted for the doctrine of a beneficent urban revolution of explosive change and expansion.

At a glance China may seem to lend itself particularly well to the symbol theory, which attaches much importance to the shape of the city plan. Some Chinese medieval towns (e.g. Ch'ang-an, P'ing-chiang, the modern Sian, and Suchow), like some but not all earlier ones, were contained within rectangular walls, and the *yamen*, or administrative office, was located more or less at the centre of a rectangular intersection of streets.[9] The streets were parallel to the walls and aligned approximately to face the cardinal points; and if there was anything resembling a palace or fort, it faced south. These are features of the design, seen in a practical light, which ensured safety from an enemy within as

[8] Paul Wheatley, *The Pivot of the Four Quarters* (Edinburgh, 1971).
[9] Cf. Andrew Boyd, *Chinese Architecture and town planning* (London, 1962).

well as an enemy without; gates and rectangularity facilitated tolls and taxes, the regular shape was thought dignified as well as convenient. Through the Chinese heritage of shamanistic lore, with its belief in a central pillar which alone allowed communication between heaven and earth—a pillar any ruler would naturally wish to keep a watch on—the notion of a ruler's cosmic centrality was never far to seek. The first use of the term Central Kingdom, *chung-kuo*, as a description of the Chinese state occurs in the Book of Songs. Its use probably goes back at least to the early decades of Chou rule, when it denoted the status of the royal Chou city and territory which claimed to dominate the many-headed confederacy. But the idea is already present in the oracular phraseology of Shang from the fourteenth century, when barbarian enemies (or insubordinate subjects) are designated by the direction in which their territory lay: it is implied that the Shang ruler was at the centre, although this is nowhere stated. *Chung-kuo* remained for long an elastic term, denoting the capital city as well as the kingdom ruled from it, and could be replaced by 'central province', 'central land', even 'central soil', when the king's demesne rather than his capital was intended. Poetically speaking the capital might be called the ridge-pole of the four quarters, as in an eulogistic poem of the Book of Songs on which ritualistic interpreters largely base their argument.[10] An epithet in the verse is a doublet repeating a character meaning 'wing', 'assist'; but the import of such doublets is far from being systematically related to the original meaning of the repeated ideograph, and in this case the unambiguous gloss accepted since Han times is 'well-ordered' or 'majestic', and no mystical role of the capital city is suggested: whatever might be said of the irresistible transforming influence radiating from an emperor without his least effort, the power was attributed to his person and not to his capital city.

The pragmatic view is represented by Kaizuka's city-state theory which sees the Shang kingdom as a virtual theocracy, and interprets the rôle of its capital, the Hsiao-t'un foundation, to be not unlike that of the great Mesopotamian cities, even to the political function of an oracle-taking priest-hood.[11] Three spheres of Shang power are defined in accordance with the indications of the oracular texts and with later tradition:

(a) the city itself and its suburbs.
(b) a larger area extending around the city.

[10] James Legge, The Chinese Classics, IV, part ii, 646.
[11] Kaizuka Shigeki, *Chūgoku kodai shigaku no hatten* (Kyoto, 1946).

(c) the independent states on the Shang borders which more or less
acknowledged Shang supremacy.

Sacerdotal control apart, similar city-rule continued in the principalities of
the Chou confederacy which emerged as independent states from the eighth
century BC onwards: the city as seat of government, centre of trade and
manufacture, and not notably a ceremonial gathering-place in the sense of the
symbol theorists. The awkwardness which the absence of a defensive wall and
the prominence of ritual features present to Kaikuza's interpretation of
Hsiao-t'un as the political nucleus of a city-state is now removed by the
discovery of the earlier foundation at Cheng-chou.[12] Although, however, the
facts furnished by excavation on this site have been known for more than a
decade, their significance for the structure of the earliest Chinese state has
perhaps not been sufficiently grasped. The contrasting characters of the two
cities can be seen as complementary.

At Cheng-chou the large enclosed area still did not contain all the population of the place. It is most unlikely, as has been suggested, that this shows
merely that the precinct was overcrowded.[13] The Bronze-Age sites lying
outside the walls appear to continue directly from Neolithic predecessors, and
such important units as bronze-foundries are not likely to have been forced
out through lack of space. On the other hand the rectangularity of the wall,
and the suggestion of rectangular insulae of building within, are aspects to
which any interpretation must give priority. The scale of the enclosure
suggests that the needs of defence—if rectangularity, in the absence of
topographical features, is accepted as militarily advantageous—were
perhaps not in this case the first concern in design. If we may take a hint from
the methods of imperial rule in Japan at a time when Chinese tradition was
enthusiastically imitated, the existence of a vast walled precinct need not
conflict with the idea that much of the enclosed space remained vacant. In the
ninth century AD the area of the new Japanese capital was vast within its
rectangular limits, and neither then nor at any time up to the present day have
the thirty-odd square kilometres of Kyoto been built upon. The northern part
of the ancient city precinct is still country and farmland, while modern

---

[12] The Cheng-chou excavations have been complicated by the modern occupation and by the wide
dispersal of the features which could be investigated. The theory of the Cheng-chou/Hsiao-t'un
succession was launched by a typological study based on material recovered at Erh-li-kang, situated
outside the wall a short distance to the south-east: cf. Tsou Keng in K'ao-ku hsüeh-pao, 1976, no. 3, 77 ff.
('Shih lun Cheng-chou hsin-fa-hsien ti Yin-Shang wen-hua i-chih'.)

[13] As Cheng Tê-k'un in his Archaeology in China, III.

industry has expanded southwards beyond the southern limit of the original plan. In Japan the imperial capital was considered less as a seat of government than as the centre of the *chi* (*kinai*), the territory recognized to be under the personal rule of the emperor, and in his gift. By the concession of estates within the city limit, no less than by conferring territories lying beyond the *kinai*, the ruler might secure the loyalty of his subject clans and exercise surveillance over his court and officers; and by a rectangular plan of streets and blocks of building land the dignity of the palace was ensured, the allotment of estates and the maintenance of the divisions were facilitated. May not the Shang capital at Cheng-chou, built in the late seventeenth century BC, have observed the same principle? The warfare which the Shang ruler conducted at some distance from his city presupposes a hierarchy of loyalty and command such as would plausibly involve the allotment of land within the *chi* to noblemen and clansmen, furnishing these with the model of administrative dependence which it was the ruler's endeavour to transplant elsewhere among populations submitting to taxation and conscription. In supposing this we do no more than assume a state of affairs for the Shang period which history records rather fully from the beginning of the succeeding Chou dynasty. We have placed defence second as motive for constructing the huge rectangular wall of Cheng-chou; but in the last resort the city was also the ruler's stronghold and military camp, and his high rampart and straight thoroughfares held a tactical advantage for meeting intruders from without and insubordination within. As to the latter, one recalls that the Shang ideograph for *yi*, city, shows an enclosure, approximately square, over a man

kneeling in submission: 𝕭

What is known of Hsiao-t'un contrasts strangely with what is suggested above regarding the design and function of the earlier city. Besides the lack of wall and of rectangular divisions, it is singular that in all the thousands of sentences written on bone and carapace none is composed outside the requirements of the oracle rite, none concerns the mundane affairs of ruler or quartermaster, unless we count as such the questions put to the spirits regarding expectation of rain or the timeliness of military campaigns. It is difficult to avoid the hypothesis that the structures traced at Hsiao-t'un, uniquely large and elaborate, served a unique ceremonial purpose, and did not form part of a citadel functioning as the fulcrum of power exercised in a city state, despite its role in oracular consultation. Hsiao-t'un would then have been a Delphi to Cheng-chou's Athens. Moreover, the proximity of tombs of royal dimensions tallies conversely with the absence of the practical features of a capital city. In a ceremonial settlement the presence of artisans and industry supplying the needs of sacrifice and funeral would find its parallel in ancient Egypt. This hypothesis, running counter to the view which has been strongly held in China for nearly half a century, admittedly entails some difficulty: we shall have to argue that the many successive Shang capitals spoken of in history, if they ever existed, were residences of the Shang kings at times when Cheng-chou and the ceremonial town at Hsiao-t'un were flourishing, for between them these occupations cover most of the duration given in history to the dynasty as a whole. Perhaps these residences, royal dwellings for a short time, were the places named 'Yin-hsü', or the Waste of Shang, so that this name was not unique to the site investigated at Hsiao-t'un, to which it may have been wrongly attributed.[14] Even if the conflict of archaeological and historical evidence as to locations may be resolved by some such hypothesis, the objection which lies in the currently accepted dating of the two Shang cities is less easily disposed of. It is generally accepted that the Hsiao-t'un foundation, answering to the historical move of Pan-keng northwards, dates from about 1400 BC, so that no part of that site has been assigned to an earlier period; while it is no less received doctrine that the occupation at Cheng-chou ceased shortly after the establishment of the Hsiao-t'un city, with a minor indeterminate overlap. If these inferences are accepted, the suggestion of a dual concurrent role of the two cities, one governmental and military, the other ceremonial, must be rejected, and could only be revived if some other town site were discovered to fit the case better. Unfortunately no such site is at present known, although one walled Shang settlement of the middle period (fifteenth to thirteenth century BC?) has recently been excavated.[15] But it must be allowed that the archaeological

[14] Local tradition held that the Yin-hsü was somewhere near the modern town of Anyang, on its west side, and this belief can be traced back to medieval times. But there are historical objections to the location of the northern and final Shang capital at Hsiao-t'un. The view that Hsiao-t'un was not Yin-hsü, and that the Shang structures there composed only a funeral city, has been advanced with special force recently in Japan: cf. Miyazaki Ichisada, 'Chūgoku jōdai no toshi-kokka to sono bochi' (The ancient Chinese city state and its burial ground), *Tōyōshi kenkyū*, no. 28 (1970); but this author does not consider the implications of the identification of the Shang city at Cheng-chou. (The author thanks Dr Sarah Allan for drawing his attention to this paper.)

[15] cf. R. W. Bagley, 'P'an-lung-ch'eng: a Shang city in Hupei', *Artibus Asiae* XXIV (1977), 165 ff. The chief interest of this excavation lies in its evidence for the southerly extension of Shang civilization. The settlement at P'an-lung-ch'eng is dated to the 'Middle Shang', a classification which follows the Chinese relegation of certain sites characterized by comparatively primitive bronze-work, to an 'Early Shang' period. By its bronze Cheng-chou is also placed in a middle phase. How this periodization is to

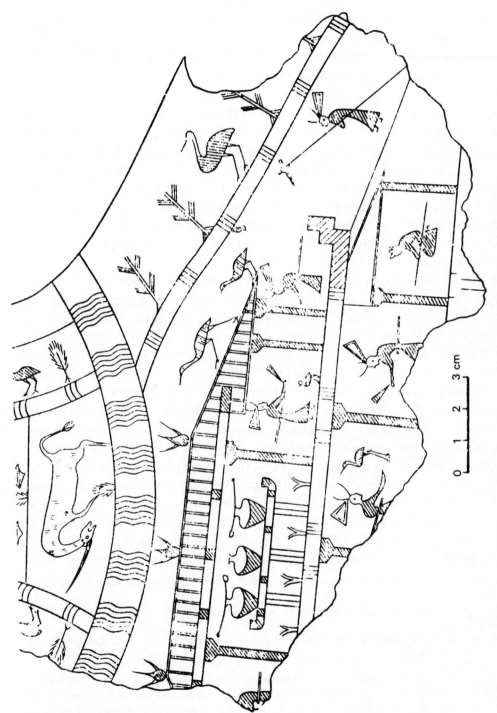

FIG. 19. Picture of a house engraved on a fragment of a bronze ladle found near Ch'ang-chih in Shansi. The illusion of an upper storey is created by the use of the terre-plein. Fifth–fourth century BC.

argument for the Cheng-chou/Hsiao-t'un succession is not wholly satisfactory, resting as it does on a typology whose dates cannot be established beyond question until more is known of the regional variation of vessel shapes and ornament during the Shang period.

It remains to say something of the appearance, in plan and from the ground, of the post-Shang capital cities. Of the first Chou city in central China, near Loyang in Honan, only part of the wall is known (Fig. 20). The north side is 3,000 metres long and has right angles at the returns. Even if it was only approximately square, the area it enclosed would have been four times that of the Han town on the same site.[16] During the following five or six centuries, from which state precincts on abandoned sites can be instanced, rectangularity was not after all the rule. Hsin-t'ien, capital of Wei, shows a rectilinear figure of seven sides; Lin-tzǔ, capital of Ch'i, spoils the rectangle with two large annexes, and Ch'ü-fu of Lu is quite irregular. T'eng, in Lu, had two rectangular walls, one inside the other. Hsia-tu, the 'lower capital' of the state of Yen, seems to have had an approximately square enclosure on the west, and another rectangle, less accurately traced, adjacent to the east. Along the junction and inside the western enclosure is a long, rampart-like feature of *pisé* which may be the foundation of a road (Fig. 21).[17]

Han-tan, capital of the state of Chao (Pl. 28), has two rectangular precincts sharing one wall, and here the internal features are well enough preserved to tell something of the elevation of the buildings (Fig. 22).[18] The subsidiary enclosures are adapted to the grandiose plan: one surmises that they did more than circumvallate a growing population. The main gate, in the south wall, was flanked by two towers, and in line with it, on a plan measuring 430 by 280 m was the dominating building, the Dragon Terrace, *Lung-t'ai*. In elevation the structure is seen to rise in five steps, so that the top surface measures only about one half of the ground trace. The whole mound is made of compacted earth, *hang-t'u*. The architecture which clothed such massive graded podia has only recently been elucidated, chiefly in the light of some

[16] cf. Ch'en Kung-ju, 'Lo-yang chien-pin Tung-Chou ch'eng-chih fa-chüeh pao-kao', *K'ao-ku hsüeh-pao*, 1959, no. 2, 15 ff.

[17] cf. Li Hsiao-tung, 'Hopei Yi hsien Yen Hsia-tu ku-ch'eng k'an-ch'a ho shih-chüeh', *K'ao-ku hsüeh-pao*, 1965, No. 1, 83 ff.

[18] cf. Harada Yoshito, *Han-Tan. Excavations at the Ruins of the Capital of Chao* (Tōa-kōko-gaku-kwai, Tokyo and Kyoto, 1954).

be affected by the radiocarbon dates now available for the Cheng-chou wall remains to be seen. It does not follow in principle that such comparatively rudimentary metallurgy necessarily indicates a much earlier date, since Shang bronze technique even in its simpler products is already well advanced.

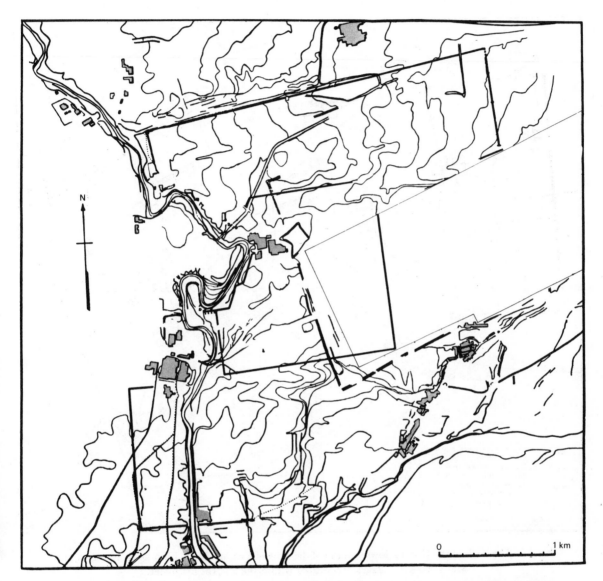

FIG. 20. The wall of the capital of the Chou state in Honan, eighth–seventh century BC. The surviving part is seen as the segment of a rectangle in the upper half of the figure. The smaller square enclosure occupying territory which lay within the Chou city marks the site of the Han dynasty prefectural town of Honan.

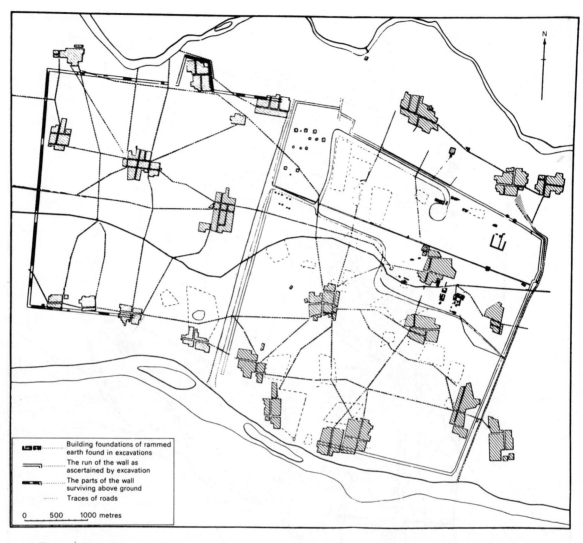

Legend:

Building foundations of rammed earth found in excavations
The run of the wall as ascertained by excavation
The parts of the wall surviving above ground
Traces of roads

0   500   1000 metres

FIG. 21. The walls of the Hsia-tu, lower capital of the state of Yen, in Hopei. Fifth–fourth century BC. Many modern villages are located within the ancient perimeter.

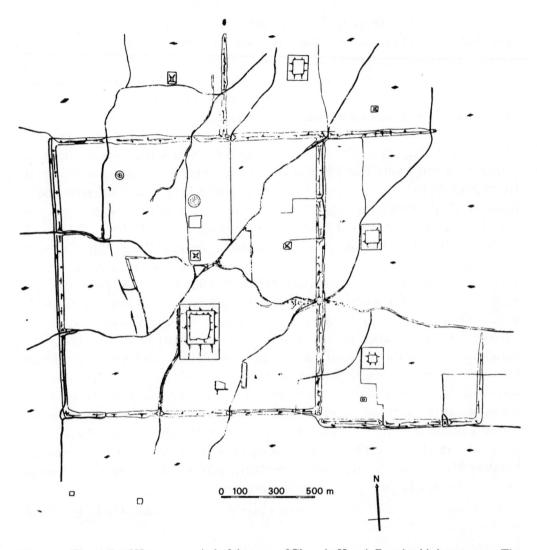

FIG. 22. The walls of Han-tan, capital of the state of Chao, in Hopei. Fourth–third century BC. The large structure at about the centre of the southern half of the main rectangle is the Lung-t'ai, or 'Dragon Terrace'.

elevations of buildings engraved on fragments of bronze recovered in excavation (Fig. 19). These show pillar-and-beam structures, typical of Chinese wooden edifices, apparently consisting of two storeys. But in the trabeate technique upper storeys were out of the question, and another explanation must be found. This is supplied by the rectangular mounds to be seen at Han-tan and some other sites: the mounds can only have served as the core, a terre-plein, on which successive galleries were raised, each set back from the one beneath (Fig. 23). The 'spirit terrace' of Chou kings was no doubt a structure of this kind. The possibility that the same method was followed in the Shang period in order to achieve impressive height was inferred above from the shape of an ideograph, and where in the Hsiao-t'un excavations one *pisé* platform appears raised on the surface of another (cf. the Yellow-earth Platform, *Huang-t'u-t'ai*, β, situated towards the middle of the elaborate foundation β5 in Sector B, and a similar eminence β21 on the very large podium β20 in Sector C) one may conclude that the same principle was adopted. At Han-tan some surviving rows of pillar footings indicate the bays which lined the terraces. Given the great length of the terraces, and on the assumption, which appears necessary, that the height of each gallery was enough to cover the vertical rise of the terre-plein, one may picture an elevation of imposing size and elaboration. The Dragon Terrace bore the largest building, but others of comparable scale were aligned on the same north–south axis, in addition to some isolated off-centre structures. Symmetry was observed in the principal elevations no less than in their location in plan. The method of terre-plein building appears to have survived into the Western Han period (second to first centuries BC), when some foundations as excavated must be interpreted on these lines.[19]

[19] cf. Wang Shih-jen, 'Han Ch'ang-an-ch'eng nan-chiao li-chih chien-chu', *K'ao-ku*, 1963, 501 ff.

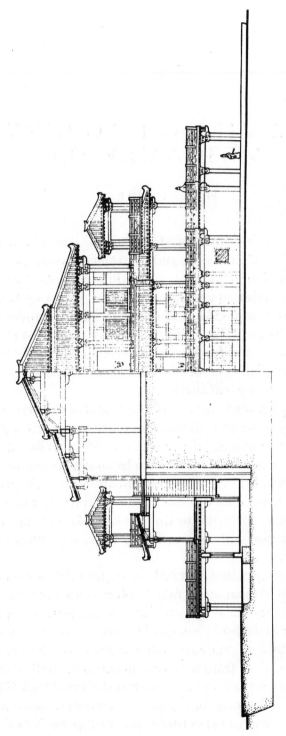

FIG. 23. Reconstruction of a house whose foundations were excavated in a suburb of Sian Shensi. First century BC. The central terre-plein rises to the level of what appears from the front to be a second storey.

V

FROM VILLAGE TO CITY IN MESOAMERICA

WARWICK BRAY

THE SUBJECT of this study is Mesoamerica—in archaeological usage, those parts of Mexico, Guatemala, and the adjacent countries which eventually became centres of high civilization. Within this area the basic ecological division is between highland and lowland zones. The highlands are arid or semi-arid, with broken topography and with mountain ranges separating the major valleys and basins. The lowlands (the coastal strips and much of the Maya zone) are hot, humid, and forested. The distinction between highland and lowland regions is one of the principal themes running through Mesoamerican archaeological literature.

In time, the story begins with the establishment of the first farming villages around 2000 or 1500 bc in radiocarbon years, or about 2500 BC in solar years—and this introduces the first problem. Why did permanent settlements appear so late in Mesoamerica by comparison with, say, the Near East, where town life had begun by 7000 BC and was widespread by 6000?

We have still no satisfactory answer to this question. There is no obvious environmental reason, nor can it be due to lack of knowledge about farming, for the first experiments with cultivation in Mexico go back to 5000 bc and perhaps long before that.

I have an uneasy suspicion, backed up by no evidence whatsoever, that village life in parts of Mesoamerica may be older than we think. In the present state of information, the most ancient farming villages, occupied on a year-round basis, appear in the archaeological record simultaneously with the first pottery. This may be a coincidence. Knowledge of the Preceramic period is limited, and comes mainly from surface collections at shallow or eroded sites, or else from excavations in caves and coastal shell middens. There has been little interest so far in looking for the flimsy remains of open-air settlements like those we have come to expect from the European Mesolithic.

All too often, excavation has consisted of deep 2 × 2 m test pits (what one of my colleagues unkindly calls 'telephone booths') designed to recover pottery stratigraphy, but not much use for anything else. We had to wait until 1969 for the first excavation of a large area, and for the first complete plan of a Mexican village of the early Ceramic period. Predictably, the work was directed by a graduate student who arrived on the scene with a fresh eye and a lack of respect for tradition. Ignoring the nearby mounds (one of them 17 m high), and amid general local scepticism, he chose a shallow site called Tierras Largas, with no surface architecture and only 30 cm of deposit. Stripping off the overburden, he found complete house floors with artefacts still in place.[1]

This kind of experiment should be repeated more often on open air *Preceramic* sites. When the stripping technique was tried at the nearby Preceramic site of Gheo-Shih, dated to the fifth millennium bc, a time when seasonal mobility was still the rule, it allowed the excavators to define flintworking, seed-grinding and butchering areas, and it also unearthed architecture of a sort, in the form of two parallel rows of boulders delimiting a clean, swept area that may have been a dance ground or something of the kind.[2] Nobody could call Gheo-Shih a village—let alone a town—but this is surely the way to find Preceramic villages if they exist.

The best place to look might be in riverine or lagoon areas, where fish and molluscs can be obtained at all seasons of the year. In this kind of locality, sedentism (based on wild resources) may be expected to precede effective agriculture.[3] Sites of just this kind have been claimed from lowland Veracruz, though the evidence for sedentism is ambiguous.[4]

By contrast, highland resources consist mainly of seasonal plant foods, and in this region what may have delayed the advent of settled life is simply the lack of a staple crop. Archaeological specimens of maize from dry caves (from 5000 bc to the Spanish conquest) show that more than three thousand years of genetic selection were needed to develop races capable of sustaining full-time

---

[1] Kent V. Flannery (ed.), *The Early Mesoamerican Village* (New York, San Francisco, London, 1976) (hereafter *EMV*), Chap. 2.

[2] K. V. Flannery, *EMV*, 51–2, 353–4.

[3] W. Bray, 'From predation to production: the nature of agricultural evolution in Mexico and Peru', in *Problems in Economic and Social Archaeology*, ed G. de G. Sieveking, I. H. Longworth, K. E. Wilson (London, 1976), 73–95.

[4] S. J. K. Wilkerson, 'Pre-Agricultural Village Life: The Late Preceramic Period in Veracruz', *Contributions of the Univ. of California Archaeological Research Facility*, 27 (1975), 111–22.

agriculture. Among modern Zapotec Indians, it is not considered worthwhile to plant maize if the yield is less than 250 kg of shelled kernels per hectare. With the large modern races this is no problem, but it was not until about 2000 bc (when cobs were still only one fifth of today's size) that this critical threshold was reached, and then only on the best land. This is just the time when the first villages of pottery-using farmers appear in the highlands, few in number and always on the most productive soils.[5]

THE NATURE OF TOWN LIFE IN PRE-SPANISH MEXICO

From these little farming hamlets, the development into towns and then into cities was continuous and fairly rapid, though the distinction between one category and another is not always easy to draw.

Even a cursory glance through the theoretical literature shows that there is still no generally accepted definition of what constitutes a town. The main division is between those writers who concentrate their attention on *formal* criteria (size, degree of nucleation, and so on), and those who give primacy to *functional* matters (diversity of services, existence of a market, specialization of labour, presence of a governing élite, and things of that sort). All of us are agreed, however, that a town is not just a large village, but something different. Archaeologically, this 'something different' ought to show up in the process of development as a kind of *discontinuity*, a sudden jump to a new level of complexity.

As a point of departure, we can begin by examining what the concept of 'the town' meant to the native Mexicans themselves.[6] It turns out to be something that would have been quite familiar to Plato, Aristotle, or even Machiavelli.

For the period covered by indigenous Mexican chronicles (i.e. the last few centuries before the Spanish conquest) the only stable political unit was the city state, consisting of a single capital town with its supporting area of rural villages and hamlets. Inter-state alliances broke up and re-formed, conquest empires rose and fell, but throughout it all the individual towns retained their identities.

This city state pattern is an old one in Mesoamerica, and can be recognized archaeologically by the first millennium before Christ. But before passing on

---

[5] A. V. T. Kirkby, 'The Use of Land and Water Resources in the Past and Present Valley of Oaxaca', *Mem. Univ. Michigan Mus. Anthropology* 5 (1973).

[6] W. Bray, 'The City State in Central Mexico at the Time of the Spanish Conquest', *Jl. Latin American St.* 4, 2 (1972), 161–85.

to the archaeological evidence we must look a bit more closely at the towns and states of the sixteenth century AD.

The state was much more than the sum of its territories. It was a focus for national loyalty; its market integrated the urban and rural sectors of the economy, and the town provided all the services we associate with government and official religion. Whatever its size and layout, the town was something functionally different from the village.

This has put the emphasis where I believe it should go—on function rather than form. To the Mexicans themselves (and this is abundantly documented) the single most important characteristic of a 'town' was a *political* one. A town was the seat of an independent ruler, the centre of his government and administration. All other criteria were secondary, including those (like population size, density of housing, and relative proportions of farmers to non-farmers) which figure so prominently in the theoretical discussions.

This is not to imply that all towns were identical in size, or were equal in power and status. Taking the Basin of Mexico alone—an area which a tourist can cover by car in a single day—there were in 1519 some fifty to sixty semi-autonomous city states, each with its own ruler. Most of these states were small, with 8,000–30,000 subjects and an average territory of 100–200 km². Few state capitals had more than 10,000 inhabitants, and most of them had no more than 5,000. In this setting, two cities stand apart from the rest: Texcoco (with 20–30,000 people packed into 4 km² and the Aztec capital at Tenochtitlan (a metropolis of 12 km² with 150–200,000 inhabitants).

All the smaller states paid tribute to one or both of these two large cities. When the Spaniards arrived, Tenochtitlan and Texcoco in alliance were extorting goods, raw materials, and services from nearly five hundred vassal states, scattered over a large part of Mexico from the Atlantic to the Pacific.

The development of these imperial superpowers adds a further dimension to the pattern. This can be expressed in the form of a diagram (Pl. 29a). At the top of the hierarchy are the few superpowers, much larger and more powerful than the other towns. Below them are the ordinary city states, more numerous but much smaller, though qualifying as towns by definition. Below these are the dependent villages, hamlets and isolated farmsteads. Each tier owed allegiance to the one above it, to which it paid taxes and labour service.

This is not just a theoretical scheme. We are talking about things which are reflected in the archaeological record, and which an archaeologist can go out and look for in the field. We should be looking for evidence of size differences and spatial patterning among sites, for the first signs of public buildings (temples and palaces), for market places and evidence of long-distance trade and craft specialization; also for differences between rich and poor, governors and governed, between those who live in stone houses and are buried with rich offerings, and those who live in cane or adobe huts and who die with little fuss.

At the same time, we are studying a landscape—not just a topographical landscape, but a social, political, and economic landscape in which the town is just one element. In terms of our pyramid model, we are looking for the moment when inequalities and discontinuities first appear, when certain settlements grow at the expense of their neighbours and turn into something larger and functionally different; into *towns*.

THE BASIN OF MEXICO SURVEY

The value of studying a total landscape rather than individual sites is best illustrated by the work of the Basin of Mexico Survey. Since 1960, teams of archaeologists have carried out a field-by-field survey of more than 6,000 km^2 (that is, about 60 per cent of the entire Basin) and have located several thousand sites, ranging from hunting camps to towns and cities, and spanning some 3,000 years.[7] Inevitably, most of these sites have not been excavated, or even tested.

Settled life began there in about 1200 bc, but before 800 bc the Basin contained only a few hamlets and small villages. Its later history can be shown through a series of maps (Fig. 24) covering the eastern half of the survey area.[8]

800–500 bc The population of the Basin is clearly growing, with new settlements established on the best farmland up to the 2,500 m contour.

500–200 bc Signs of differentiation are evident. Some sites are larger than others, and Cuicuilco may have had about 7,500 inhabitants. Town life is well established. In terms of relative size and ranking, the two lowest tiers of our pyramid are clearly recognizable.

[7] Eric R. Wolf (ed.), *The Valley of Mexico: Studies in Prehispanic Ecology and Society* (Albuquerque 1976) (hereafter *VM*) with full refs.; P. Tolstoy, 'Settlement and Population Trends in the Basin of Mexico', *Jl. Field Arch.* 2 (1975), 331–49; P. Tolstoy, S. K. Fish, M. W. Boksenbaum, K. B. Vaughn, 'Early Sedentary Communities in the Basin of Mexico', *Jl. Field Arch.* 4 (1977), 91–106.

[8] Based on J. R. Parsons, 'The Development of a Prehistoric Complex Society: A Regional Perspective from the Valley of Mexico', *Jl. Field Arch.* 1 (1974), 81–108.

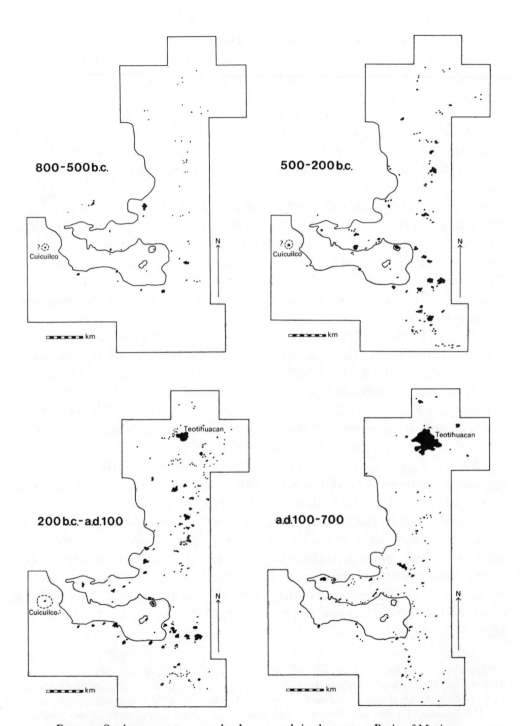

800-500 b.c.

Cuicuilco

500-200 b.c.

Cuicuilco

200 b.c.-a.d.100

Teotihuacan

Cuicuilco

a.d.100-700

Teotihuacan

FIG. 24. Settlement patterns and urban growth in the eastern Basin of Mexico.

200 bc–ad 100   Cuicuilco grows to its maximum size of *c*.400 ha and 20,000 people, and has several large, stone-faced platforms. Since the town was subsequently buried under a lava flow, its precise nature remains uncertain, though it has irrigation canals which may be of this age.

In the northern part of the Basin a new centre of power begins to emerge at Teotihuacan, now a town with several thousand inhabitants, with small-scale public architecture and indications of obsidian workshops. From the first century BC, with Cuicuilco destroyed by a volcanic eruption, Teotihuacan was left without a serious rival.

By the end of this period, around AD 100, Teotihuacan had grown into a city spread over 17 km^2, with an estimated 30–60,000 people.[9] Buildings were laid out according to a grid plan that allowed for future growth, and one of the largest temple pyramids in Mesoamerica (the 'Pyramid of the Sun') was almost finished. The superpower status of Teotihuacan is now beyond doubt, and our three-tier settlement hierarchy is archaeologically documented.

The mature city of Teotihuacan is described in a later section. As a final methodological point, what the series of maps shows (and what could never have been demonstrated from individual sites studied in isolation) is that the rapid growth of Teotihuacan was at the expense of the rest of the Basin, most of whose population was drawn into the growing metropolis. Between AD 100 and 600, almost 90 per cent of the total population in the eastern part of the Basin was concentrated at Teotihuacan.[10]

This is a truly massive restructuring, and it makes a complete break with the former pattern. The old power centres were eliminated and the rural population was relocated thinly but evenly over the Basin in small settlements, rarely larger than 10 ha or 500 people. Many of these little settlements were new foundations. Where, previously, ecological considerations had governed the choice of site locality (with the biggest settlements on the best land), we now see something new: a landscape created by planners, with the natural course of development overridden by political considerations. Teotihuacan is a bureaucrat's dream—a planned city in a planned landscape.

---

[9] R. Millon, 'Social Relations in Ancient Teotihuacán' in *VM*, 205–48; id., 'The study of urbanism at Teotihuacan, Mexico' in *Mesoamerican Archaeology: New Approaches*, 335–62, ed. N. Hammond (London, 1974); G. Cowgill, 'Quantitative studies of urbanism at Teotihuacan' in N. Hammond, op. cit., 363–96.

[10] J. R. Parsons, 'Teotihuacan, Mexico, and its impact on Regional Demography', *Science* 162 (1968), 872–7.

And, with this, we are back to where I began—with the town as a political phenomenon.

FROM HAMLET TO CITY IN THE VALLEY OF OAXACA

The most complete information comes, of course, from a combination of landscape survey with selective excavation. These two approaches were used simultaneously in a study, directed by Kent Flannery, of the Valley of Oaxaca.[11] Like the Basin of Mexico, Oaxaca is in the semi-arid highlands, though at a lower altitude ($c.$ 1550 m). The Valley is Y-shaped, formed by the meeting of the Atoyac and Salado rivers, and offers one of the largest expanses of level farmland in southern Mexico (Fig. 25).

Settled life may have begun in Oaxaca before 1600 bc, but the picture does not become clear until about 1300. Over the next thousand years we can trace, though not completely explain, the development of town life and the emergence of large, centralized political states.

By about 1300, the Valley contained more than a dozen permanent agricultural hamlets of three to ten households. Those in the northern arm of the Valley were spaced evenly along the river, situated on low spurs adjacent to the best farmland, in this case alluvial soils with the water table less than 3 m below the surface, allowing simple pot irrigation. In the south-east branch of the Valley, where the main river is less reliable, the settlements were on higher ground where piedmont tributaries could be tapped to provide irrigation water.

Tierras Largas at this stage is typical of the group as a whole. It consisted of ten rectangular wattle and daub houses, each of a size to accommodate a single nuclear family. Around each house were earth ovens, bell-shaped storage pits, and a number of burials. There were no public buildings, and no obvious differences in wealth or status. Each family engaged in farming and hunting, and made its own tools from local chert or from obsidian imported from up to 400 km away. In addition, most households engaged in part-time craft activities, in particular the manufacture of ornaments from shells brought in from the Pacific coast.

Sites of this period are uniformly small, and none of them could be called a town. But there are already signs of that differentiation which is to be a feature of the next five centuries. Only two communities (Tierras Largas and San

[11] *EMV*; K. V. Flannery and J. Marcus, 'Formative Oaxaca and the Zapotec Cosmos', *American Scientist* 64, 4 (1976), 374–83.

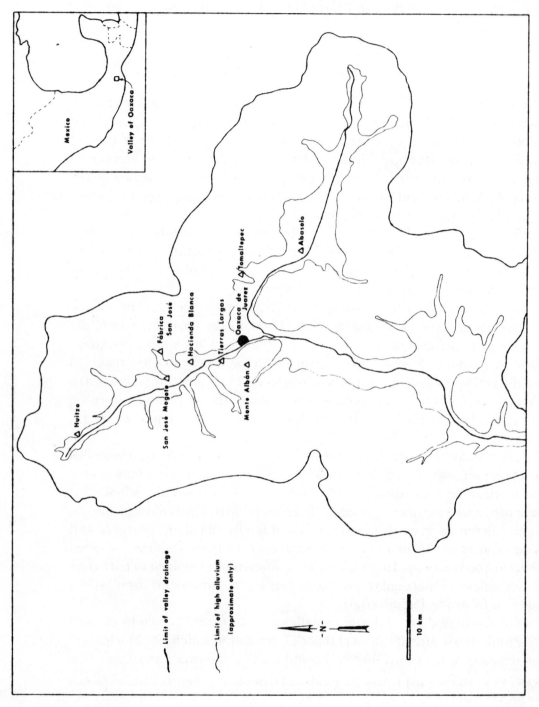

FIG. 25. The valley of Oaxaca, showing the modern city of Oaxaca de Juarez and archaeological sites mentioned in the text.

Jose Mogote) have archaeological evidence of shell working, and only the largest village (San Jose) has public buildings of any form.

At San Jose was found a substantial one-room structure (Pl. 30). Its walls had a core of pine posts, interspersed with wattle and daub, and it was set on a low platform. Walls and floor were covered with lime plaster, renovated several times. Against the southern wall stood a low bench or altar, and in the middle of the floor was a pit filled with powdered lime of the kind used to make the wall plaster.

At this time there was no discontinuity in site size. All were small, and San Jose was only fractionally larger than its neighbours, but—whatever this slight difference may have meant in terms of power or prestige—it was enough to set the pattern for subsequent development in the Valley.

In the period between 1150 and 850 bc we find just the kind of sudden discontinuity that we have been looking for. All the other Valley settlements remained small, but San Jose grew rapidly. From the original nucleus, it expanded to cover an area of 20 ha (45 acres), with 80–100 households. By 850 it was ten times the size of the next largest site, and by 550 it was fifteen times the size of the average settlement in the Valley. By this time we have clear evidence of a two-tier settlement hierarchy, and can reasonably call San Jose a 'town'. And San Jose retained its dominant status throughout. As the excavators point out, 'Nearly half the *regional population growth* of the Valley of Oaxaca between 1500 and 500 BC can be attributed to the growth of a single large nucleated village. That village [San Jose] added 5 ha. to its size every century for roughly 700 years.'[12]

San Jose in 950 was not only larger than its rivals, but it offered a greater range of services. It had the only public buildings in its arm of the Valley, and also a greater variety of craft trades. Design similarities in pottery decoration suggest that the outlying hamlets of Tierras Largas, Abasolo, and Fábrica San Jose were more closely linked to San Jose than to any competing centre, and were perhaps dependent on the services it provided.[13]

The town itself was physically divided into wards separated by unoccupied gullies, and there are strong indications that the population of San Jose Mogote was divided into two descent groups, each with its own symbols. At this time the finest pottery in Oaxaca is decorated with incised designs originating from the Gulf Coast, the homeland of Olmec civilization. Most of the patterns are stylized representations of two supernatural beings: the

[12] M. C. Winter, *EMV*, 229.   [13] S. Plog, *EMV*, 262–72.

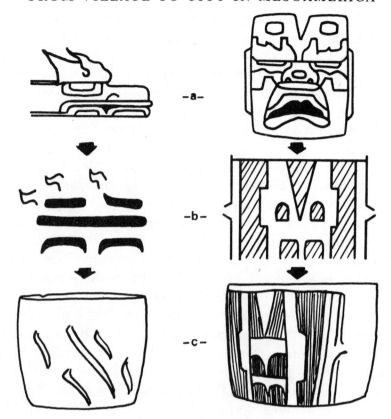

FIG. 26. Olmec fire-serpents and were-jaguars. (a) realistic version (b) stylized, abstract form (c) pottery from Oaxaca: left, with an infant burial at Abasolo; right, from a house at Tierras Largas.

fire-serpent and the *were-jaguar* (Fig. 26). The distribution of these two motives is mutually exclusive. Fire-serpent designs, on black or grey pots, dominate at the hamlets of Tomaltepec and Abasolo, and in the houses of the east and west wards at San Jose; were-jaguars, on white or yellow vessels, predominate in the southern ward at San Jose and in the outlying hamlets of Huitzo and Tierras Largas.[14] The were-jaguar and the fire-serpent seem to have been spread all over Mesoamerica under Olmec influence, and they occur together, carved in stone, as far away as Tzutzuculi on the Pacific coast of Chiapas.[15]

At this time, too, social distinctions are recognizable within San Jose itself.

[14] N. M. Pyne, *EMV*, 272–82; Flannery and Marcus, op. cit., 1976.
[15] A. J. McDonald, 'Two Middle Preclassic Engraved Monuments at Tzutzuculi on the Chiapas Coast of Mexico', *Am. Antiq.* 42, 4 (1977), 560–6.

People of high rank lived in houses raised on platforms, but the ordinary families occupied one-room structures with walls of cane covered by mud and whitewashed plaster (Fig. 27). Floors were strewn with clean sand and covered with mats made of woven reeds. The distribution of artefacts suggested that each sex had its traditional work area—women at the north end (where there is a concentration of cooking pots, grinding stones, and corn huskers), men at the south end (with chipping waste and the debris of craft activities).

One house, for example, belonged to a part-time shell worker. In a corner of the hut was his workspace, littered with cut and drilled fragments of imported sea shells, and with chert drills and burins that he knapped on the spot.

The surface of one small field on the east edge of San José produced more than 500 pieces of iron ores (ilmenite and magnetite) of the kinds used to make little polished mirrors about the size of a thumb-nail. These raw materials came from sources some distance away in the Valley, and the finished mirrors were exported to several parts of Mexico.[16] Although San José is not the site closest to the ore deposits, it seems to have had a monopoly of the industry, for it is the only site in Oaxaca to have produced manufacturing waste.

Trade networks now linked centres of production and consumption all over Mexico. San José imported its obsidian from seven different sources scattered from highland Guatemala to central Mexico. In return for the mirrors and Fine Grey pottery which it exported, all kinds of materials flowed into San José. From the Gulf Coast came turtle-shell drums, and the conch shells which the people of San José made into ceremonial trumpets. The Tehuantepec region of the Pacific coast sent pearl oysters, conch shells, thorny oysters, and ritual paraphernalia such as the stingray spines and shark teeth used in bloodletting rituals, or the blue macaws whose wing feathers were used in dance costumes. It is probably no coincidence that Laguna Zope, in the shell-exporting region of Tehuantepec, was one of the biggest sites of its time in Mesoamerica, and covered about twice the area of San José.[17]

The social stratification recognizable at San José can also be seen (albeit to a lesser degree) at other sites in Oaxaca. To the north of San José, at Barrio

[16] J. W. Pires-Ferreira, *EMV*, 311–28.

[17] R. N. Zeitlin, 'Long-Distance Exchange and the Growth of a Regional Center: An Example from the Southern Isthmus of Tehuantepec, Mexico', in *Prehistoric Coastal Adaptations: The Economy and Ecology of Maritime Middle America*, eds B. L. Stark and B. Voorheis (New York, San Francisco, London 1978), 183–210.

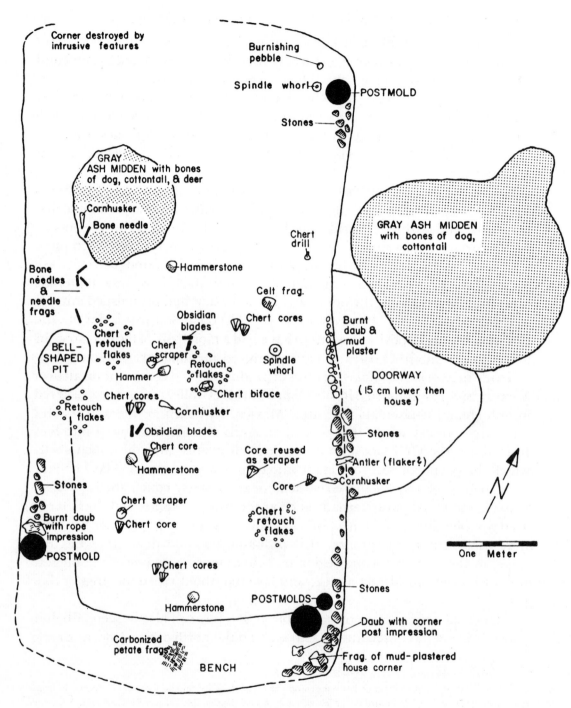

FIG. 27. Plan of a house at Tierras Largas, Oaxaca, with select artefact categories plotted on the floor. Late San Jose period, about 900 bc.

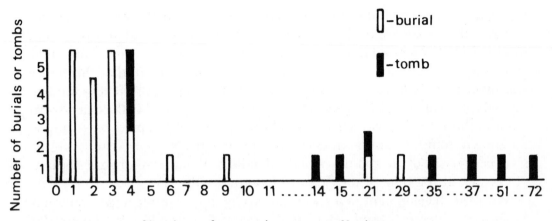

FIG. 28. Late Formative burials in Oaxaca. The range of wealth and status is reflected by the number of funerary offerings. Richer individuals tend to be buried in stone-built tombs, while the poor are interred in simple graves.

Rosario Huitzo, a minor centre of power (and possible competitor) had emerged by 900 bc. Here, a large mound was sectioned, and proved to contain superimposed floors, platforms, and adobe walls. Although the site is much smaller than San Jose, 13 per cent of its total area was given over to public buildings of one sort or another.

During the succeeding Guadalupe phase (850–550) the processes of growth and differentiation continued, with power passing more and more into the hands of an élite class. Rich burials start to appear, and some of these were of children. Since these infants had not lived long enough to *earn* prestige in the community, their wealth and status must derive from family position—an indication that rank may now have been inherited.

By the sixth century (the Rosario phase), burials range from simple interments with one or two pots, to masonry tombs containing jade trinkets and large numbers of vessels[18] (Fig. 28).

At San Jose Mogote, a natural hill in the centre of the town was covered with a group of masonry buildings orientated to the cardinal points. Limestone blocks weighing up to two metric tons were transported from the other side of the river, but the most significant feature of this acropolis was a carved stone that served as a threshold in a passage between two of the main

[18] M. C. Winter, 'Late Formative Society in the Valley of Oaxaca and the Mixteca Alta', paper to XLI Int. Cong. Americanists, Mexico, 1974.

buildings.[19] Carved on the stone is a naked and awkwardly spraaled human being, with closed eyes. On his chest is a scroll-like pattern that may represent flowing blood. Among later Mesoamerican peoples these conventions indicated slain or sacrificed captives, and it is surely no accident that this figure was placed where it would be trampled underfoot. Beneath the legs are two hieroglyphs which may be read as One Earthquake, probably the calendrical name of the individual carved on the slab. This is the oldest piece of writing so far known from the Americas, and it is also evidence for the existence in the sixth century bc of the 260-day ritual calendar still in use among the Indians of Oaxaca at the time of the Spanish Conquest (Pl. 32).

With the development of a social hierarchy, large public and ceremonial buildings, literacy, and the mathematical–astronomical knowledge embodied in the calendar, we have come a long way from the tiny farming hamlets of a thousand years earlier. The final jump, into true city life and a state level of organization, took place over a few centuries, starting about 500 bc.

To accommodate the Valley's growing population, many new sites were founded, some of them (like Hierve El Agua) in the foothills close to perennial streams which provided irrigation water (Pl. 33). Other new foundations were hamlets specializing in salt-boiling or other localized crafts. The single most important act was the creation of a new Valley capital at Monte Alban, on a previously unoccupied hill rising from the plain at the point where the three arms of the Valley meet.[20]

The site does not fit the usual pattern. It was not an old-established centre; it has relatively poor soils and no raw materials. Although central to the Valley, it seems perverse to put the main regional market on top of a 400 m hill, where everything has to be carried up. What Monte Alban really looks like is an artificial, political creation (like Brasilia or Washington D.C.) designed to administer a federation of second-order state capitals.

Where sites like San Jose may have controlled a part of the Valley, Monte Alban probably controlled it all. It is a superpower, of a different order of magnitude from anything seen before in Oaxaca. From a settlement of less than 7,000 people in 500 bc, it grew into a metropolis with between 22,000 and 45,000 inhabitants, living on hillside terraces surrounding a nucleus of governmental and religious buildings. Check dams and canals distributed

[19] Flannery and Marcus, op. cit., 1976.
[20] R. E. Blanton, 'The Origins of Monte Alban' in C. Cleland (ed.), *Cultural Change and Continuity: Essays in Honor of James Bennett Griffin* (New York, San Francisco, London, 1976) 223–32.

water to terraced fields on the slopes. By AD 200, the city covered more than 4 km², and was surrounded by a defence wall. True literacy is demonstrated by a pair of stelae with long hieroglyphic inscriptions incorporating day signs, bar-and-dot numerals, and still undeciphered glyphs. In contrast to the single 'captive' from San Jose, Monte Alban has more than three hundred such slabs. If these scenes do in fact depict conquests, Monte Alban must have been the capital of a militaristic empire like those documented for later times.

At very least, our pyramid model now has the required three levels of settlement, and Monte Alban has all the archaeological signs of an imperial state.

OLMEC CULTURE IN THE GULF COAST LOWLANDS

The previous case studies have been taken from the highland zone, where techniques of intensive farming allow large populations and encourage grouping into towns and cities. The lowlands of Mesoamerica are another world entirely. Under natural conditions they are rainy and forested. Sherds are hidden under forest humus, and even large buildings are masked by vegetation. In these conditions, accurate estimates of site size and population are not easily obtained.

The tropical soils lose their fertility after a few years of cropping, and slash-and-burn, shifting cultivation is the norm over much of this area. A field is cleared from the bush, planted for a year or two, then allowed to revert to forest. Each family therefore needs a good deal of land, most of which lies fallow at any one time, and settlement therefore tends to be less dense and more dispersed than in the highlands.

Whether or not one calls the great lowland centres 'urban' is largely a matter of semantics. Ignoring for the moment what these places *looked like*, and concentrating instead on *how they worked*, the development of lowland civilization parallels that of the highlands in almost every respect.

Between 2000 and 1500 bc in radiocarbon years, villages of pottery-using farmers were established on the Gulf Coast, the Pacific coast plain, [21] and in the eastern Maya lowlands. [22] By 1300 we begin to get signs of differentiation into larger and smaller sites, with communal planning, small public build-

[21] G. W. Lowe, 'The Mixe-Zoque as Competing Neighbors of the Early Lowland Maya' in R. E. W. Adams (ed.) *The Origins of Maya Civilization* (Albuquerque, 1977), 197–248.
[22] N. Hammond, 'The Early Formative in the Maya Lowlands' in *Social Process in Maya Prehistory* (London, New York, San Francisco, 1977), 77–101.

ings, and hints of craft specialization. After 1100 we can see, in parts of the lowland zone, just that kind of discontinuity or quantum jump that we have already identified in Oaxaca—and at just the same time.

The best documentation for this stage of development comes from the Gulf Coast plain of Veracruz and Tabasco, the homeland of Olmec civilization. Wherever extensive surveys have been carried out in this area, the majority of sites consist of little groups of houses, often on river levees.[23] Against this background of small-scale village life, certain sites stand out as centres of organization and as concentrations of wealth.

San Lorenzo is the prime example.[24] By the tenth century before Christ, a huge artificial platform had been built there, with 7 m of fill covering over and masking a natural eminence. Associated with this structure were man-made ponds and more than 200 m of stone drains. Set around the plateau were some 60 stone monuments, including single-piece colossal heads weighing 40 tons or more and made of andesite brought from outside the region. San Lorenzo does not look like a town, but it covers nearly 53 ha and had about 200 house mounds—say, 1,000 residents. This makes it one of Mexico's biggest sites—more than twice the size, and double the population, of San Jose Mogote at the same date.

At San Lorenzo, the size distinction and the vast investment of social effort (in the form of earth-moving and stone-carving), plus the concentration of wealth (in the form of imported raw materials) represent something new on the local scene. They are the outward signs of centralized authority, the end of village self-sufficiency, and the transfer of power into the hands of a controlling élite.

The same phenomena can be recognized at La Venta, which replaces San Lorenzo as the principal Olmec site some time around 800.[25] Situated on an island surrounded by swamps, with neither farmland nor building stone, its main feature is a fluted pyramid with a complex of courtyards and platforms stretching for one and a half miles. Much of the community's wealth was used for non-utilitarian ends. Stone sculptures like those of San Lorenzo were scattered over the site; expensive jade figurines disappeared from sight into

[23] E. B. Sisson, 'Settlement patterns and land use in the north-western Chontalpa, Tabasco, Mexico', *Cerámica de Cultura Maya* 6 (1970), 41–54.

[24] M. D. Coe, *America's First Civilization* (New York, 1968); M. D. Coe, *Map of San Lorenzo, an Olmec site in Veracruz, Mexico* (Dept. of Anthropology, Yale Univ., 1968).

[25] P. Drucker, R. F. Heizer, R. J. Squier, 'Excavations at La Venta, Tabasco, 1955', *Bull. Bureau of American Ethnology, Smithsonian Institution* 170 (1959); R. F. Heizer, J. A. Graham, L. K. Napton, 'The 1968 Excavations at La Venta', *Contributions, Univ. of California Research Facility* 5 (1968), 127–54.

offerings and caches; some three thousand tons of imported serpentine were laid out in the form of pavements which were immediately buried at the bottom of deep pits. As at contemporary sites in Oaxaca, rich burial was granted to infants as well as adults.

And yet—La Venta can hardly be called a town. The resident population was small (not enough to have built the site without help), but La Venta was clearly a centre of government, serving the same purpose as the more nucle-ated capitals of Oaxaca and the Basin of Mexico. Perhaps the phrase 'service centre' might be appropriate for sites of this kind.

THE MATURE CIVILIZATIONS: TEOTIHUACAN AND TIKAL

By the start of the Christian era, the future pattern of Mesoamerican history was well and truly set. The distinction between the mature forms of highland and lowland civilization can be demonstrated by comparing two of the best known archaeological sites of Mesoamerica: Teotihuacan in the Basin of Mexico and Tikal in the rainforest of the central Maya lowlands. These two sites, both of them superpowers, are the culmination of their respective patterns of civilization.

Teotihuacan is one of the few cities in Mesoamerica to have been com-pletely mapped.[26] At the time of its maximum importance, around AD 600, it covered about 20 km^2, about the size of imperial Rome, and much larger than any European city of its day. The estimated population (based on a count of the number of 'sleeping rooms' in the city) is about 200,000 inhabitants. Building conformed to a regular grid plan, with two major avenues intersect-ing at right angles (Fig. 29). Along the north–south axis, the so-called Avenue of the Dead, were more than one hundred shrines and temples, including the pyramids of the Sun and Moon. The Sun Pyramid alone contains about one million cubic metres of fill.

The city's residents lived in single storey apartment compounds, more than 2,000 of which have been mapped. Each compound is a self-contained unit surrounded by windowless walls, and separated from its neighbours by narrow streets. The internal layout incorporates sleeping quarters, halls, kitchens, and one or more small temples, all arranged round open patios with subfloor drains to carry off rainwater from the courtyards. The number and

---

[26] See note 9 above. Also R. Millon, 'Teotihuacan: Completion of Map of Giant Ancient City in the Valley of Mexico', *Science* 170 (1970), 1077–82; id., *Urbanization at Teotihuacán, Mexico: Vol. 1, The Teotihuacán Map* (Austin, 1973).

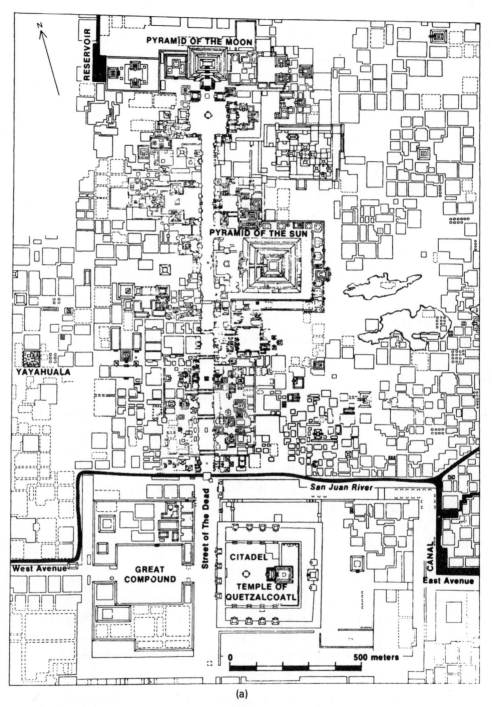

FIG. 29. A highland Mexican city and a lowland Maya centre. The central zones of (a) Teotihuacan and (b) Tikal.

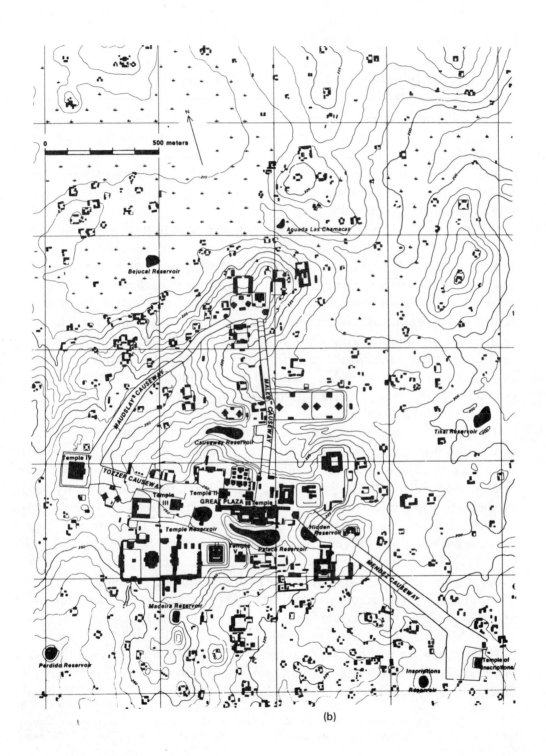

(b)

arrangement of rooms indicates that these compounds were multi-family residences, perhaps occupied by some kind of kin group or by a number of related households.

The walls of the richer compounds were covered with frescoes in a distinctive style, incorporating richly dressed personages, and also birds, jaguars, and gods (among them the Feathered Serpent and Tlaloc the Rain God—both of whom were still being worshipped a thousand years later). Rather surprisingly, there are no carved and inscribed stelae, and no unambiguous evidence for writing.

A quarter of the city's population was engaged in manufacturing, and more than 500 workshops were identified during the survey. Their products included objects of clay, basalt, slate and shell, but most numerous were obsidian workshops, drawing on local quarry sources and producing for export all over Mesoamerica. As the major political, religious, and commercial city of highland Mexico, Teotihuacan was in contact with the whole of civilized Mesoamerica, from Oaxaca and the Gulf Coast to the Maya lowlands, where highland obsidian and pottery are common on all major sites.

The differences between Mexican and Maya notions of town planning are not therefore the result of physical isolation, but of cultural choice influenced by environmental considerations.

The past ten years of research have completely changed our view of Maya civilization during its Classic period (c. AD 300–900). Not so long ago, it used to be said that the Maya were simple slash-and-burn farmers, peaceful and rather unworldly, devoting their intellectual efforts to philosophy and mathematics, and raising their beautifully carved stelae merely to commemorate the passage of time. Every one of these propositions turns out to be false. We now have fortified sites and numerous depictions of warfare, capture, and sacrifice. We have drainage works, raised fields, and terraces to prove that the Maya were as concerned as anyone else with maximizing production. And we find that they were as preoccupied with power politics as any of their highland neighbours. This comes as a great relief; the inscrutable Maya turn out to be normal Mesoamericans after all.

In date, the growth of Tikal coincides closely with that of Teotihuacan. Work started on the main acropolis in about 200 bc, and Tikal rapidly developed all the symptoms of a stratified and centralized society.[27] Vaulted

[27] W. R. Coe, *Tikal, a Handbook of the Ancient Maya Ruins* (University Museum, Univ. of Pennsylvania, 1967); W. A. Haviland, 'The Ancient Maya and the Evolution of Urban Society', *Univ. of N. Colorado, Mus. Anthropology, Misc. Ser.* 37 (1975).

tombs were introduced for the interment of richer individuals, sometimes accompanied by retainer burials, and from about 25 bc these burials were all male. Since women had previously figured among the richer corpses, it seems that important positions were gradually becoming a male monopoly. Soon afterwards, the bone evidence shows that the occupants of the rich tombs, concentrated in the central area of Tikal, were bigger, lived longer, and were better fed than the common people. Hieroglyphic writing (a good indicator of bureaucracy) makes its first appearance in the Maya lowlands on a Tikal stela bearing a date equivalent to 6 July AD 292.

Figure 29 shows the central areas of Teotihuacan and Tikal at more or less the same scale,[28] and illustrates the difference between a Mexican city and a Maya capital. Instead of the densely crowded suburbs of Teotihuacan, Tikal has a more dispersed pattern of settlement, which is not entirely due to topography. There is a good deal of open space, and the grid plan of Teotihuacan is replaced by a more haphazard arrangement of buildings—though the planning is not random. Studies of access patterns and traffic flow show that, in Maya centres, the areas of public activity (temples and plazas) are easily accessible, while palaces and élite residences are more secluded.[29] The apartment compounds of Teotihuacan have no counterpart in the Maya zone, where the normal residential unit is a little cluster of two to five houses around an open patio.

Architecturally Tikal and Teotihuacan are different kinds of site, but it can be demonstrated that Tikal carries out all the functions, and offers all the services, of a highland city state.

The first line of approach is epigraphic, something denied to us at Teotihuacan. Although we can read only a fraction of the 800 or so Maya hieroglyphs, we can decipher dates, calendrical information, and the symbols for such events as conquests, marriages, and royal accessions. The inscriptions make it clear that Tikal was the seat of a royal lineage with succession in the male line, normally—though not invariably—from father to son. Individual named rulers have been found buried in tombs below the main temples, and marriage patterns indicate dynastic alliances with neighbouring centres.[30]

[28] W. T. Sanders and B. J. Price, *Mesoamerica, the Evolution of a Civilization* (New York 1968), Figs 6–7.
[29] N. D. C. Hammond, 'Locational Models and the Site of Lubaantún: a Classic Maya Centre' in D. L. Clarke (ed.) *Models in Archaeology* (London, 1972), 757–800.
[30] C. Jones, 'Inauguration Dates of Three Late Classic Rulers at Tikal, Guatemala', *Am. Antiq.* 42, 1 (1977), 28–60; W. A. Haviland, 'Dynastic Genealogies at Tikal, Guatemala: Implications for Descent and Political Organization', *Am. Antiq.* 42, 1 (1977), 61–7.

Tikal is also one of the few Maya sites for which we can make reasonable calculations of size and population. To the north and south, just where the density of house mounds falls very sharply, are defensive earthworks. To the east and west are *bajos*, seasonal swamps. The area enclosed within the earthworks and *bajos*, what we can perhaps call Greater Tikal, is some 120 km², with a population in the 40,000 to 50,000 range.[31]

If we think of this Greater Tikal as a *state*, rather than as a *site*, and compare it with its highland equivalent, the fit is remarkably good. In size and population Greater Tikal ranks with all but the largest highland states. Like them, it has a nucleus of more densely packed housing which contains about 25 per cent of the total population, as well as all the principal temples, mausolea, and palaces. In function, and as a concentration of political, economic, and religious power, this central zone is the equivalent of a highland capital town. Around the central nucleus is a less densely settled hinterland, equivalent to the dependent territories of a highland city state.

In the context of the Peten rainforest, Tikal ranks as a superpower and, again like its highland counterpart, exerts its influence over a wide area outside its own territory. Two kinds of evidence make this clear:

The first of these takes us back to questions of ranking and spacing. It has long been realized that Maya centres come in different sizes. At the top are the really large sites (like Tikal, Copan, and Palenque), few in number but rich in temples, palaces, ball courts, and inscribed stelae. Secondary centres are much more numerous, but smaller and with fewer monuments or public buildings. They seem to have functioned as second-order state capitals, and they had their own royal dynasties—though they probably owed allegiance to one or other of the regional capitals. Below the secondary capitals are many house groups with no carved monuments or public architecture. These constitute the dependent settlements, the lowest tier of our pyramid (Pl. 29a).

In the Maya lowlands, too, the spacing of sites comes closest to the ideal lattice model predicted by locational geographers, in which major service centres are surrounded by hexagons of secondary service centres, and these in turn by lower order ones serving local needs (Pl. 29b–c).

---

[31] W. A. Haviland, 'Tikal, Guatemala, and Mesoamerican Urbanism', *World Arch.* 2, 2 (1970), 186–98; D. E. Puleston, 'Intersite areas in the vicinity of Tikal and Uaxactun' in N. Hammond (ed.) *Mesoamerican Archaeology: New Approaches* (London, 1974), 303–11

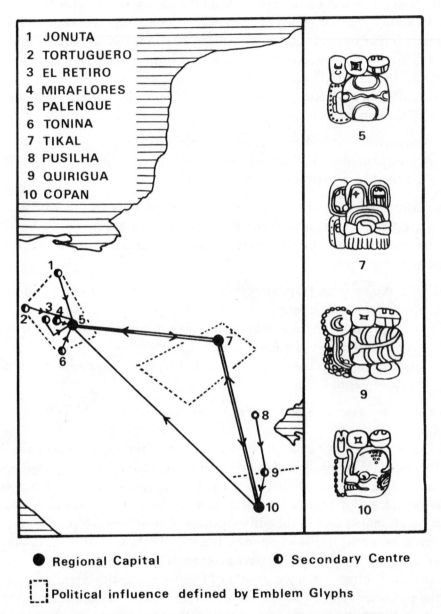

1 JONUTA
2 TORTUGUERO
3 EL RETIRO
4 MIRAFLORES
5 PALENQUE
6 TONINA
7 TIKAL
8 PUSILHA
9 QUIRIGUA
10 COPAN

● Regional Capital   ◑ Secondary Centre

[¦ ¦] Political influence defined by Emblem Glyphs

FIG. 30. Political influence inferred from the distribution of Maya Emblem Glyphs. Left: the Palenque 'sphere of influence' defined by secondary centres whose inscriptions incorporate the Emblem Glyph of Palenque. Centre: the Tikal sphere, defined on the same basis. Right: Quiriguá was at first a satellite of Copan. Later it became independent, and gained dependencies of its own.

The final piece of evidence comes from the inscriptions again.[32] Since 1958 we have known that a certain category of hieroglyph represents the emblem of a state capital or its royal house. These glyphs share the same suffix and affix, but each site has its own main sign—a tied bundle for Tikal, the head of a leaf-nosed bat for Copan, etc. (Fig. 30).

When a 'foreign' Emblem Glyph appears at a particular site, it is normally in one of three contexts:

1. Associated with other foreign Emblem Glyphs.
2. Accompanied by a marriage glyph or a female head.
3. Attached to a captured warrior.

These inscriptions, in other words, deal almost entirely with political events: inter-state agreements, marriage alliances, and conquests.

If the distribution of Emblem Glyphs is examined statistically, an interesting pattern emerges.

(a) The major sites (the 'superpowers') receive the greatest number of mentions at other sites.
(b) Inscriptions from these major sites more often mention each other than they do their own dependencies.
(c) Inscriptions at secondary sites most often refer to a single major site or regional capital.

This allows us to define spheres of political influence on the basis of Emblem Glyph distribution.

In Fig. 30 this exercise has been done for two of the regional capitals: Tikal and Palenque. We end up with a good tight clustering, and with polygons of roughly comparable areas (between 15,000 and 26,000 km²). Each polygon contains one major regional capital, and a number of secondary capitals which mention its name in their inscriptions. There thus is a good correlation between power and status as inferred from Emblem Glyph studies, and size and complexity as revealed by archaeological field survey.

In political terms, we have another of those three-tier pyramids, and an internal structure typical of Mesoamerican states in general. Looked at in this way, from the point of view of function rather than of form, that favourite controversy of Mesoamerican archaeology—*Was Maya civilization urban or not?*—becomes a time-wasting irrelevance.

[32] J. Marcus, *Emblem and State in the Classic Maya Lowlands: An Epigraphic Approach to Territorial Organization* (Washington, 1976).

VI

THE RELIGIOUS DEVELOPMENT OF SOME EARLY SOCIETIES

N. K. SANDARS[1]

TO TALK about the religions of early societies, in the twentieth century, is not only a great presumption, it is virtually impossible. It demands mental qualities unattainable by the historian. In a recent essay on Vico and Herder, both men much concerned with this subject, Isaiah Berlin writes of the creative activity of men to be conceived 'not as reproduction of objects for use or pleasure or instruction ... but as voices speaking, as expressions of individual visions of life', and that this activity is to be understood 'not by exhaustive classification under concepts, incorporation into logically coherent systems, or the use of other technical devices, but by what Herder calls *Einfühlen*, empathy, the gifts of an artist endowed with historical insight, imagination'. 'Each society', he concludes, to be 'understood in terms of its own values and outlook, and not by any universal scale of values'.[2] If that is not daunting enough it must be added that 'objects of use, pleasure and instruction' cannot be ignored by an archaeologist.

The first question is, of course, where to begin. Obvious alternatives are the beginning of literacy in the ancient orient rather less than five thousand years ago, or the appearance of *homo sapiens* around forty thousand years ago. There is much to be said for either starting-point, and consideration of both together may provoke some rather disconcerting thoughts. It is arguable that we *can* know next to nothing about the earliest sapiens men, our remote ancestors. We will certainly never be able to 'understand them in terms of their own values'; but the point is that they *are* our ancestors. Physically they were identical with ourselves, and in no way inferior to us. When we look at these bones we can only say 'This is my father.' Paradoxically when we read the

[1] For their generous help and guidance on various points that arose in the preparation of this lecture, I have to thank Drs J. K. Campbell and O. R. Gurney, Mrs K. R. Maxwell-Hyslop, Drs Roger Moorey and Kenneth Oakley, and Father John Tillett; and also Mrs W. H. Burnett thanks for her expert typing.
[2] Isaiah Berlin, *Vico and Herder, Two Studies in the History of Ideas* (London, 1976), xxii.

writings of the ancient Egyptians and the Sumerians of southern Iraq, we see at once a hundred ways in which they are different from ourselves. There is no difficulty in recognizing a great part of the life of third millennium man as religious; can we in any way infer the same of that other starting-point, forty or so thousand years before? What I think we can see, and this is of great value, is a matter of scale, the perspective which that remote past gives to everything we learn about more recent centuries, including our own.

We cannot for a start expect to find anything particularly primitive still around in the ancient world in three thousand BC. What we find are already very old, very advanced societies with complicated structures including those of a religious nature. It is also beside the point to talk of absolute beginnings or 'firsts ever'. That great Sumeriologist Samuel Kramer, at least in his more popular writings, is apt to present us with 'The First Moral Ideas', 'Man's First Cosmogony' and so on;[3] but in the history of ancient societies there are no 'firsts', there are only the first recordings that have survived.

The materials for any inquiry of this sort are in the main literary, but they also come from art, whether this was gratuitous activity, or the tool of a cult; and they come from architecture where surviving monuments can indicate the outward forms of worship, though very little about its content. I do not include among helpful materials ethnographic studies of contemporary primitive societies. Perhaps I should include them, but the omission is deliberate. These studies provide not too little, but too much and too heady material which, if applied to the remote human past, can intoxicate and mislead. One instance is the argument that has been going on now for a long time concerning hunter–gatherers and whether, as an older generation believed, such societies are by nature (or through need) violent and aggressive, possessed of what has been called a 'carnivorous psychology', or whether, as recent field studies seem to show, they tend to be notably unaggressive, like the Mbutu pygmies of central Africa studied by Colin Turnbull, who apparently kill without any aggressive spirit at all, and even, it is claimed, with a sort of regret.[4] The same is said of other hunter–gatherers, but not of all, for there are exceptions. Or there are the Hadza of northern Tanzania, and the disconcerting conclusions of J. Woodburn, that these particular hunter–gatherers manage to conduct their lives with an almost

[3] S. N. Kramer, *History Begins at Sumer* (revised ed., London, 1961), *passim*.
[4] C. M. Turnbull, *The Wayward Servant or the Two Worlds of the African Pygmies* (London, 1965); also Erich Fromm, 'Analysis of Thirty Primitive Tribes', *The Anatomy of Human Destructiveness* (London, 1974), 167–81.

total absence of ritual and hierarchy within the society. Social relations are carried on without rites of passage or other ceremonies and with little or no concern with time past; while other groups, Australian aborigines and native west-coast Americans, live within a social structure extremely well-furnished with rituals, hierarchies, and a sense of time dominated by 'the present in the past'.[5]

Which of these is likely to be more relevant to stages in man's early social development? There is no way of knowing, nor need one necessarily eliminate the other. The same doubt adheres to the religious capabilities of hunter–gatherers as to their aggressiveness, or its lack. The point, I think, is that all these contemporaries of ours: Australian aborigines, pygmies, Hadza, American Indians, have experienced the same long past with all its changes and chances. We are not justified in supposing that *their* ancestors, because of their mode of life, were locked in a motionless trance, unchanged throughout millennia, while our own ancestors possessed the dynamic to evolve. It is, I would maintain, unsafe to project the social systems or religious ideas belonging to one or other of these contemporary societies, back into a common past.

The great value of ethnographic studies for the prehistorian is the help they give in understanding the uses, applications and, to a lesser extent, social implications, of the artefacts that he finds. They give us a range of possibilities, of choices and limitations, that are of a physical and practical kind. They do not give solutions, but they provide something like a field of force within which solutions may be sought.

Comparatively sparse and unsatisfactory as are the lights that archaeology and art throw on to the remote past, they may be treated with a little more confidence. For instance there are virtually no representations in Paleolithic art of men killing men, but in the Mesolithic there are such representations.[6] One is a supposed 'execution scene' from eastern Spain (Fig. 31). The archaeologist also suffers from the temptation to see the past as flat and unchanging, except for those points at which it can be recorded by stone, bone, clay, and by other artefacts, plans of buildings, interference with the environment. But what lies between is not a featureless blank; the unrecorded years, centuries, millennia, were as sensitive to the passage of time as our own

[5] J. Woodburn, various writings on the Hadza referred to by Maurice Bloch, 'The Past and the Present in the Past', *Man* 12, 2 (1977) 278–92.

[6] N. K. Sandars, *Prehistoric Art in Europe* (Harmondsworth, 1968), 96 and Pl. 89 with further references. Although the work of 'Mesolithic' hunter–gatherers, these small-scale paintings may be contemporary with the beginnings of urban life in the Near East.

FIG. 31. 'Execution Group', painting at Castellón, east Spain, 1.14 cm.

age; only our instruments are too coarse to pick up the signals. I know that I am labouring this question of the brute passage of time, but although it is obvious and fundamental, its consequences are surprisingly neglected.

Faced by those nebulous and anything but empty expanses of prehistoric time we set about constructing patterns to fill them. This needs no apology, it is the natural thing to do since pattern-making is a basic characteristic, not only in the life of human beings, but of life itself from the double helix up. The history of early man has led to a particularly prolific outbreak of pattern-making. Marx, Jung, Freud, have all been at it; archaeologists and sociologists make their 'models', which are another sort of pattern. In the course of this lecture I shall refer to two quite recent systems.

In 1976 Thorkild Jacobsen, a distinguished scholar in the field of Sumerian and Assyrian studies, and the translator of many texts, published a comprehensive interpretation of early Mesopotamian religions, which he called *The Treasures of Darkness*.[7] Jacobsen is a man of Vico's kind, broad in his sympathies and with great depth of imaginative insight. 'In its choice of central metaphors,' he writes, 'a culture, or cultural period, necessarily reveals what it considers essential in the numinous experience . . . our present enquiry accordingly will focus specifically on the major religious metaphors of ancient Mesopotamia.'

An even more comprehensive system is sketched in *The Anatomy of Human Destructiveness* by the social philosopher and psychologist Erich Fromm, published in 1974.[8] The danger with these, as with all systems, is that they may be taken for universals, when in fact much of the evidence used is peculiar to one locality and one situation. I shall have more to say about both systems later on.

[7] Thorkild Jacobsen, *The Treasures of Darkness, A History of Mesopotamian Religions* (New Haven and London 1976), 4.

[8] Erich Fromm, op. cit. (note 4 above).

In the prehistoric centuries before literacy, and before the construction of permanent buildings, perhaps only art can help us to recognize those religious metaphors in which the literatures are so rich. Art may give a little help even in the old Stone Age when the last great ice-sheet covered northern Europe. The image of the human being, as we see it represented from around 28,000 BC, will tell us something about early man's estimate of himself, and so of his own species, and so perhaps something also about his gods. At the same time his portrayal of animal subjects will tell us about his relationship with the beasts. This relationship has passed through extraordinary revolutions from one of total parity to total alienation. The first revolution is too remote to be seizable, but the change from hunter to farmer will concern us later on. So profound an alteration must have had its religious connotations.

In the earliest surviving old Stone-Age art one is struck immediately by how unlike the art of children it is. Paleolithic man was not a child; nor is his art at all like that of contemporary primitive societies. It is peculiar to one tradition which embraces China as well as Egypt, Greece, and Renaissance Italy. This underlines the argument against ethnographic comparisons; inappropriate to the arts, they are equally inappropriate to religious interpretation.

Two images probably dominate any generally held view of Upper Paleolithic art: the image of the naturalistic animal, and of a fat, not very naturalistic, woman. From this may follow thoughts about mother-goddesses, sympathetic magic and hunter's rituals. On these topics I can only make the briefest of comments. Paleolithic art, as we know it, begins with sculpture in the round, and with naturalistic human figures.[9] It is rather unfortunate that the so-called 'Venus of Willendorf' should have been one of the earliest figures found, as well as one of the earliest in date; for it has fixed this image as though it were the prevailing type. A small limestone carving of around 28,000 BC, it is full of vitality, but it is far from typical. There is a very damaged mammoth ivory figure of a man found at Brno, Czechoslovakia, which is much the same age (Pl. 34). Beardless and with cropped hair, it is certainly no caricature or stylization. Around 26,000 BC from Ostrava Petřokovice, comes a tiny woman's torso carved in haematite, a hard material; although only 4·5 cm tall, it has the proportions of one of the classical Graces

[9] P. Graziosi, *L'Arte della antica età della pietra* (Florence, 1956; English edn., London, 1960). A very comprehensive presentation of Paleolithic art; the best illustrations of the Moravian carvings are in J. Poulík and B. Forman, *Prehistoric Art* (Prague and London, 1956); see also N. K. Sandars, op. cit. (note 6), Chaps. 1 and 2, and Pls 2, 3, 5.

(Pl. 35). Later again, and still in Czechoslovakia, an ivory head from Dolní Věstonice, 48 mm long, is very beautiful, and quite individual (Pl. 36). With these figures and faces we are already confronting our own criteria of comeliness and propriety.

Two half life-size reliefs carry on what I am calling a 'Classical tradition' of representation. They were found in a shallow cave at La Magdaleine, Tarn, and may be dated around 12,000 BC (Pl. 37). The technique of carving and choice of pose show a surprising mastery of perspective, which foreshadows a long line of reclining figures.[10] In Czechoslovakia and in south Russia semi-permanent houses were built with mammoth bones in place of timber; the small figures were found near the hearths and one building has even been taken for a shrine.

The naturalistic sculpture of animals is almost as old as that of human figures, with a carving from the Lontal in South Germany among the earliest (Pl. 38).[11] In view of these carvings it is simply not true that some sanction or taboo prevented Upper Paleolithic man from portraying himself as he portrayed the animals. There is no difference in the treatment of either. Further than that we cannot go. We do not know what these figures meant to their makers beyond the fact of a truthful vision of human and animal nature. This is already quite a lot; but whether the carvings were also vehicles for spirits, for gods, for ancestors, for powers of nature, for physical needs or psychological desires, or whether they were just plain likenesses, there is no way of knowing.

If we try to follow one of these images, the so-called 'mother-goddess' figure, downwards, a gap of several thousand years separates the Old Stone Age figures from those of Epipaleolithic and early Neolithic sites with which historians of art and religion have connected them. There is in fact very little to connect them at all, and little or nothing to suggest that they represent the same ideas. Female figurines are not found, on the whole, in the pre-agricultural sites of the eighth millennium in the Near East. They begin in pre-pottery Neolithic sites from the seventh millennium, that is to say among crop-growing farmers; and they continue from then on. Cultivation seems to have started with the collection and sowing of *wild* grains, and some of the earliest carbonized grains from a settlement were found at Mureybet on the upper Euphrates in the two lowest levels. In these levels there are no figurines,

[10] Sandars, op. cit. (note 6), 42, and Pls 30, 31.
[11] W. Kimmig and H. Hell, *Vorzeit an Rhein und Donau* (Lindau and Konstanz, 1958), Pl. 7 from the Vogelherdhöhle, and many more illustrated by Graziosi, op. cit. (note 9).

but in level three, second half of the eighth millennium, ox-horns and the jaw of a large carnivore were stuck into house-walls, and a stone object with indistinctly anthropomorphic features, was also found. Game was still the chief source of food at Mureybet, but at Cayönü, a site just south of the Taurus mountains, the change from wild to domesticated grains, and from wild game to domestic animals, can be followed through five levels dated between 7600 and 6800; and here female figurines modelled crudely from clay begin to appear.[12] At Catal Hüyük in Anatolia, from the later seventh into the early sixth millennium, we have the most ample record of a community that, while it still hunted wild game, depended chiefly on domesticated grains, while domesticated cattle provided 90 per cent of meat eaten. There are also a great number and variety of carved and modelled human figures, and of painted, modelled, and carved animals which, in themselves, seem to show a change of viewpoint actually taking place.[13]

Wall-paintings of large bulls begin in almost the lowest levels (level IX), with plaster reliefs of bulls' heads in X and of a birth-giving female goddess or mother from VII. Female figurines also begin with level VII midway through the life of the settlement. It is at first a slim figure carved in stone, and linked often to a leopard or bull, like the 'Mistress of Animals' of a later age (Fig. 32). There are also some male figures, linked to animals but they are not found in late levels. In level II, on the other hand, the woman or goddess appears modelled in clay, fat, often pregnant, sometimes giving birth, and sometimes found actually in the grain bins (Fig. 33).[14] So here at Çatal Hüyük, and at other Neolithic sites in the Near East, we have our first indications of a goddess of grain and of the earth. The primordial Jungian 'Earth-Mother' may be no more than eight or nine thousand years old, which is a short span seen against the ages of our hunting ancestors. That comfortable metaphor of a fruitful earth who is wife and mother, made fertile by a sky husband, may seem obvious and appropriate to us, but it is in fact only one among many metaphors. Even in the Levant, in nearby Egypt, everything is topsy turvy, the earth is a god and the sky a goddess. It has been too easily assumed that an archetypal earth-mother has a certain right to our collective unconscious; but why should hunters regard the earth as female? Their prime source of food,

[12] J. Mellaart, *The Neolithic in the Near East* (London, 1975), 42–9, Mureybet; 52–4, Cayönü; P. J. Ucko and D. Dimbleby, *The domestication and exploitation of plants and animals, Proceedings of the Research Seminar in Archaeology and related subjects, Institute of Archaeology* (London, 1970).

[13] J. Mellaart, *Çatal Hüyük, A Neolithic Town in Central Anatolia*, (London, 1967).

[14] See particularly, Pls IX, 67, 68, and Fig. 52, from a grain bin, level IIA, clay, but the 'throne' is composed of two leopards, compare Pls X, 73–6, 84, 85, stone, level VIA.

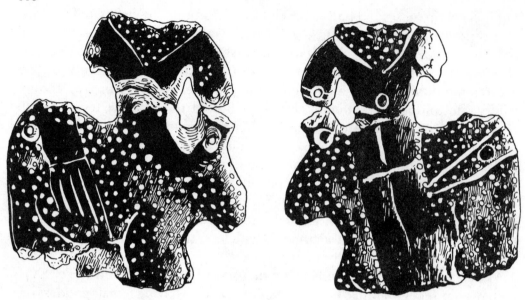

FIG. 32. Carving of a woman with a leopard from Çatal Hüyük, Turkey, level VI, steatite, h. 11 cm.

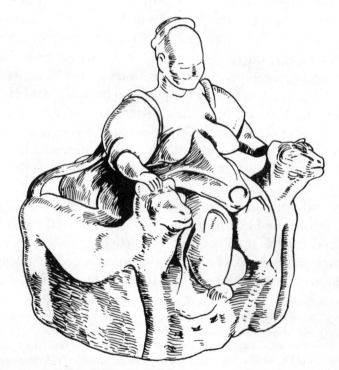

FIG. 33. 'Goddess' on leopard throne, Çatal Hüyük, from a grain bin, level II, clay, h. 16.5 cm.

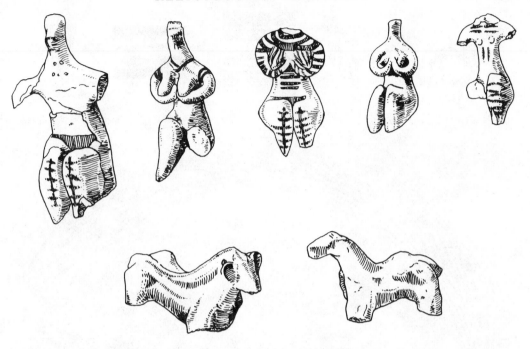

F IG. 34. Figures of women and quadrupeds from Chagar Bazar, Syria, level 11 and later, clay.

the animal prey, did not rise out of the earth like grain, but came on its own legs through the forest or over the horizon, like the caribou and mammoth. As gatherers of roots and berries, men and women might feel grateful towards a sometimes benevolent earth; but it was the mammoth that was the great provider of warmth, clothing, fuel, even house-materials, as well as food for Upper Paleolithic man, just as the bison were for the plains Indians.

Those female figurines that are found in some numbers in early agricultural communities are generally small and roughly modelled in clay; they belong in fact to the kitchen, and their existence does not imply a dominating position in any hypothetical hierarchy of gods (Fig. 34). The same people who made clay models of fat women, painted quite different subjects on their pots: bull's heads and friezes of birds and ibex (Fig. 34a, b).[15]

[15] See for example 'Chagar Bazar', M. E. L. Mallowan, *Iraq*, 3 (1936) 1–87, Pl. 1, 1–3, Fig. 5, clay figurines of women and animals from levels 11 and later. cf. Figs. 26 and 27, painted sherds, various levels. Oddly the same distinction occurs in the Neolithic of Romania where Cucuteni farmers made small clay figures of bovines but painted on their pots a prick-eared wolfish animal.

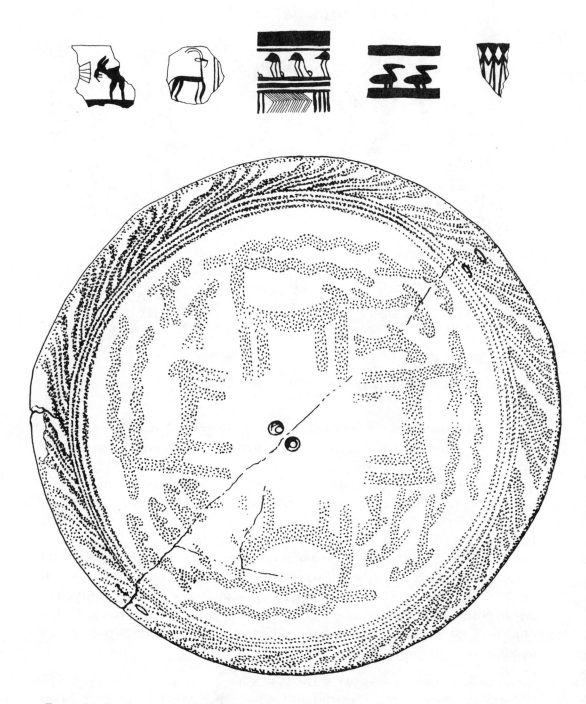

FIG. 34(a) Sherds painted with animal motifs from Chagar Bazar, Syria, various levels. (b) Painted 'Samarra' style dish from Tell Hassuna, Iraq.

There is a popular 'myth' concerning Old World western civilization according to which it passed through a longish Neolithic phase during which society was peaceful, egalitarian and dominated by a benevolent mother-goddess. This was followed by a Bronze Age dominated by warrior kings and chieftains worshipping equally warlike male deities. This may be quite harmless, and even contain a fragment of truth, but it is worrying to find a writer of the stature and rigorous training of Erich Fromm using very much the same scenario for his study of Human Destructiveness. He quotes much from Çatal Hüyük: its lack of walls and of houses showing differences in social status, its lack of obvious sackings, and above all he stresses the central role of the mother, shown in the decoration of shrines, and the burial of young children beside their mothers, which is described as a 'characteristically matriarchal trait'.

Too much depends on one site, which is in many ways exceptional. Contemporary Jericho was defended by a great wall and tower; and the 'mother-goddess' at Çatal Hüyük has a far from benevolent aspect. Fromm goes on to cite Engels and a handful of Soviet scholars who have written of matriarchy, and claims that 'the excavations of Neolithic villages in Anatolia offer the most complete material evidence for the existence of matriarchal cultures and religion postulated by J. J. Bachhofen.' This refers to *Die Mutterrecht*, published in 1861 where, even according to Fromm himself, the argument is based on a study of Greek and Roman myths, symbols, and dreams.[16] Not surprisingly anthropologists have remained sceptical. Indeed they now tell us that matriarchy of the sort envisaged is not known, and has never been known. The whole concept seems to have arisen from a misunderstanding of different institutions, such as matrilineal inheritance in which, though property may be inherited through the mother, in the division of labour men play all the public roles and have jural authority. These societies have evolved different systems especially designed to safeguard male rights and status.[17] If matriarchy is a myth today it does not follow that it can never have existed in the past, but very strong reasons must be brought forward in its support, certainly stronger than any that have yet appeared.

The relationship of the hunter to the game he pursues and which is sovereign and free, is quite different from that of the farmer and herdsman to

[16] Fromm, op. cit. (note 4), 151–66, especially see 158–9.

[17] R. Fox, *Kinship and Marriage* (Harmondsworth, 1967), 16–22, 111, 114, etc. I am grateful to Dr J. K. Campbell for this reference and for help with present anthropological thinking on 'matriarchy' and on primitive hunter–gatherers.

the enslaved beasts over which he rules with an absolute authority. To understand this we only have to compare the painted bulls of Lascaux, (Pl. 39), or a shivering pony engraved on bone from Schweizersbild,[18] with the humble little clay ex-votos and toys that are found on Neolithic sites. When those early farmers put fences round their crops they made enemies of the foraging herds for the first time in history. When the forests were cleared with axe and fire the wilderness became hostile and frightening. This 'crime' converted wild nature from ally into enemy. It is remarkable how few really frightening animal images there are in Paleolithic art. Animals are alert, or galloping off or, in some later representations, probably already dead.[19]

The hunched bison on the roof of the Altamira cave in north Spain are trussed for carrying. In another late cave, Trois Frères, Ariège, the only really live figure is one that is half human and half bison, surrounded by a *battu* of dead beasts. The relationship was, I suggest, already changing.[20] On a small

FIG. 35. Engravings from Raymondan, Dordogne, France, bone.

engraved bone from Raymondon there is the majestic head of a dead bison, the dislocated forelegs are stretched out in front, and on either side of the backbone, which has been picked bare, are anonymous little human figures, participants in the ceremonial feast (Fig. 35). The relationship and scale of man to animal are like that of the hunt scene at Çatal Hüyük (Fig. 36).

At Çatal Hüyük the painted griffin-vultures snapping off the heads of tiny insect-like human figures are frightening in a way that the Paleolithic mammoth and bison are not (Fig. 37). There is cruelty here which is absent there. James Mellaart sees them as symbols of death.[21] Whether this could account

[18] Sandars, op. cit. (note 6), Pl. 34 and very many more.

[19] Convincing and reasoned arguments for the use of dead models were put forward by P. Leason, *Proceedings of the Prehistoric Society* N. S. 5 (1939) 51, though rather too much was claimed at the time.

[20] Sandars, op. cit. (note 6), pp. 63, 72, Fig. 24 and Pl. 74.

[21] J. Mellaart, op. cit. (note 13), Pls 45, 48, 49, Fig. 47. The fearful full-face lions of Trois Frères are an exception in cave art, Sandars op. cit. (note 6), Fig. 18.

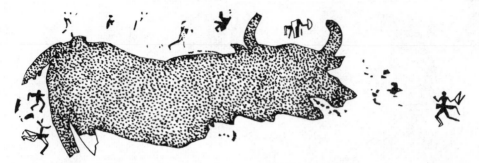

FIG. 36. Wall-painting of hunt-scene, Çatal Hüyük in Turkey, level III, l. of bull 2.05 m.

FIG. 37. Wall-painting of men and griffin-vultures, Çatal Hüyük, level VII.

for the new element of horror I do not know. Even if Paleolithic hunters respected the game, it does not follow that they worshipped animals, or worshipped gods in animal shape.

It might, I think, be helpful now to move down to the standpoint of the early literate inhabitants of the Near East, especially Mesopotamia, for this is one of the many subjects discussed in his latest book by Thorkild Jacobsen. He puts forward a progression from gods in animal form to the same gods in human form, but carrying, standing on, or even attacking, their old animal shapes, now reduced to emblems. The power of the storm was at one time visualized as a great bird with a lion's head, its spread wings the black cloud of torrential rain. This is how we see it on a mid-third millennium silver vase from Telloh (Pl. 40), where the storm-god was worshipped as Ningirsu. Third

FIG. 38. Relief from Nimrud in Iraq.

millennium seals show the god growing a human body and keeping only the wings of the storm-bird Imdugud; while in first millennium Assyria, in Ninurta's temple at Nimrud, the man-like god is shown menacing with a thunderbolt his old persona (Fig. 38).[22]

Samuel Kramer has claimed that the Sumerians are among the best known people of the Near East.[23] The recognition of a non-Semitic language among the archives at Nineveh had led to their identification in the first place, and the title 'King of Sumer and Akkad' suggested a name for this language and for its Semitic sequel. After the first attempts at writing in the early third millennium the script had become flexible enough, by its second half, to express literary and historical matters; but although tens of thousands of

[22] Jacobsen, op. cit. (note 7), 6–9; H. Frankfort, *The Art and Architecture of the Ancient Orient* (Harmondsworth, 1954), Pl. 32, vase from Telloh (Lagash); see also the famous copper relief from Al 'Ubaid, Pl. 27a; also Fig. 38 relief from Nimrud; Frankfort is more cautious in his ascriptions than Jacobsen.

[23] S. N. Kramer, 'Sumerian Literature, A General Survey' in F. Wright (ed.), *The Bible and the Ancient Near East. Essays in honour of W. F. Albright*, 249–66 (London, 1961); id., *The Sumerians, their history, culture and character*, (Chicago, 1964).

economic and administrative texts have come down from the early period, there are only a handful of literary documents among them. It is not until the first half of the second millennium that we get large numbers of Sumerian literary compositions. These include myths, lamentations, historical records, wisdom, proverbs, and fables. But although Sumerian grammar is well understood there has been no equal advance in lexicography. Much has been achieved with the help of bilingual texts, Sumerian and Akkadian, but there are many expressions for which no Akkadian counterpart is known, and meanings have to be guessed from context, while some Sumerian words seem to have more than one Akkadian equivalent.

In spite of these difficulties, and starting from the assumption that a long oral tradition lies behind the written documents, Jacobsen has set out a boldly chronological scheme. The chapter-headings show the shape of his thinking.[24] He starts with 'Fourth Millennium Metaphors: The gods as providers, dying gods of fertility'. This is followed by 'Third Millennium Metaphors: The gods as rulers, the cosmos a polity'. In the second millennium we find 'The gods as parents and the rise of personal religion', with which goes a greater concern with world origins and world order. Finally in the first millennium personal religion persists and develops, but there is also a growing brutalization. These changing religious metaphors are seen as the counterpart of developing social structures.

The 'earlier' gods, those projected back into the fourth millennium, are called 'intransitive' because they are innate powers representing the prime economic needs of a people living in village settlements and small towns, among marshes, orchards, and lagoons, surrounded by desert. A favourite metaphor was fixed in the figure of the god Dumuzi as Amaushangalanna, 'the one great source of the date-clusters'; and he is linked to a goddess, Inanna, who stands for the communal store-house represented as a stylized door-post with its matting door bundled round it.

The lighthearted courtship of these two is celebrated in a number of songs; and is followed by marriage rituals in which sometimes the human king took the place of Dumuzi with the goddess, like Iddin Dagan of Isin around 1950 BC, of whom the texts state 'after the raising of the marriage dais for Inanna, the king being a god, will unite with her upon it'. According to Jacobsen it was through such rituals as this that the date-harvest was secured for the year, with universal rejoicings. The songs, prayers, and fragments of ritual belong

[24] Jacobsen, op. cit., *passim*. What follows is necessarily a very incomplete summary of a quantity of extremely rich and concentrated material.

to a particular place, city, or temple. The names are not important. For the shepherds and herdsmen Dumuzi was a shepherd, and in this character he had a tragic side, dying in the dry heat of summer when lambing and calving were at an end and the pastures withered. The beautiful laments for a lost Dumuzi are forerunners of those of the women weeping for Tammuz and Adonis.

The early dynastic period in the third millennium saw open villages giving place to heavily fortified towns; and the character of the gods changed from 'intransitive' to 'transitive'. Enlil is no longer 'Lord Wind', the innate power of wind, but a god who *commands* the winds. Other gods, while retaining some of their 'older' social and economic character, now possess transitive functions as judges and war-leaders. It follows that this is the time of the institution of kingship when, according to the language of the day, kingship 'came down from heaven'. Population grew and so did pressure on the land, power was concentrated and the state became far more complex with professionals controlling all the principal departments of life. Continuity was maintained in the concept of gods as 'manorial lords' administering their great temple estates through their human deputies.

Then in the second millennium we find a new religious development which is, I think, the most interesting to come out of ancient Mesopotamia: personal religion and the relationship of man to god as of child to parent. To quote Jacobsen again, personal religion meant 'a particular easily recognised attitude in which the religious individual sees himself ... in close personal relationship to the divine, expecting help and guidance in his ... affairs and divine anger and punishment if he sins, but also expecting divine compassion, forgiveness and love.'[25] The personal god is older than personal religion, which probably sprang from this peculiar Mesopotamian development. To begin with it was probably no more than a man's 'luck', the sudden, and not uncommon, sense of some power 'taking over', or taking a hand in one's affairs. The god is always a clearly identified member of the pantheon, male or female. He, or she, inhabits the body of the individual and protects him. The formula used is 'So-and-so, son of his god'. But his relationship to the other gods remains the same. Personal religion finds its expression in prayers and penitential psalms. But there is another side to 'luck' which is the equally mysterious visitations of misfortune; the sense that a power, whatever it is, has departed. Though apparently unique to Mesopotamia at this early period, it is a feeling not unknown in later ages. Shakespeare used it through

[25] Jacobsen, op. cit. 147.

Plutarch, when the defeat and death of Antony are presaged by signs and strange music, and the 'second soldier' announces:

> It is the god Hercules whom Antony loved
> Now leaves him ...[26]

Side by side with the humility and self-abasement of the suppliant before his god, there is a paradoxical element of self-importance. Jacobsen notes that 'the unlimited ego of the penitent monopolises the god and holds the centre of the stage'. Some of the individual complaints strike near home.

> I, a literate person, have been changed
> From one who knew things into a clod.
> My hand has been stayed from writing,
> My mouth has had its discourse lessened.

And I think we all probably know this subject:

I am a young man, I am knowledgeable, but what I know does not come right with me.

> What I truthfully say turns into falsehood.
> ....
> The wrong-doer says shaming things to me
> But you, my god, do not answer them back.[27]

It is clear that his long-suffering god has lost interest in the young man.

As early as 2000 BC there are hints, in some of the laments, that personal religion might have developed into a great cry of all humanity to its god, to stay him from his more terrible actions, but this nationwide supplication did not emerge until Israel transcended the self-importance of the individual into the reconciliation of Job; while at the national level the relationship of Yahveh to Israel, his compassion, his anger, his forgiveness, is in all essentials the same as the relationship of god and the individual in Mesopotamian personal religion.

It was in the second millennium that men began to take a special interest in world origins and the construction of theogonies. Stories of beginnings became the concern of the organized priesthood, but there is great variety in the choice of protagonists, each city promoting its own particular god. Thus

---

[26] *Antony and Cleopatra* IV. iii; see also a poem by the Alexandrian poet C. P. Cavafy, 'The God abandons Antony'. (English trans. in E. Keeley and P. Sherrard, *Six Poets of Modern Greece* (London, 1960), 40).

[27] Jacobsen, op. cit. 154, 153.

in the best known of all, the Babylonian cosmogony of the later second millennium, contained in the Enuma Elish, Marduk, the city's patron god, is given prime authority, and eventually endowed with the qualities and powers of all the other gods.[28]

Some theogonies belonged to special occasions such as the curing of diseases, or to certain classes of persons such as midwives. One theogony recently published by Kramer, and dated around 2000, begins with the goddess Nammu who is called 'the ancestress who gave birth to all the gods'. Kramer thinks that the place of this goddess of the sea and the sweet waters was usurped by Enki, the numinous power in rivers, marshes, and rain.[29] Yet other lists start with An, heaven, and Ki, earth, whose first-born offspring was Enlil, the storm-wind, who separated heaven and earth. Around 2300 the usual order seems to have been An, Enlil, Ninhursag (queen of the mountain), and Enki.

It is tempting to treat these lists as schematized versions of some real order of precedence with older gods fading into the background as their children succeed to their places; or as the Babylonian cosmogony has it, 'grow taller than their fathers'. But I do not think that this really works.

The brutalization of religious ideas and practices in the first millennium was partly due to the deterioration in the conditions in which life was lived, with constant wars, famines, and the rise of the terrible Assyrian Empire. Art as well as religion is marked by cruelty and violence. The warrior gods of the third millennium had been heroes, such as Enlil and Ninurta, but in the first millennium the ruler metaphor is taken over by Erra, god of riot and indiscriminate slaughter. Assyrian rituals have a new crudeness and brutality, as when king and priest advance bouncing, like a football, a loaf which represents the heart of An, the once supreme sky-god, which has been torn from his body. We might be among the Incas.

Gods now are pawns of politics and the god of an enemy state is himself an enemy. A more interesting development in first millennium religious ideas was the delegation of powers to one particular god, matching the absolutism of the human sovereign. All gods may appear as aspects of one god; but Jacobsen warns us, 'The line between epithets and names of a deity had been

---

[28] The *Enuma Elish*, sometimes called the Babylonian Creation, though it is as much a hymn in praise of Marduk as a true creation story.

[29] S. N. Kramer, *The Legacy of Sumer, Invited Lectures on the Middle East*, University of Texas, Austin, ed. D. Schmandt-Besserat (Malibor, 1976), 12–21. I owe this reference to Mrs K. R. Maxwell-Hyslop. An example of a special purpose 'creation' is the Atrahasis Epic for the use of midwives.

fluid, and the decision as to whether one or more gods were involved must already have been a difficult one for the ancients'.[30]

This attractive and persuasive system will probably be adopted and adapted for some years to come, so it is well to remember how much it depends on inspired guesswork, as well as its very localized geographical scope, tied to one landscape and its inhabitants. The problem is aggravated by the late date of the texts. Writing in 1963, when he had already formulated his central ideas, Jacobsen said that the written sources, that only begin late in the early dynastic period, 'do not in fact constitute an autonomous body of evidence ... left to stand by themselves they would be largely meaningless and incoherent'. So recourse has to be made to later evidence and to the proposition that these later sources contain some 'elements directly surviving from earlier times, others that survive more or less altered, and others that are altogether new developments'. 'Before they can be used in this way internal criteria of relative age must be considered and the various strata of tradition distinguished. Only then can they be used without obvious danger of anachronism.'[31] This leaves much room for subjective judgements, but when applied by a scholar of Jacobsen's unique qualities, for the most part they may be accepted with confidence.

I said earlier that, given our long adult history, it is no good looking for anything very primitive in the societies of the fourth and third millennium BC. But the use of this term 'primitive' is itself highly subjective. There are some very 'primitive' elements in our own coronation service; and the wording of a profound and very beautiful prayer used by the church on Holy Saturday, could, taken literally, be very primitive indeed. The waters of the font are blessed with these words, 'He fertilizes the water prepared for the regeneration of men by the hidden intermixture of His light, that by a heavenly conception a holy offspring may rise up out of the spotless womb of the font'.[32] The words contain a theological mystery, but they are common English. When you add the difficulties and ambiguities of the Sumerian language, we find ourselves on very precarious ground indeed. We have no *real* knowledge of what the Sumerians, or any other ancient people meant by, or made effective in, the words of their religious texts.

[30] Jacobsen, op. cit. 234–5.

[31] Jacobsen, 'Ancient Mesopotamian Religion—the Central Concerns', *Proceedings of the American Philosophical Society*, 107:6 (1963), 473–84, with detailed apologia for the method of deduction employed. This reference I owe to Dr Oliver Gurney.

[32] This part of the very ancient prayer is taken from the *Sarum Missal* in the translation of A. Harford Pearson, 2nd edn (1884), 169.

With all sorts of races of men, and with most animals, we can recognize a cry of pain for what it is; a shout of joy and another shout of rage; but the moment we become tangled with those arch-symbols, those charged, loaded, contorted, intricate counters—words—we are drifting from probability to possibility to doubt. Thorlief Boman has written of the problems of the Book of Genesis, that the psychological mystery is perhaps explained by the fact that, for the ancients, the word was more substantial and matter more spiritual than for us.[33]

The 'primitive' is really the timeless, like those courtship songs in which the young god Dumuzi is invited by Inanna as a beautiful young girl. Dumuzi speaks,

> As I walked out, as I walked out
> As I walked by the house
> My dear Inanna saw me;
> O brother mine what was it then she told me?
> O brother mine, it was of love and loving
> And the sweetest of sweet things ...
> ... into her house she brought me
> And made me to lie down
> On the sweet soft, honey-soft bed.

And another song,

> As I walked out one spring morning fair,
> To view the fields and take the air,
> There I heard a pretty maid making her complain,
> And all she wanted was the chiefest grain.
>
> I said to her, 'My pretty maid,
> Come tell me what you need?'
> 'O yes kind sir, you're the man to do my deed,
> For to sow my meadow with the wanton seed.'[34]

If we did not know that the second song could be heard till recently in the West Country, we might have turned it into a pretty piece of mythology, with a goddess of the cornland inviting a young god, just like Inanna and Dumuzi.

[33] T. Boman, *Hebrew Thought Compared with Greek* (London, 1960), 92; see also the chapter on 'Impression and Appearance', pp. 74–90.

[34] Sumerian song, Jacobsen, op. cit. (note 7), 27, with minor rewording; and A. L. Lloyd, *Folk Song in England* (London, 1969), 201.

Yet these Sumerian songs have been called by both Kramer and Jacobsen some of the earliest surviving compositions. So they may be, but they also belong to the timeless placeless world of popular song.

Where all the texts are comparatively late, and so uncertain, archaeology may occasionally provide a corrective. In the texts the god of sweet waters and of the deep, Enki, 'Lord Earth', is usually one of the younger gods; but the city of Eridu in southern Sumer, which was Enki's own city, is one of the earliest excavated Sumerian sites. It is now 150 miles from the Persian Gulf, but formerly it was much closer, it had a quay and stood on one of the many interconnecting lagoons. A series of eighteen very early temples have been excavated, underlying a great unfinished ziggurat built by Amar-Sin who died of a septic foot about 2039 BC.[35] The two earliest temples of around 5200 were simple rectangular one-room buildings, not very different from the mud-brick and reed houses of the first inhabitants, who lived on fish and molluscs (Fig 39). The third temple, No. 16, had a bay or apse and an altar, and the remains of burnt offerings were found. From the beginning of the fifth millennium the buildings become more complex with separate rooms around a central nave or hall, and with stairways and corridors. A temple plan was established that remained typical of Sumerian centres for a very long time. Since Eridu was Enki's city, these must have been his temples, and his claim to antiquity antedates by some two thousand years the earliest literary theogony.

This does not, of course, prove that he was 'the oldest' Sumerian god. That would be a meaningless statement anyhow. The personality of Enki is the personality of the landscape and the life of these men of the lagoons and marshes, whose well-being depended on irrigation with canals, and the management of the flood-water of rivers, annually swollen by melting snows in the faraway mountains. The personalities of most of the other Sumerian gods are equally at home here, and would be equally alien among the mountains of Iran or Anatolia, or in the Nile valley. Their names may travel but the gods themselves do not.[36]

Temple-building continued to increase in grandeur. Another important early site is Tell 'Uqair fifty miles south of Baghdad.[37] The so-called 'painted

[35] M. E. L. Mallowan, *Cambridge Ancient History*, rev. edn., I Chap. VIII, part 1 (Cambridge, 1967), Fig. 1.

[36] For an attempt to emphasize this rather neglected facet see N. K. Sandars in J. V. S. Megaw (ed.) *To Illustrate the Monuments, essays presented to Stuart Piggott*, 277–82.

[37] M. E. L. Mallowan, loc. cit., Fig. 8; and S. Lloyd and E. Safar, *Journal of Near Eastern Studies* 2 (1943), 132–58, Pls X, XIV, etc.

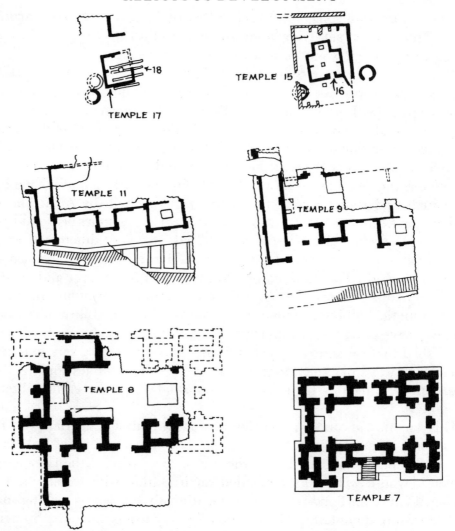

FIG. 39. Ground-plans of early temples at Eridu (Abu Shahrein) in Iraq.

temple' stands on a platform, has a buttressed façade, and is approached by three ceremonial flights of stairs flanked by parapets (Fig. 40). The inside walls of the temple, which is of the usual Sumerian tripartite plan, have paintings of men bringing offerings of cattle to the god, and of a seated leopard (Fig. 41); the same domestic and wild beasts, incidentally, that were so prominent at Çatal Hüyük. If the painted temple belongs to the end of the fourth millennium it is one and a half millennia later than Çatal Hüyük.

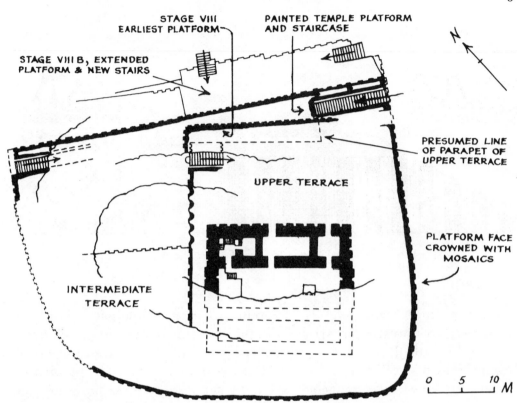

FIG. 40. Ground-plan of 'Painted Temple', Tell'Uqair, Iraq.

Another millennium later still the temple complex of third dynasty Ur is the setting for still more magnificent ceremonial, as well as housing a large administrative officialdom.[38] There is a regular progression from the hugger-mugger village plan at Çatal Hüyük with its jumble of shrines and private houses, iconographically rich, but lacking any provision for the entry of sacrificial animals or for the larger gestures of public worship; from this through the simplicities of early Eridu, to the later temple buildings with their stairways, platforms, and raised altars, the stages for more magnificent rituals, leading to Ur and eventually to Babylon itself.

Architecture reflects changes in ritual observance, but these outward shows need not imply significant changes in the objects of worship, any more than do the different emphases in the formal worship of the Christian church

[38] e.g. Ur at the end of the third millennium, C. L. Woolley, *Antiquaries Journal* XIV (1934), 355–82 and Pl. 49.

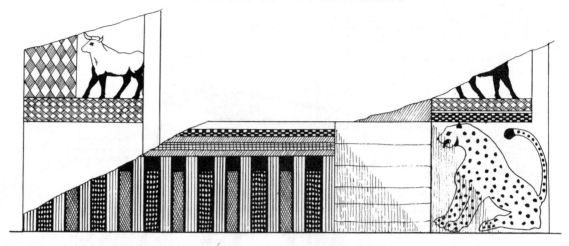

FIG. 41. Wall-painting in 'Painted Temple', Tell'Uqair, Iraq.

at various times, which we also see reflected in the buildings. The large baptisteries of the early centuries, the imperial basilicas, the noble gradations of a Gothic cathedral lifting to its great east end, and the eighteenth-century compromise between concert hall and lecture-room dominated by pulpit and organ—an unwitting archaeologist might suppose these to be houses of totally different creeds.

So here we are, brought up short again by discouraging reflection on the limitation of the archaeological evidence which, while it may tell us something about the social and outward aspects of religion, is quite silent upon all the things that matter most. Literary evidence, archaeological evidence, art, are all limited, all defective. Those 'voices speaking, expressions of individual visions of life . . . that need the gifts of an artist endowed with historical insight and imagination to understand them', they escape us and probably always will.

I am afraid that what I have been saying may appear very negative, even defeatist; but we should be profoundly grateful to the constructors of interpretive systems, the pattern-makers. Without their creative activity there would be nothing really to talk about. So even if the sum of the achievement by the end of the day, is only to tell us a little more about ourselves, this is still worth doing. After all, many a poorish painter can produce a very passable self-portrait.

There are so many things that I have not mentioned and they include perhaps the most central of all, death: so I will end with some words of J. S. Dunne. In *The City of the Gods* he wrote, 'The history of hitherto existing society is the history of a struggle for life. This struggle though, has not been the struggle among the races, or among classes, which it is supposed to have been . . . Rather it has been a struggle of all human beings against the common nemesis of every human life, a struggle to overcome death. The shadowed figure of Gilgamesh roaming over the wasteland . . . is the figure of man himself wandering through these many centuries in quest of immortality'.[39]

[39] J. S. Dunne, *The City of the Gods* (New York 1965, London 1974), 217.

VII

THE ORIGIN AND DISSEMINATION OF WRITING IN WESTERN ASIA

J. D. HAWKINS

INTRODUCTORY

The questions

THE PRESENT study of the origins of civilization, in its survey of the rise of cities in four parts of the world, has suggested various criteria which distinguish human societies qualifying as 'cities' and as 'civilized'. The development of agriculture, technology, and trade has been seen to have enlarged the economic base of communities, and permitted them to expand. In the archaeological record, evidence for this is found in the larger and more elaborate buildings excavated, the improvement of metalworking techniques and the appearance of goods of distant origin. Another criterion of the advance of civilization is often held to be literacy, with all its implications of the ability to account, record, and administer, to transmit and to perpetuate knowledge through space and time. It was indeed peculiarly a feature of the civilization of the Ancient Near East, and its origin, dissemination, and character may appropriately be considered in the present context.[1]

In speaking of the origin and dissemination of writing in the Ancient Near East, one risks begging the question. While it is conceded that the earliest systems of writing yet discovered belong to the Near East, we may ask

[1] In venturing to tackle this very wide-ranging subject, I have received invaluable help from a number of scholars. I wish particularly to thank Professor John Baines, to whom I owe Egyptological advice and references; Professor Anna Morpurgo Davies, for her help and criticism in the Aegean sphere; and Dr Michael Weitzman for his reading of the manuscript and apposite comments.

Short, general bibliographies on Writing and Decipherment and a Map are given at the end of the article. Otherwise in providing references, I have attempted to confine myself to the accessible and the recent: to the revised *Cambridge Ancient History*, hereafter *CAH*, vols I/2–II (3rd ed., Cambridge, 1971, 1973, 1975) and its bibliographies, for the historical background and discussion where available; and to recent Symposia and other works with comprehensive bibliographies where possible.

whether within this area there was only one origin of writing, from which all systems were disseminated, or whether writing arose independently in a number of different centres. Similarly, were there independently originating centres outside this geographical area, or were they all ultimately dependent on dissemination from the earliest known centre? To pose the question so starkly is to court failure to answer it. Nevertheless these questions must be borne in mind while we review the evidence, and certain general conclusions may be permissible. It is possible, for example, to construct a hypothetical tree tracing the descent of all writing systems from a Mesopotamian origin (see Fig. 42).

Our inquiry will extend until the beginning of the Alphabet, but will not follow the triumphant progress whereby this system of writing was disseminated, sometimes in almost unrecognizable forms, to become the script of the vast majority of written modern languages. It is useful in our examination of earlier scripts to recall that while the Alphabet has been borrowed directly and adapted by a new language from an older one, sometimes also it has been substantially remodelled in the process, usually in the external appearance of its sign forms but occasionally also in its internal characteristics.[2]

Preservation of ancient scripts

A preliminary question should be considered, whether the recovered corpuses of ancient inscriptions adequately represent the whole range of ancient literacy, and whether new discoveries may not radically alter our present perspectives. Among the most durable of ancient writings are those inscribed on rock faces or dressed stone, and these are therefore common survivors. However the laborious nature of such writing has restricted the type of document so inscribed to those for which special permanence was desired—largely religious and commemorative dedications—and if we were dependent on these for our knowledge of ancient literacy, we should indeed have a very unbalanced view of it. Chance has preserved other ancient corpuses written on other materials. Of these the most outstandingly durable is clay, which when baked rivals the permanence of stone, and which even unbaked is usually archaeologically recoverable. Clay was the principal writing material of ancient Mesopotamia and of areas under its cultural influence. The surviving Mesopotamian corpus is thus likely to be truly representative, though much

[2] e.g. the Kharosthi and Brahmi scripts, which substantially remodelled the Semitic Alphabet from which they are presumed to derive.

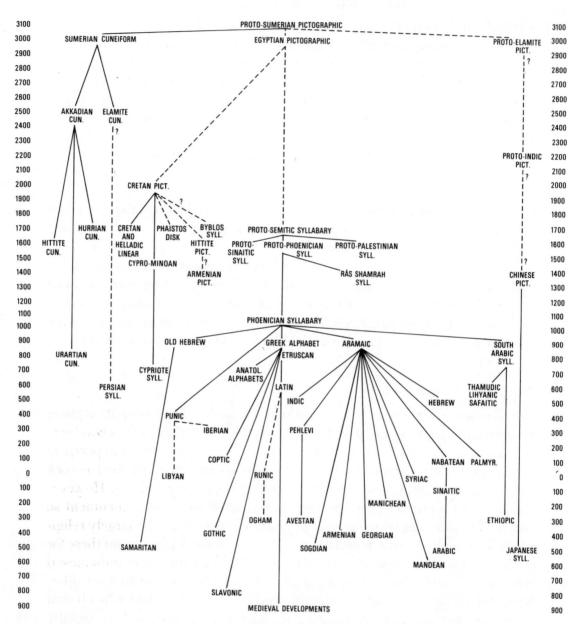

FIG. 42. The Diffusion of Writing (hypothetical).

more essentially comparable and complementary material is known to await discovery.

In Egypt on the other hand the principal writing material was papyrus, the survival of which is very rare other than in those extremely arid conditions which fortuitously but fortunately obtain in Egypt. A proportion of Egyptian papyrus literature has thus survived, though not in quantities to rival that of the Mesopotamian clay tablet. On the other hand, places under Egyptian cultural influence, such as the Levant, which may be presumed to have seen the circulation of Egyptian papyri, have preserved hardly a trace.

The Hittite sphere of literacy offers an instructive example of survival. Their palace archives written on clay tablets adopted from Mesopotamia have survived in fair proportion in spite of deliberate and random destruction, and their monumental inscriptions on stone in Hieroglyphic script have also been transmitted in small numbers. However their texts also refer to documents and scribes 'of wood' (see below, page 155 and note 73), but of these not a single example has been recovered, nor are the prospects good for the future. We shall see below that other such lost corpuses are known or may be inferred, while yet others may be unsuspected. This advises caution in evaluation of the evidence.

Nature of early writing

We shall see that one of the earliest stages of writing is 'pictography', in which the 'pictographs' are to be 'read' as the object they portray—a picture of a MAN, read 'man', or a COW, read 'cow'. Pictograms readily become 'ideograms' which represent not only the concrete object portrayed but also associated 'ideas'—a picture of a FOOT read not only 'foot' but also 'stand; walk; go', etc., or SUN not only 'sun' but also 'day; bright; white' etc. Pictograms and ideograms, together termed generally 'logograms' (word signs), may be combined in a system which has obvious limitations: if each word is to be represented by one sign, the number of signs required is likely to be very large. Thus the student of the modern Chinese script, which retains its original logographic character, needs to learn about 3,000 characters to achieve even a modest competence. We may also note that logograms as such do not render any specific language but may be read in the language of the reader; thus COW may be read 'cow', 'vache', 'Kuh', 'vacca', etc.

An important advance over logography was achieved when a method of representing not words but the sounds of a language was devised. We shall consider in detail below how this was done; essentially 'syllabograms' were invented, signs to represent the constituent syllables of words. The advantage of this over the theoretically limitless demands of logography is that a complete series of syllabograms, a 'syllabary', only requires some 80–100 signs, an immense economy. Theoretically the adoption of a syllabary would permit the elimination of logography, since any word could be written syllabically, but in practice this was seldom carried out. Logograms continued to be used in combination with the syllabary as a kind of shorthand. It was perhaps considered easier to write a word with one sign, a logogram, rather than several syllabograms. The disadvantage lay of course in the initial memorization of the repertory of logograms. However it is clear that ancient writing was in the hands of a small literate élite, the scribes, who manifested great conservatism in the practice of their craft, and, so far from being interested in its simplification, often chose to demonstrate their virtuosity by a proliferation of signs and values which borders on the cryptographic. Thus most ancient scripts retained a mixed logographic–syllabographic character.

However we shall see how a momentous advance beyond this stage of development did occur, which led to the supersession of the cumbrous logographic–syllabic systems. Where the syllabaries wrote words in syllabic signs, a system was invented whereby signs were used to represent the individual phonemes of words. This system, the Alphabet, was superior to syllabaries in requiring only some twenty to thirty signs, and thus being much easier to master and more flexible to use. The Alphabet's place and date of origin and the manner of its development will be considered in this paper.

Decipherment[3]

The decipherment of ancient scripts is bound up with their natures as outlined. A sign count will suggest the nature of an undeciphered script. As a rule of thumb, a repertoire of over 100 signs (and some ancient corpuses show over 500) suggests the presence of logography, one of 50–100 suggests a syllabary, and one of 20–30 an alphabet. The process of decipherment consists partly in identifying the logograms, but much more important, in attributing to the phonetic signs, syllabic or alphabetic, their correct phonetic value, after which they may be transcribed into a modern Alphabet. Only thus can the underlying language be penetrated.

Most of the main corpuses of ancient inscriptions are more or less completely deciphered, though many lesser corpuses remain unpenetrated,

---

[3] See general bibliography at the end of the article.

perhaps impenetrable, while the decipherments claimed for others remain still *sub judice*. In these cases it is usually an insufficiency of material which rules out the penetration or the decisive confirmation or rejection of a plausible hypothesis. A number of these uncertain scripts will be considered below, though naturally much less can be said with confidence about them than about those more fully deciphered.

Dissemination

Cuneiform writing, developed in the Sumero–Akkadian symbiosis in Mesopotamia, was disseminated to other linguistic groups, passing to Syria (Ebla), the Elamites and the Hurrians in the third millennium BC, to the Assyrians and Hittites and also the Canaanites and Egyptians in the second, and to the Urartians and the Achaemenian Persians in the first. The Elamites before their borrowing of Mesopotamian Cuneiform had a linear script of their own (i.e. one in which the signs are rendered in drawn lines), and the possible connection of this with Mesopotamia, as also that of the more distant Indus Valley script, must be considered below. The other great centre of literacy, Egypt, may also have arisen under Mesopotamian influence. Egyptian Hieroglyphic writing had its own area of dissemination, directly to the Syro-Palestinian coastlands and perhaps indirectly to the Aegean (the Cretan syllabaries) and to Anatolia (Hieroglyphic Luwian). Much more important than these transmissions however is the question of the possible links between Egyptian writing and the early Canaanite alphabet, for which the rock inscriptions of Sinai are suggestive. This paper will follow the story down to the end of the second millennium BC and the appearance of the Canaanite Alphabet. The transmission of Cuneiform to Urartian and the Achaemenian Persians and of Egyptian Hieroglyphic to Meroitic, and the spread of the Alphabet to Greece and the West, to South Arabia, and by the medium of Aramaic to the East, lie beyond the present purview.

THE MESOPOTAMIAN SPHERE

The rise of the Cuneiform script

Mesopotamia's long-standing claim to be the home of the earliest writing and probably also of its ultimate origin, is still not seriously contested. That is, all other systems present at least the possibility that they originated ultimately under Mesopotamian influence. One caveat should be borne in mind:

Mesopotamia from the first wrote on that material most conducive to survival, namely clay, and it might be that earlier experiments elsewhere on other materials have been lost for ever. However other considerations still do not suggest that this is likely.

Mesopotamia's 'Cuneiform' script is so called from the characteristic wedge-shaped strokes of which the signs are composed, the impressions left by a reed stylus on clay, later imitated in stone and metal. The script in its earliest recovered stages however was not cuneiform but linear and pictorial. Its external cuneiform appearance as well as its essential internal characteristics resulted from a process of development which will be briefly traced.

The period of the earliest-known writing, termed Protoliterate from this most important innovation and conventionally dated c.3200–2800 BC,[4] is marked by the discovery of groups of archaic clay tablets at the site of Uruk level IV, followed by others from level III[5] and the contemporary site Jemdet Nasr.[6] The tablets are small and bear linearly drawn signs, mostly of a recognizably pictographic character, as well as impressed markings denoting numerals, oblique almost triangular strokes for units and circles for tens. Often the surface of the tablets is divided up by horizontal and vertical linear rulings, and the signs and numerals are grouped within the compartments. The signs, many of which can be identified with their later known, descended cuneiform shapes, may recognizably represent parts of the human body, animals, plants, artefacts or astral phenomena. They cannot actually be 'read' because they provide no indication of the underlying language, but as a very limited system of writing they can be partially understood, mostly as inventories listing issues or receipts of commodities to or from named individuals. One for example (Fig. 43) registers on one side 50+4 cow ox, a total broken down on the other into individual entries against one or two signs each of which is doubtless to be interpreted as a personal name.

The stage of writing represented by these documents shows on the one hand more or less recognizable pictograms, and on the other the numeral system. The writing of the presumed personal names however must represent a more advanced device than either pictograms or numeral notation, since it may be assumed that few would lend themselves to pictographic representa-

---

[4] See in general *CAH* I/2³, Chap. XII with bibliography, 892 ff.

[5] A. Falkenstein, *Archaische Texte aus Uruk* (Berlin, 1936).

[6] S. H. Langdon, *Pictographic inscriptions from Jemdet Nasr*, OECT 7 (Oxford, 1928).

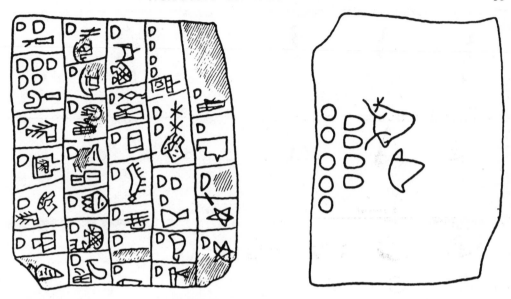

FIG. 43. Archaic Uruk tablet.

tion. These writings cannot at present be penetrated, but it is likely that the names were rendered on some sort of 'rebus'-principle, i.e. the representation of an undrawable word by one or more drawable objects to suggest its sounds. Such a postulated divorce of sound from meaning would have been a significant step in the development of the script.

A forerunner of this earliest stage of writing has recently been sought in the clay 'calculi' discovered on many Near Eastern excavations.[7] Particularly common examples of these are clay spheres and cones, sometimes found in connection with hollow clay balls bearing numeral markings on their exteriors, into which the calculi can be put. It is suggested that the spherical and conoid calculi were later represented two-dimensionally by the impressed triangles and circles of the protoliterate numerical system, and perhaps even that the idea of linear pictograms went back to some three-dimensional models used as calculi; thus for example, the sign SHEEP (circle with internal cross) might be associated with the clay discs with incised crosses. See Fig. 44 for table of suggested correspondences. As has been noted a pictographic–logographic script affords no evidence of the underlying

[7] D. Schmandt-Besserat, 'An Archaic Recording System and the Origin of Writing', *Syro-Mesopotamian Studies* 1/2 (1977), 1–32.

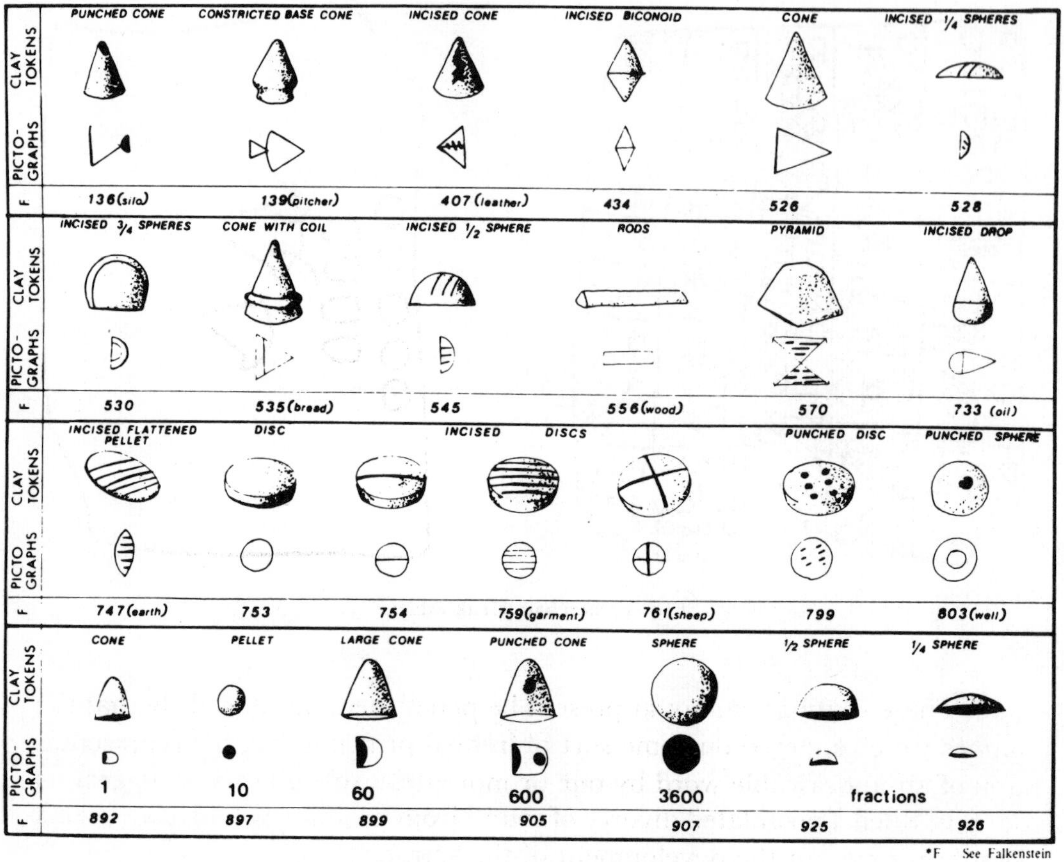

CLAY TOKENS	PUNCHED CONE	CONSTRICTED BASE CONE	INCISED CONE	INCISED BICONOID	CONE	INCISED ¼ SPHERES
PICTO-GRAPHS						
F	136(silo)	139(pitcher)	407 (leather)	434	526	528
CLAY TOKENS	INCISED ¾ SPHERES	CONE WITH COIL	INCISED ½ SPHERE	RODS	PYRAMID	INCISED DROP
PICTO-GRAPHS						
F	530	535 (bread)	545	556(wood)	570	733 (oil)
CLAY TOKENS	INCISED FLATTENED PELLET	DISC	INCISED DISCS		PUNCHED DISC	PUNCHED SPHERE
PICTO-GRAPHS						
F	747(earth)	753	754	759(garment)	761(sheep)	799	803(well)

CLAY TOKENS	CONE	PELLET	LARGE CONE	PUNCHED CONE	SPHERE	½ SPHERE	¼ SPHERE
PICTO-GRAPHS	1	10	60	600	3600	fractions	
F	892	897	899	905	907	925	926

*F   See Falkenstein

FIG. 44. Warka (Uruk) pictographs and suggested corresponding clay tokens.

language since only when phonetic signs can be identified can this be penetrated. However a purely logographic script is subject to severe limitations; besides the difficulty in rendering personal names, logograms having more than one potential reading cannot be distinguished, nor can sentences which require number, case and tense markers for nouns and verbs be rendered unambiguously. All these call for the invention of at least a limited number of phonetic signs. A very few such devices have been identified in the later archaic tablets (Uruk level III and Jemdet Nasr),[8] one of the most notable being an ARROW (Sumerian TI) being used to write the word LIVE/LIFE (Sumerian TI(L)) in a name to be read EN.LÍL-TI (Sumerian '(the god) Enlil

[8] Falkenstein, *Archaische Texte aus Uruk*, 37 ff.

(gives) life') a typical later name form. Besides being one of the earliest clear examples of rebus-writing, this certainly points to the inventing language, i.e. the language of the late archaic texts, being Sumerian, the later known language of lower Mesopotamia. Since in the following 'Early Dynastic' period, the Sumerians are found as the main population group and the users of the developing script for their own language, it seems likely that they were indeed its original devisers in the archaic period, though incontrovertible evidence is absent.[9]

Certainly the Sumerian language was the first and most important detectable influence on the development of the phonetic elements of the script.[10] Sumerian, an agglutinative language of unknown affiliations, is characterized by monosyllabic roots of the type single-vowel (e.g. A, 'water'), consonant-+vowel (e.g. KA, 'mouth'), vowel+consonant (e.g. AN, 'sky') and consonant-+vowel+consonant (e.g. SAG, 'head'). The existence of such roots readily led to the formation of a rudimentary syllabary from common, drawable words used as rebus-writings. Since Sumerian also possessed many homonyms, the script early acquired a number of 'homophones' (signs with the same phonetic value), which are one of its later characteristics.

In the Early Dynastic period (c.2800–2400 BC), the recovered documents suggest a dramatic expansion in the use of writing.[11] Substantial groups of tablets have been found at Ur, Fara, Lagash and most recently at Abu Salabikh.[12] These are predominantly administrative and economic texts, but the recent discoveries also show that the foundations of Sumerian written literature were laid in this period. In addition the tradition of royal inscriptions begins, usually short dedications on stone or other artefacts.[13] This was the age of the first flowering of recognizably Sumerian culture.

The script of the period was still basically logographic, but began to be supplemented by phonetic elements written more or less sparingly as 'phonetic complements' to the logograms and as grammatical elements; e.g. STAR +na, read an-na, 'heaven', as opposed to STAR +ra, read dingir-ra, 'god'. As

---

[9] A. Falkenstein, *Das Sumerische* Handbuch der Orientalistik (Leyden, 1959), B. Die Keilschrift. For the idea of a pre-Sumerian substratum as inventors of the script, see I. J. Gelb, 'Sumerians and Akkadians in their ethno-linguistic relationship' (IXe Rencontre Assyriologique Internationale, Geneva, 1960; published, *Genava* N.S. 8 (1960), 258–71, esp. 261–4).

[10] Falkenstein, *Das Sumerische*, 14 ff.

[11] See in general *CAH* I/2³, Chap. XIII, esp. § 1, with bibliography, 894 ff.

[12] R. D. Biggs, *Inscriptions from Tell Abū Salābīkh*, *OIP* XCIX (Chicago, 1974); R. D. Biggs and J. N. Postgate, 'Inscriptions from Abu Salabikh 1975', *Iraq* 40 (1978).

[13] E. Sollberger and J.-R. Kupper, *Inscriptions royales sumériennes et akkadiennes* (Paris, 1971).

a further aid to reading 'class determinatives' were introduced, common word signs written before (or, less commonly, after) logograms and thereby assigning them to a class and signalling the correct reading option. Common examples include the signs GOD (for deities), MAN (for professions or nationalities), WOMAN (for female names); CITY, COUNTRY, PLACE; FLESH (for parts of the body), WOOD (for trees and wooden artefacts), and others. Hereafter three elements of the script are normally present throughout its history, (i) logograms, (ii) syllabograms and (iii) determinatives.[14]

Besides these internal developments, the script also underwent some characteristic if less significant external changes. From being linear and pictorial, the signs were simplified into groups of characteristically wedge-shaped strokes, and as they became more 'cuneiform', their original pictographic content was forgotten. Also the direction of writing changed. Scribes writing signs in vertical columns arranged from right to left, found their right hands smudging what they had written. They therefore swivelled their tablets 90° anticlockwise so that they were writing in horizontal lines from left to right, arranged from top to bottom. This practical device gradually became the accepted norm and the old orientation was forgotten. It had the effect of turning the increasingly unrecognizable pictograms on to their backs.[15]

The last great indigenous development in the formation of the script arose from the ethnic composition of the population of Mesopotamia. Beside the predominantly Sumerian south of lower Mesopotamia, the northern area Akkad was largely inhabited by speakers of a Semitic language, Akkadian. Evidence for the presence of these Semites appears in the written records almost as early as that for the Sumerians, in the shape of Akkadian names and loan words into Sumerian. The Dynasty of Akkad (c.2400–2250 BC) terminated the Early Dynastic period by seizing the political hegemony of the land and uniting a widespread though precarious empire.[16] Thereafter the Sumerian language declined and gave way to Akkadian, and after a Neo-Sumerian cultural revival (Third Dynasty of Ur, c.2120–2000 BC), it apparently died as a spoken language. Even when dead however, it was maintained as a learned language and a cultural medium of Mesopotamia and by a fusion with Akkadian produced a remarkable bilingual cultural tradition.[17]

[14] Falkenstein, *Das Sumerische*, 18 ff.

[15] R. Labat, *Manuel d'épigraphie akkadienne* (2nd ed. Paris, 1976), esp. Introduction, sections I–IV.

[16] *CAH* I/2³, Chap. XIX.

[17] W. von Soden, *Zweisprachigkeit in der geistigen Kultur Babyloniens*, Österreichische Akademie der Wissenschaften, Phil.-Hist. Klasse, Sitzungsberichte 235/1 (Vienna, 1960).

The Semitic Akkadian language differed widely from Sumerian, particularly in its phonology. Already during the Early Dynastic period the script began to be adapted for Akkadian to write its personal names. With the rise of the Dynasty of Akkad to political power, Akkadian became an official written language and a thorough-going adaptation of the script was demanded.[18]

Since pure logograms could be read in either language, the whole logographic system of the script could be instantly borrowed, and the logograms rendered bilingual, e.g. Sumerian SAG=Akkadian rēš-, 'head'. The rudimentary syllabary based on monosyllabic Sumerian roots was also adopted, but it was necessary to expand and supplement this. New syllabograms were devised in the same way as the older ones, this time utilizing monosyllabic Akkadian roots as the basis, e.g. Sumerian GIŠ=Akkadian is-, 'wood'; syllabic value is/iš/iz. From this early developing bilingualism of the culture, it can be seen how single signs, besides having a double logographic value, could also acquire two or more syllabic values from them, e.g. Sumerian ú=Akkadian šamm-, 'plant'; syllabic values ú, šam. The 'polyphony' (single signs with multiple values), which was such a marked feature of the later script, was built into it from the start.

With the adaptation of the script to write Akkadian the formation of the writing system was essentially complete, and it continued in use in substantially the same form for more than two millennia. Only comparatively minor modifications occurred during this long period, both external (changes of sign forms) and internal (developments of logographic and syllabic values).[19] No consistent attempts were made either to discard the superfluous logography or to reduce the number of syllabograms to the workable minimum of perhaps one hundred. Indeed the reverse is true: the course of time saw an accumulation of extra and rare values for many signs, which led in the script's latest stages to a bewildering polyvalency which proved such an obstacle to modern decipherers.

Dissemination from Mesopotamia: Elam

Other steps in writing contemporary with those in Mesopotamia were being made elsewhere, which suggest that the idea of writing was early disseminated from the older centre. The closest neighbour is a large group of archaic tablets from the site of Susa in Elam, and from a number of other sites

[18] I. J. Gelb, *Old Akkadian Writing and Grammar*, *MAD* II; 2nd edn., Chicago, 1961, esp. parts I and II.
[19] Labat, *Manuel*; R. Borger, *Akkadische Zeichenliste*, *AOAT* 6 (Neukirchen–Vluyn, 1971); W. von Soden and W. Röllig, *Das Akkadische Syllabar* (An.Or.42; 2nd edn., Rome, 1967).

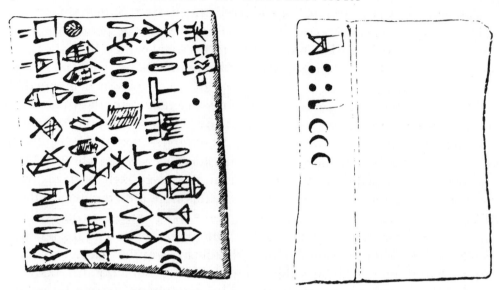

FIG. 45. Proto-Elamite tablet.

extending all across the Iranian plateau, archaeologically datable to a level contemporary with Mesopotamia's late Protoliterate (Uruk III–Jemdet Nasr).[20] Indeed these documents closely resemble the archaic Mesopotamian documents especially in their similar numeration system, which implies that they are of a comparable, primarily actuarial character. The signs however, though partially pictorial, are not generally identifiable with the Protoliterate repertory (see Fig. 45). The proximity in time and space between the two corpuses and the evidence of archaeological contact between the cultures preclude a totally independent origin, and since a margin of priority of perhaps two centuries may be claimed for the Uruk IV tablets, present knowledge would lead us to suppose that this 'proto-Elamite' script was locally devised under the influence of the Mesopotamian system.

Proto-Elamite remains essentially undeciphered, or perhaps more exactly impenetrably logographic like the earliest Mesopotamian documents. In the late third millennium BC it appears to have developed into another script, 'Linear Elamite',[21] surviving in a few inscriptions on stone and other artefacts

---

[20] See most recently C. C. Lamberg-Karlovsky, 'The Proto-Elamites on the Iranian Plateau', *Antiquity* 52 (1978), 114–20—with bibliography.

[21] *CAH* I/2³, Chap. XXIII, esp. § i, iv; P. Meriggi, *La scrittura proto-elamica*, Incunabula Graeca, Rome, 1971; W. Hinz, 'Problems of Linear Elamite', *Journal of the Royal Asiatic Society* (hereafter JRAS) 1975/2, 106–15. Hinz reads PUZUR- as *Kutik-*.

belonging to the king Puzur-Inshushinak (*c*.2240 BC) (Plate 41a). By this time however the Elamites had already borrowed the Akkadian cuneiform script for writing inscriptions both in their own language and in Akkadian.[22] In this borrowing they discarded nearly all logograms and employed an almost exclusively syllabic form of cuneiform. A probable short bilingual of Akkadian and Linear Elamite exists,[23] but in spite of this the latter script is substantially undeciphered, largely on account of its very scanty transmission. It was not destined to survive, and from the late third millennium onwards, the Elamites used exclusively their own adaptation of the cuneiform script for their inscriptions.

Indus Valley

A more distant ancient civilization with attested archaeological links with Mesopotamia is that of the Indus valley, perhaps designated by the Mesopotamian term 'Meluhha'.[24] This advanced civilization with its brick-built cities and regular town planning, produced another characteristic feature, its stamp seals, typically rectangular in form, bearing representations of various animals and frequently a short inscription.[25] (Plate 41b.) Of these inscriptions some 3,000 are known, averaging only five signs each and the longest containing only seventeen signs. Examples of such seals have been excavated in Mesopotamia too, and the period of contact between the two centres appears to be the mid-third millennium BC.[26] A consideration of other known glyptic corpuses strongly suggests that the inscriptions are likely to identify the owners of the seals by name, and perhaps also patronymic and title.[27] In spite of recent claims the script remains undeciphered,[28] and in view of its presumed severe limitation of content, may well be regarded as

[22] E. Reiner, 'The Elamite Language' (in J. Friedrich (ed.), *Altkleinasiatische Sprachen*, Handbuch der Orientalistik (Leyden, 1969), 57 ff.

[23] Hinz, *JRAS* 1975/2, 108–11 (inscription published *Mémoires Délégation en Perse* VI, 8 ff. and Pl. 2=Plate 41a here).

[24] J. Hansman, 'A *Periplus* of Magan and Meluhha' *Bulletin of the School of Oriental and African Studies* 36 (1973), 554–87; *RlA* V, s.v. Industalkultur.

[25] B. B. Lal, 'The Indus Script: some observations based on Archaeology' *JRAS* 1975/2, 173–7, with bibliography; A. Parpola, 'Tasks, Methods and Results in the study of the Indus script', ibid. 178–209—with bibliography.

[26] C. J. Gadd, 'Seals of Ancient Indian style found at Ur' *Proceedings of the British Academy* 18 (1932), 1–22.

[27] cf. e.g. D. O. Edzard, 'Die Inschriften der altakkadischen Rollsiegel', *Archiv für Orientforschung* 22 (1968–9), 12 ff.

[28] Parpola, *JRAS*, loc. cit. (note 25)—the 'tasks' and 'methods' are well defined, but the 'results' are illusory.

indecipherable. Although its origins are obscure, it appears to be an indigenous device. The fact that it appeared more than 500 years after the Mesopotamian invention of writing, in a period of known Mesopotamian contact suggests that it was created under Mesopotamian influence rather than that it was a completely independent and original invention. The question should perhaps be regarded as still open, until future archaeological discovery can throw more light on its origins or perhaps even identify a means and route of transmission from Mesopotamia.[29]

Ebla

Besides these two early possible examples of the dissemination of the idea of writing from Mesopotamia, direct borrowings of the Cuneiform script were comparatively frequent throughout its history. A new example, the earliest so far, is in process of being revealed by the dramatic discovery of the royal palace archive of Ebla (Tell Mardikh, in Syria).[30] The Italian excavations of 1975–7 have recovered some 15,000 tablets, mostly well preserved. The bulk of this vast hoard is written in the Cuneiform script borrowed from Mesopotamia, but although the writing is preponderantly logographic, there is sufficient evidence, in the form of phonetic elements, to show that the texts were read not in Sumerian but in the local language. The native population of Ebla was not Sumerian but, as may be seen by their names, spoke a Semitic language, provisionally termed 'Eblaite', which is the language in which the texts are to be read. Many bilingual Sumerian–Eblaite word lists, the vocabularies, attest the means by which the local scribes mastered their borrowed script. While analysis and classification of Eblaite are still in the early stages, it is becoming clear that it is *not* Akkadian, and that it shares many features with Hebrew and Phoenician.[31] The time span of the archive, also not exactly established, appears to bridge the late Early Dynastic and early Akkad Dynasty periods (thus perhaps *c*.2550–2350 BC), and the civilization of Ebla was certainly terminated by destruction by one of the early Akkad kings.

The importance of this new material for the history of writing is that it attests the dissemination of Sumerian cuneiform from Mesopotamia 500

---

[29] cf. now Lamberg-Karlovsky, loc. cit. (note 20).

[30] For the most up-to-date bibliography at present available, see P. Matthiae, *Ebla, un impero ritrovato* (Turin, 1977), 257–9.

[31] I. J. Gelb, 'Thoughts about Ibla: a preliminary evaluation, March 1977', *Syro-Mesopotamian Studies* 1/1 (1977), 1–30.

years earlier than previously supposed, and its adaptation for the writing of another Semitic language at least as early as for Akkadian. Thus a detailed study of the composition of its syllabary will be of prime importance, and substantial publication of the material is eagerly awaited.

Protoliterate Syria

As it is, other recent archaeological research has been casting new and welcome light on the early history of Syria and its place in Ancient Near Eastern civilization. In the rescue excavations for the Euphrates Tabqa dam project, the sites of Habuba Kabira and Jebel Aruda revealed briefly, before their inundation, large settlements showing strong Mesopotamian influence of the Protoliterate period.[32] Though none of the characteristic archaic inscribed tablets were found, very comparable tablets bearing numerical registrations and seal impressions were recovered,[33] attesting a wide dissemination of this archaic accounting system as early as the late fourth millennium BC, and even suggesting the possibility that Protoliterate written documents may await discovery outside Mesopotamia.[34]

THE EGYPTIAN SPHERE

The rise of the Hieroglyphic script

From the consideration of Mesopotamian writing and its dissemination, we turn to the other great centre of ancient literacy, Egypt. Here, the main writing material, papyrus, does not survive so well as Mesopotamian clay; the earliest surviving inscribed papyri probably date to the Fourth Dynasty (c.2600–2500 BC), though uninscribed papyrus rolls of the First Dynasty (c.3100–2900 BC), and the use of the pictogram portraying the roll, attest to its earlier employment.[35] Thus the earliest preserved inscriptions from Egypt are

[32] E. Strommenger, 'Habuba-Kabira-Sud 1974', *Les Annales Archèologiques Arabes Syriennes* 25 (1975), 155–64 with references to earlier reports); S. E. van der Leeuw, 'Jebel 'Aruda', in *Antiquités de l'Euphrate: exposition des découvertes de la campagne internationale de sauvegarde des antiquités de l'Euphrate*; Musée national d'Alep, November 1974.

[33] E. Töpperwein, *Mitteilungen des Deutschen Orient-Gesellschaft* 105 (1973), 21 ff.; E. Strommenger, ibid., 65 ff.

[34] For the curious Tartaria tablets, see most recently J. Makkay, *Orientalia* 37 (1968), 272–89.

[35] P. Posener-Kriéger, 'Les papyrus de Gébélein. Remarques préliminaires (*Révue d'Égyptologie* 27 (1975), 211–21); W. B. Emery, *Archaic Egypt* (Harmondsworth, 1961) 235; for an early use of the papyrus-roll Hieroglyph, see e.g. a sealing of Peribsen (2nd dynasty)—Flinders Petrie, *The Royal Tombs of the Earliest Dynasties*, II (London, 1901) Pl. XXI, no. 164.

largely restricted to stone with its limitation of text type, and it must be borne in mind that these may not be as representative of the general literacy of their age as are their Mesopotamian counterparts.

The term 'Hieroglyphs', originally coined to describe the supposedly sacred nature of the Egyptian signs, is usually maintained for convenience, and has a certain appropriateness to the most striking external feature of the monumental form of the script, namely its highly pictorial charcter and the conservatism which maintained this substantially unchanged from earliest to latest phases (see e.g. Fig. 46). Besides this monumental script, two cursive versions normally written in ink on papyrus or ostraca came into use, Hieratic and (later) Demotic. These were essentially graphic simplifications, and differ from the monumental script largely in external appearance rather than in internal characteristics. By contrast with Mesopotamian writing which was originally designed for practical purposes to write on clay and was only later adapted for display inscriptions on stone, Egyptian writing gives the impression of being a decorative monumental script, later adapted for more commonplace needs.

The earliest known phase of Egyptian writing is found on stone and other artefacts, palettes, mace-heads, pottery, and cylinder seals and sealings belonging to the transitional age bridging the Predynastic and Early Dynastic periods (c.3000 BC).[36] On the palettes and mace-heads,[37] scenes of conquest are rendered by symbolic scenes in which the king may be represented as the Falcon or other royal beast and the provinces by their emblems (Plate 42). Figures portrayed are identified by their names presumably written on rebus-principles as in Mesopotamian Protoliterate documents, as CAT-FISH + CHISEL (n'r-mr(?), 'Narmer'). Some signs of the later signary are already identifiable. Further signs also appear as the main motif on the seals and sealings,[38] presumably identifying the owner, but as with Mesopotamian names of the Protoliterate period, not yet readable with any certainty.

Following these preliminary stages, a developed system of writing appears in the Early Dynastic period surviving almost entirely in the form of tomb inscriptions on stone and other artefacts, such as wooden and ivory labels,

[36] *CAH I/2³*, Chap. XI.

[37] Flinders Petrie, *Ceremonial Slate Palettes*, British School of Egyptian Archaeology, 66(A) (London, 1953); S. Schott, *Hieroglyphen. Unterschungen zum Ursprung der Schrift*, Akademie der Wissenschaften und der Literatur in Mainz, Abhandlungen der Geistes- und Sozialwissenschaftlichen Klasse, Jahrgang 1950, Nr. 24, Abb. 1–12.

[38] P. Kaplony, *Die Inschriften der ägyptischen Frühzeit*, I (Wiesbaden, 1963), I. Teil. Rollsiegel und Lehmverschlüsse.

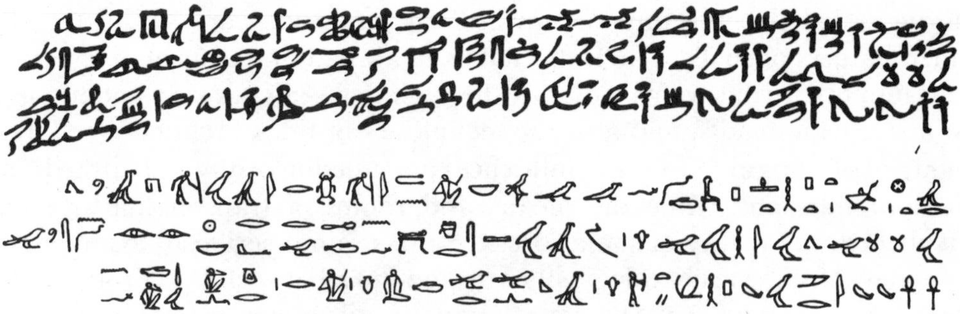

LITERARY HIERATIC OF THE TWELFTH DYNASTY (*Pr.* 4, 2-4),
WITH TRANSCRIPTION

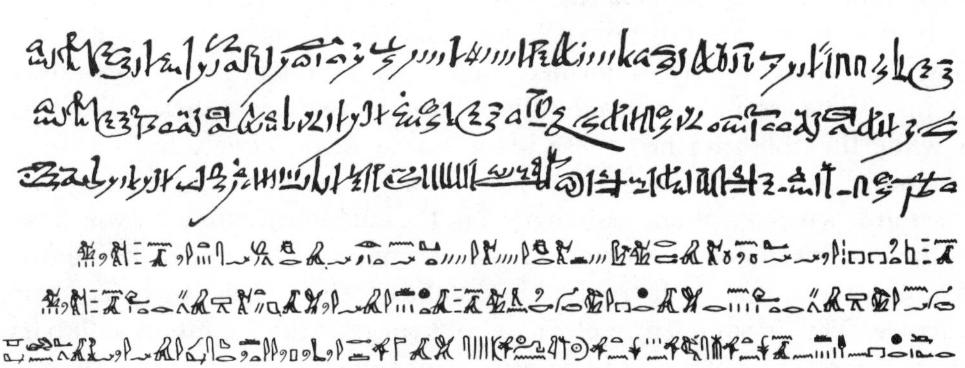

OFFICIAL HIERATIC OF THE TWENTIETH DYNASTY (*Abbott* 5, 1-3),
WITH TRANSCRIPTION

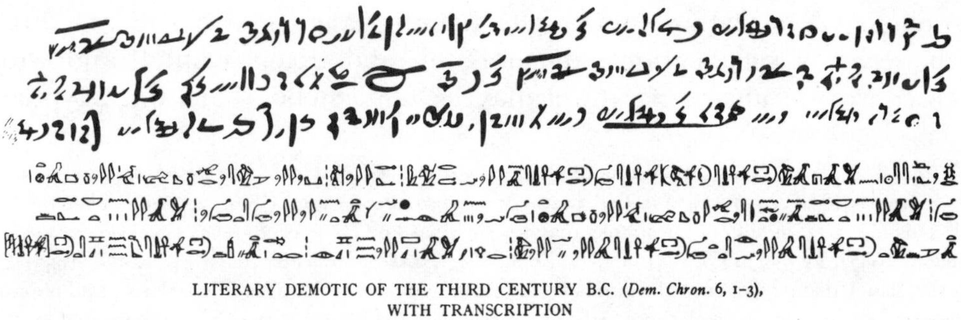

LITERARY DEMOTIC OF THE THIRD CENTURY B.C. (*Dem. Chron.* 6, 1-3),
WITH TRANSCRIPTION

FIG. 46. Specimens of Egyptian Hieratic and Demotic, with transcriptions into Hieroglyphic.

and especially clay sealings. The script is already used here in essentially the same form as in later periods, and the seeming suddenness of its appearance has suggested that the impetus towards its formation came from outside. Other features of civilization imported from abroad in this formative period lend support to this view, notably the cylinder seals already mentioned, various artistic motifs, and also the techniques of brick architecture.[39] The country of origin of this influence is unequivocally identified as Mesopotamia, and while the means and routes of transmission are not established, the reality of some sort of contact is not seriously disputed.

In view of these archaeologically attested links between late Protoliterate Mesopotamia and Early Dynastic Egypt, it still seems probable that the Egyptian script was devised with a more or less detailed knowledge of that of Mesopotamia. In internal character the two scripts show an overall similarity, in that they are both mixed logographic–syllabographic scripts, both using class determinatives formed from common logograms as aids to reading.[40] The essential internal difference of the two lay in their syllabaries; for while they both formed these in the same way (namely by the rebus-principle of stripping a logogram of its semantic content and using it to write the syllable which its phonology suggests), the cuneiform syllabary was based on the monosyllabic structure of Sumerian, supplemented by similar Akkadian roots, but the hieroglyphic syllabary reflected the Egyptian word structure. This is sufficiently clear to confirm that the Egyptian syllabary, like its signary in general, was of purely indigenous construction. Its most distinctive feature, the way in which Egyptian syllabograms represent only the consonantal skeleton of the syllable without reference to the vowels, is presumably to be explained by the instability of the vowels in Egyptian morphology,[41] a feature common to Semitic languages. There are three main series of syllabograms, the uni-, bi- and triconsonantal, and with each consonant any or no vowel may be understood. Thus the Egyptian

[39] *CAH* I/2³, Chap. XI, § vi; for a more sceptical survey, see W. Helck, *Die Beziehungen Ägyptens zu Vorderasien im 3. und 2. Jahrtausend v. Chr.* (2nd edn., Wiesbaden, 1971), Chap. 2, 'Die Frühzeit'.

[40] This observation follows the simple analyses by Sir Alan Gardiner, *Egyptian Grammar* (3rd edn., London, 1957), §§ 5–7, 17, 22–5), and E. Edel, *Altägyptische Grammatik*, An.Or.34 (Rome, 1955) §§ 24–107, which distinguish only ideograms including generic determinatives (logograms), and phonograms (syllabograms). A much more elaborate analysis of the usages of the signs is suggested by W. Schenkel, 'Zur Struktur der Hieroglyphenschrift', *Mitteilungen des Deutschen Archäologischen Instituts: Abteilung Kairo* 27 (1971), 85–97; id., The structure of hieroglyphic script (*Royal Anthropological Institute News* 15 (August 1976), 4–7).

[41] cf. Gardiner, *Egyptian Grammar*³, § 7; Gelb, *A Study of Writing*², 80 ff.

syllabary is made up of signs on the following patern (C=consonant, x any (or no) vowel):

$$Cx : CxCx : CxCxCx.$$

e.g. p, 'stool' (syllabic px); $ḥr$, 'face' (syllabic $ḥ$xrx); $ḫpr$, 'scarab' (syllabic $ḫ$xpxrx).

This may be compared with the Mesopotamian syllabary composed of the following syllables:

$$Ca-aC : (Ce-eC) : Ci-iC : Cu-uC$$
$$CaC : (CeC) : CiC : CuC$$

While the Mesopotamian syllabary renders vowels and consonants fairly unambiguously within limits, our apprehension of the nature of Egyptian vowels is restricted to more or less controversial reconstructions based on such evidence as the transcription of Egyptian into Cuneiform, and the known vocalization of Coptic, the latest form of the Egyptian language.[42] The Egyptian uniconsonantal series (Cx) is often, but incorrectly, referred to as an 'Alphabet'[43]—it should formally be regarded as syllabographic, although the syllabogram which does not determine the vowel differs from those that do in a very significant aspect. Compare:

Mesopotamian Ca, (Ce), Ci, Cu
Egyptian   Cx

Later in the history of Hieroglyphic, when Cuneiform influence was very strong (second half of the second millennium BC), Egyptian scribes did develop, especially for writing foreign names, a system known as group-writing, which seems to be modelled on the Cuneiform practice of *scriptio plena* (the 'full writing' of the vowels);[44] compare:

Mesopotamian C$a+a$,   C$i+i$,   C$u+u$
Egyptian   Cx+'x,   Cx+yx,   Cx+wx

Hieroglyphic has selected a weak-consonantal syllabogram to represent a vowel. Both the existence of uniconsonantal syllabograms and this method of marking vowels are important steps towards the development of Alphabetic

---

[42] e.g. Gardiner, *Egyptian Grammar*³, Appendix A, 'The vocalization of Middle Egyptian'; Edel, *Altägyptische Grammatik*, §§ 151–73.

[43] e.g. Gardiner, *Egyptian Grammar*³, 27.

[44] Gelb, *A Study of Writing*², 168 ff.; and, for a more recent examination of new examples, E. Edel, *Die Ortsnamenlisten aus dem Totentempel Amenophis III* (Bonn, 1966), Chap. II.

writing. But the Egyptian scribes never consistently adopted this graphic practice in connected texts, nor attempted to discard the more complex features of the established system in its favour—to them indeed it would have doubtless seemed more cumbersome.

Unlike Mesopotamian Cuneiform, Egyptian Hieroglyphic was never borrowed for writing another language (though it was adapted for writing alphabetic Meroitic in the first millennium BC).[45] Hieroglyphic did however circulate widely over the Levant from an early period in the form of inscribed artefacts exported from Egypt[46] and also papyri, though none have survived, and occasional ostraca. Thus the idea of Egyptian writing must have been familiar in this area, yet when the local peoples required a script, they normally adopted Cuneiform Akkadian.[47] This was perhaps because Hieroglyphic was too idiosyncratic in form and firmly tied to the language of its origin, while Cuneiform, with its early history of borrowing and adaptation by Akkadian, offered a syllabary more flexible and readily adapted to other languages.

Dissemination from Egypt: The Aegean

It may be that the idea of writing was transmitted from Egypt to the Aegean as from Mesopotamia to Elam and Egypt itself. Excavation in Crete shows evidence of Egyptian influence in the form of artefacts from at least Early Minoan II onwards (c. 2500 BC).[48] Contemporarily an indigenous glyptic was also developing, preserved as signets carved with animal figures and other motifs.[49] Early in the second millennium BC, from Middle Minoan I onwards, signs conventionally termed 'Hieroglyphs' begin to be found on the seals,[50] and seem to have been gradually developed into a limited script found also on a few clay dockets. Parallel to this essentially glyptic script, a linear form,

[45] See e.g. Diringer, *The Alphabet*³, 140 f.; Jensen, *Sign, Symbol and Script*, 78 ff.

[46] See B. Porter and R. Moss, *Topographical Bibliography of Ancient Egyptian Hieroglyphic Texts, Reliefs and Paintings* VII (Oxford, 1951), Chap. XVIII. Western Asia and Europe (including objects found in Palestine, Transjordan, Syria, Iraq, Persia, Turkey).

[47] Notably in the Amarna period; see *CAH* II/1³, Chap. XX, § i. Other Amarna letters have now been found at Kamid el-Loz (Kumidi)—D. O. Edzard *et al.*, *Kamil el-Loz—Kumidi. Schriftdokumente aus Kamid el-Loz* (Bonn, 1970), Chap. 5; also from Tell Nebi Mend (Qadesh)—A: R. Millard, publication forthcoming; and most recently from Aphek (cf. below, note 86). The early second-millennium kings of Byblos however wrote Egyptian Hieroglyphic—see below, note 109.

[48] *CAH* I/2³, Chap. XXVI (*a*), 801 ff.; *CAH* II/1³, Chap. IV (*b*), and Chap. XII.

[49] *CAH* II/1³, Chap. XIII, with bibliography, 801 ff.

[50] Ibid., 587, where the term 'Pictographic' is preferred· 'Hieroglyphic' and 'Linear' terminology introduced by Sir Arthur Evans, *Scripta Minoa* I (Oxford, 1909).

known as Linear A, was developed for use on clay tablets and other artefacts—these stem mainly from the transitional Middle Minoan IIIb to Late Minoan Ia period (*c*.1700–1550 BC). A substantial proportion of the Hieroglyphic and Linear sign forms are closely similar, though it would be premature to assume that therefore they must have the same values (see Fig. 47). Clay tablets inscribed with a further linear script, Linear B, have been discovered in much larger quantities, not only at Knossos but also at sites on the Greek mainland, and are apparently to be dated *c*.1400–1200 BC.[51]

Linear B, being the only deciphered script of the three,[52] is the only one about which much can be said. Its underlying language has been shown to be an archaic form of Greek, for the rendering of which the script is unsuitable, presumably because its prototype was devised for a non-Greek language. Linear B comprises a syllabary of some ninety signs (see Fig. 48), and over one hundred often pictographic logograms, of which a few have also a syllabic value.[53] The syllabary is made up of syllabograms of the single-vowel (V) and the consonant+vowel (CV) type (with a few two-consonants+vowel, CCV), and shows an almost complete five-vowel series C*a*/*e*/*i*/*o*/*u*. A notable characteristic is that in rendering the stops the script does not distinguish voiced, voiceless and aspirate (thus *b*/*p*/*ph* and *g*/*k*/*kh* are represented by only one series each) except for the dentals where there are separate *d* and *t* series. Also one series only represents *l*/*r* and *h*, is not normally expressed.

In spite of the fact that a proportion of the sign forms of Linear A (and Hieroglyphic) closely resemble those of Linear B (see Fig. 47) and may thus have the Linear B values at least hypothetically attributed to them, no claims to the decipherment of the former script have won acceptance, and consequently the underlying language also remains unidentified.[54] This failure is

[51] Recent editions include J. Chadwick, J. T. Killen and J.-P. Olivier, *The Knossos Tablets* (4th edn., Cambridge, 1971); E. L. Bennett and J.-P. Olivier, *The Pylos Tablets Transcribed*, I–II, Incunabula Graeca, LIX (Rome 1973, 1976); J. Chadwick, 'Linear B Tablets from Thebes', *Minos* (1970), 115–37; T. G. Spyropoulos and J. Chadwick, *The Thebes Tablets* II, Suplementos a *Minos*, no. 4 (Salamanca, 1975); A. Sacconi, *Corpus delle iscrizioni in Lineare B di Micene*, Incunabula Graeca LVIII (Rome, 1974); ead., *Corpus delle iscrizioni vascolari in Lineare B*, Incunabula Graeca LVII (Rome, 1974); cf. also J.-P. Olivier, L. Godart, C. Seydel, and C. Sourvinou, *Index Généraux du linéaire B*, Incunabula Graeca LII (Rome, 1973). See also below, p. 165, Additional Items.

[52] J. Chadwick, *The Decipherment of Linear B* (2nd edn., Cambridge, 1967).

[53] A. Morpurgo, *Mycenaeae Graecitatis Lexicon*, Incunabula Graeca III (Rome, 1963), XXV–XXXI for the Signary. For the logograms, see also below, p. 165, Additional Items.

[54] For recent statements on the limits of accepted present knowledge, see J. Chadwick, 'Introduction to the problems of "Minoan Linear A"', *JRAS* 1975/2, 143–47; J. T. Hooker, 'Problems and methods in the decipherment of Linear A', ibid. 164–72; and for an unacceptable recent claim, C. H. Gordon, 'The Decipherment of Minoan and Eteo-Cretan', ibid. 148–58.

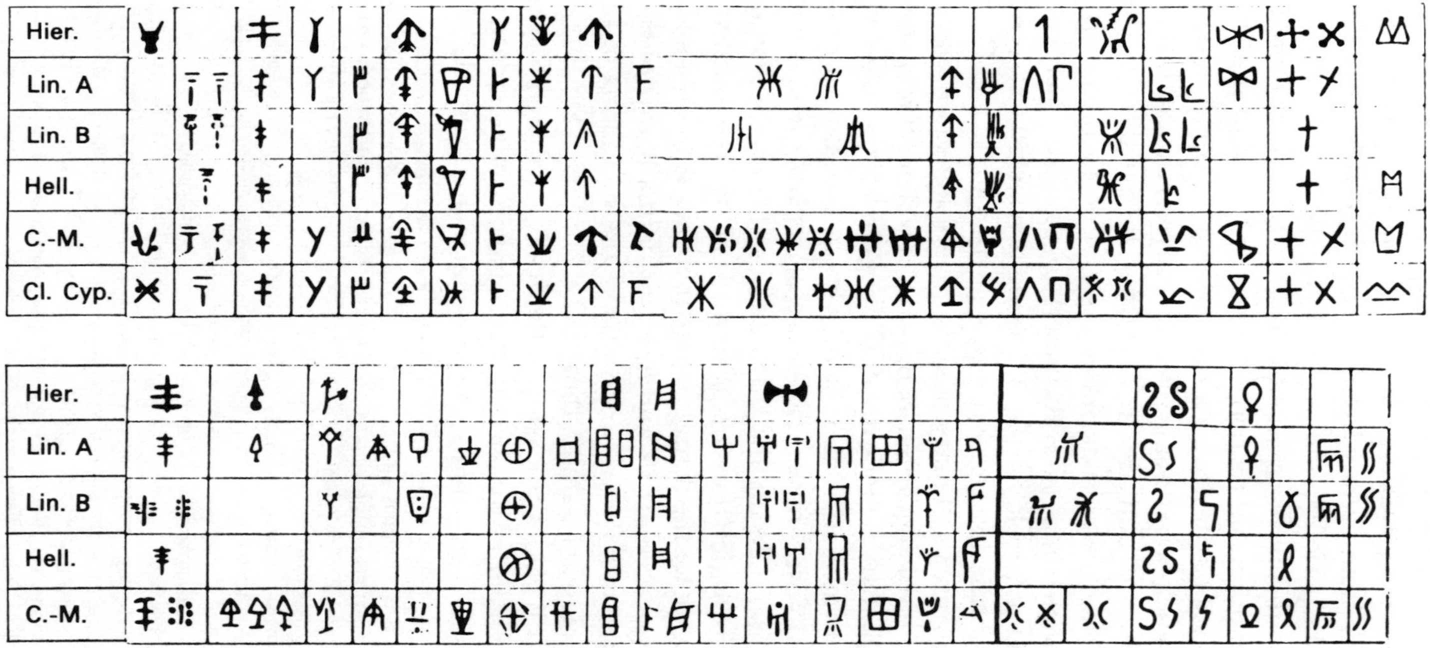

Fig. 47. Cypro-Minoan characters with Minoan and Classical Cypriot parallels.

a		e		i		o		u		a₂		a₃	
da		de		di		do		du		dwe		dwo	
ja		je		—		jo		—					
ka		ke		ki		ko		ku					
ma		me		mi		mo		mu					
na		ne		ni		no		nu		nwa			
pa		pe		pi		po		pu		pte		pu₂	
qa		qe		qi		qo							
ra		re		ri		ro		ru		ra₂		ra₃		ro₂
sa		se		si		so		su					
ta		te		ti		to		tu				two	
wa		we		wi		wo		—					
za		ze		—		zo		—					

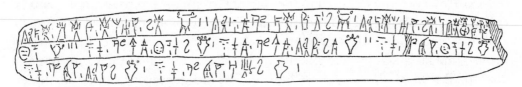

FIG. 48. The Linear B syllabary and a Pylos tablet.

certainly due in part to the paucity of Linear A documents though more are becoming available at present.[55] A substantial influx of material may be hoped to lead to a better insight.

The archaeologically attested Egyptian influence on Crete is generally considered to have provided the stimulus for the formation of the Cretan

[55] L. Godart and J.-P. Olivier, *Recueil des inscriptions en Linéaire A*, 1 and 3, Études crétoises XXI (Paris, 1976).

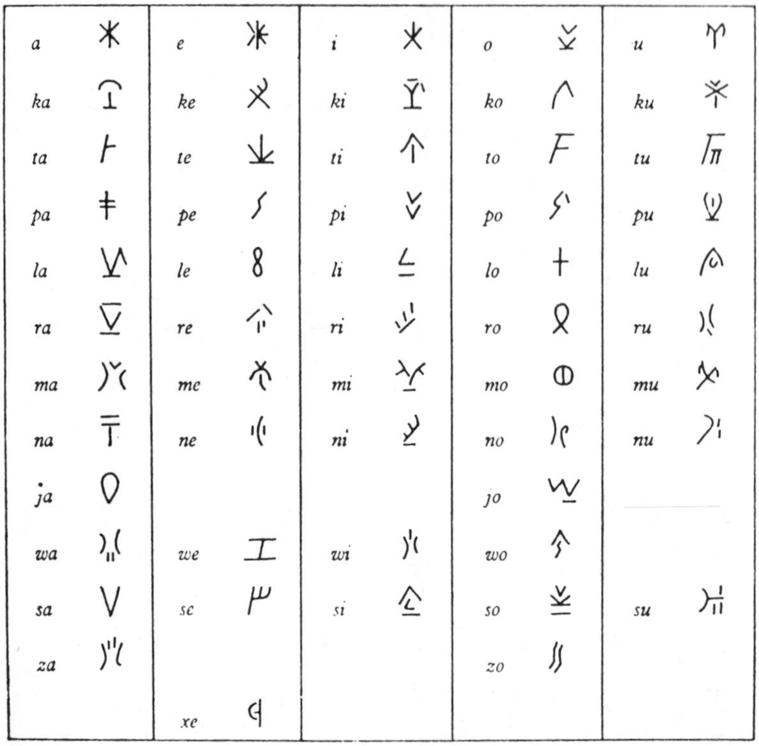

a	✳	e	✳	i	✳	o	˘	u	⋔
ka		ke		ki		ko		ku	
ta		te		ti		to		tu	
pa		pe		pi		po		pu	
la		le		li		lo		lu	
ra		re		ri		ro		ru	
ma		me		mi		mo		mu	
na		ne		ni		no		nu	
ja						jo			
wa		we		wi		wo			
sa		se		si		so		su	
za						zo			
		xe							

FIG. 49. The Classical Cypriot syllabary.

scripts. However any detailed modelling of Cretan on Egyptian sign forms is rarely observable.[56] Nor do the internal characteristics of Linear B point to any close dependence on Egyptian original values. Thus while the nature of the original language(s) and the method of construction of the script remain obscure, it seems that here too we have scripts indigenously originating under a general external stimulus.

A small group of inscribed tablets and artefacts of the Late Bronze Age (c.1500–1200 BC) have been discovered on Cyprus and similar documents have come from the excavations of Ugarit.[57] The script appears to be ances-

---

[56] cf. Evans, *Scripta Minoa* I, Table XVI.

[57] *CAH* II/2³, Chap. XXII (*b*), § x, with bibliography, p. 945; see especially O. Masson, 'Répertoire des inscriptions chypro-minoens', *Minos* 5 (1957), 9–27; also id., 'Documents chypro-Minoens de Ras Shamra', *Ugaritica* III VI (Paris, 1969), 379–92; E. Masson, 'Étude de vingt-six boules d'argile (Paris, 1956) 234–50; inscrites trouvées à Enkomi et Hala Sultan Tekke', *Studies in the Cypro-Minoan Scripts* I (*Studies in Mediterranean Archaeology* XXXI: 1, Göteborg, 1971).

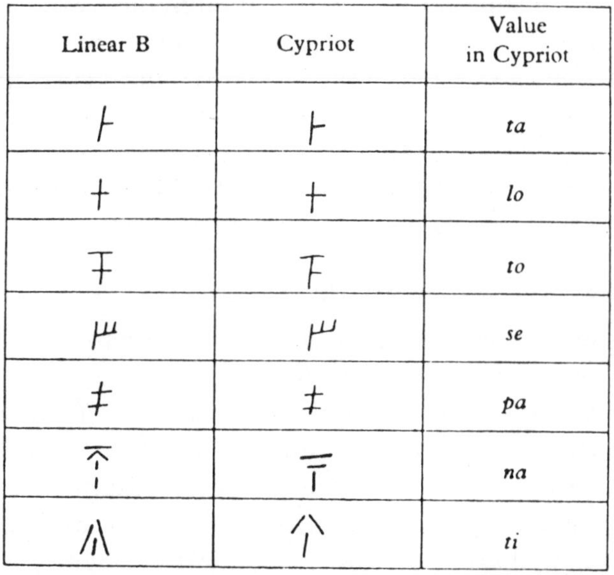

Linear B	Cypriot	Value in Cypriot
⊦	⊦	*ta*
✝	✝	*lo*
∓	⊤̄	*to*
⊍	⊍	*se*
⧧	⧧	*pa*
⊼	⊤̄	*na*
⋀	↑	*ti*

FIG. 50. Comparison of forms of signs of identical values in Linear B and Classical Cypriot.

tral to the syllabic Cypriot script of the Classical period,[58] for a proportion of the sign forms of these two may be identified with fair certainty (see Fig. 47). The Classical Cypriot syllabary (Fig. 49), deciphered in the last century, was used to write inscriptions principally in Greek (for which it was as unsuitable a vehicle as was Linear B), as well as a few in a still unknown language. The decipherment and identification of the language(s) of the Bronze Age inscriptions are not yet achieved though a plausible approach has been recently suggested.[59] Comparison of the Bronze Age sign forms with those of the Cretan scripts (see Fig. 47) suggests a borrowing by Cyprus from Crete (hence the designation Cypro-Minoan) or from elsewhere—though the means of transmission are obscure.[60]

Comparing known with known, we may note that both Linear B and the Classical Cypriot syllabary were used for writing Greek, and while the latter does not employ logograms,[61] the two syllabaries show marked similarities (cf. Figs 48–49). Both have a fairly complete series of syllabograms of the

[58] O. Masson, *Les Inscriptions chypriotes syllabiques* (Paris, 1961).

[59] E. Masson, 'Cyphrominoica', *Studies in the Cypro-Minoan Scripts 2 (Studies in Mediterranean Archaeology XXXI: 2*, Göteborg, 1974); summarized, *JRAS* 1975/2, 159–63.

[60] The comparison goes back to Evans, *Scripta Minoa* I, 68 ff.

[61] For the character of the Cypriot syllabary and its local variants, see Masson, *Les Inscriptions chypriotes syllabiques*, Introduction § iv, 'Remarques générales sur le syllabaire chypriote'.

single-vowel and consonant+vowel type, though there are some differences of detail. As to sign forms, only those of similar values may usefully be compared at present and while a number of the forms do indeed correspond (Fig. 50),[62] the majority do not. The separation of the two corpuses in space and time is perhaps too great for such comparisons. Thus further comparison of signs of unknown value from the Linear A and Cypro-Minoan corpuses should only be advanced as hypotheses for independent testing.

SPREAD OF WRITING IN THE SECOND MILLENNIUM

While logographic–syllabic scripts were circulating in the Mediterranean in the second millennium BC, the Cuneiform script was being ever more widely borrowed by Mesopotamia's neighbours. Such borrowings were usually made in two stages, first the adoption of the Sumero-Akkadian literary language and scribal tradition, followed by the adaptation of the script to write the native language. We have already seen the transmission to Ebla in the mid-third millennium BC, and the somewhat later passage to Elam. A unique document, the foundation tablet accompanying the 'Urkish Lion', shows that the Hurrians had already adapted the script for their own language by the same date,[63] although the bulk of Hurrian texts, like the Elamite, are known much later.[64] Both Hurrians and Elamites considerably simplified the borrowed script in the direction of discarding most of the logograms and reducing homophony and polyphony.[65] They wrote with almost pure syllabaries but never quite achieved the total minimal Cuneiform syllabary.

In the early second millennium BC, besides the differentiation of Akkadian into the dialects Assyrian and Babylonian each with distinct orthographies, schools of provincial Akkadian have been found, notably at Mari and Alalah,[66] 'Amorite' states, where the large-scale writing of the native personal names shows how readily, almost casually, Cuneiform could be adapted for writing another language.[67]

[62] Chadwick, *The Decipherment of Linear B*, 23 f.; cf. the attempt to utilize these comparisons to assign values to Cypro-Minoan—Masson, *Studies in Mediterranean Archaeology* XXX1/2, 39.

[63] F. W. Bush, *A Grammar of the Hurrian Language* (Brandeis University Ph.D.; University Microfilms, Ann Arbor, 1964), § 1.25; J. Friedrich, 'Churritisch', in J. Friedrich (ed.), *Altkleinasiatische Sprachen* (Handbuch der Orientalistik; Leyden, 1969) § 2(1).

[64] Bush, op. cit., § 1.2; Friedrich, op. cit., § 2.

[65] Hurrians—Bush, op. cit., part II; Elamite—see above, note 22.

[66] J. Bottéro and A. Finet, *Répertoire analytique*, ARM XV (Paris, 1954), for the palaeography, syllabary, and list of ideograms; G. Giacumakis *The Akkadian of Alalah* (Mouton, 1970).

[67] I. J. Gelb, 'La lingua degli Amoriti', *Atti della Academia Nazionale dei Lincei, Rendiconti*, Serie 8, XIII (1958), 143–64, especially § 1. 'Il sistema di scrittura'.

The Hittites

An important transmission of Cuneiform in the second millennium BC was to the Hittites, who shortly before 1600 BC both borrowed, through the presumed intermediacy of some Hurrian or Syrian scribal school, Cuneiform Akkadian as the international diplomatic and literary medium, and adapted the script for their own language.[68] Akkadian and Hittite are the main languages found in the Hittite palace archives written on clay tablets excavated at Boğazköy (ancient Hattusa), but no less than five other languages are represented here by small corpuses of ritual and cultic texts,[69] namely Luwian and Palaic (Anatolian languages related to Hittite); Hattian (a pre-Hittite language of Anatolia); Hurrian; and 'Mitannian' (an Indo-Iranian language scantily represented by a few divine and personal names and some horse-training terms).[70]

In adapting the script, the Hittites, like the Elamites and Hurrians, simplified the syllabary, but unlike them retained large numbers of logograms as well as 'allograms' (Akkadian phonetic spellings, to be read in Hittite), which in the texts were used as 'shorthand' for full Hittite phonetic spellings.[71] If this is consistently done, as it is for a number of common words, we are denied knowledge of the Hittite word; thus, e.g. the Hittite for 'woman', 'son', 'slave', 'gold', 'ox', 'sheep', 'dog', and almost all the numerals, is unknown.[72]

Besides this Cuneiform corpus written on clay, the Hittites used another script, mainly surviving on monumental stone inscriptions and seals. This is conventionally termed 'Hieroglyphic' by reference to the largely pictorial appearance of its signs.[73] References in Cuneiform texts to 'wooden documents', none of which has survived, indicate a lost corpus perhaps also

---

[68] T. V. Gamkrelidze, 'The Akkado-Hittite Syllabary and the problem of the origin of the Hittite script', *Archiv Orientální* (Prague) 29 (1961), 406–18.

[69] For an analysis of the text material, see E. Laroche, *Catalogue des textes hittites* (Paris, 1971).

[70] For Hittite, Luwian, Palaic, Hattian, and Hurrian see J. Friedrich (ed.), *Kleinasiatische Sprachen*; For Akkadian, R. Labat, *L'Akkadien de Boghaz-Köi* (Bordeaux, 1932); for the language of Mitanni, A. Kammenhuber, *Die Arier im vorderen Orient* (Heidelberg, 1968).

[71] For a signary, see J. Friedrich, *Hethitisches Keilschrift-Lesebuch*, part II, 'Schrifttafel' (Heidelberg, 1960).

[72] J. Friedrich, *Hethitisches Wörterbuch* (Heidelberg, 1952); see under *Ideogramme* (264 ff.), SAL, DUMU, ÌR, GUŠKIN, GUD, UDU, UR.ZÍR and *Zahlwörter*.

[73] P. Meriggi, *Hieroglyphisch-Hethitisches Glossar* (2nd edn., Wiesbaden, 1962); E. Laroche, *Les Hiéroglyphes hittites, Première partie. L'écriture* (Paris, 1960)—detailed examination of the signary.

written in Hieroglyphic.[74] The decipherment of this script has shown that the language usually written in it was not Hittite itself, but a dialect of Luwian.[75]

This script and language are much better known from the corpus of inscriptions of the 'Neo-Hittite' states of the Iron Age[76] (c.950–700 BC) than from the very few, poorly preserved or unpublished stone inscriptions of the Empire period[77] (c.1400–1200 BC). Besides the monumental stone inscriptions of the former corpus, a precious handful of strips of lead with letters or economic texts written in a cursive form of the script[78] attest to its otherwise lost vernacular use. The script at this period is quite developed, comprising a body of over 200 logograms but, more important, a regular syllabary with vowel syllabograms *a/i/u* and a fairly complete set of consonant+vowel syllabograms in three-vowel series, C*a/i/u*.[79] The origin of some of the syllabograms can be determined and is usually in the first instance a monosyllabic or reduplicated Luwian–Hittite root (the two languages are too closely related to isolate one or other) used with a correspondingly syllabic value.[80]

This script in the Late Bronze Age was, so far as we may judge, preponderantly logographic. Though most of the syllabograms seem to have been already known, they were used sparingly, mostly as single phonetic complements to nouns and verbs, and also to write words difficult to render logographically. Though no inscriptions have been found in a Luwian as opposed to a Hittite context, we may suppose that the script was devised by the Luwians (since all linguistically identifiable inscriptions—apart from short epigraphs—are in Luwian), and borrowed by the Hittites for decorative monumental and glyptic usage. It is clearly an indigenous Anatolian construct, and its earliest stages, though not recovered, probably date back to

---

[74] E. Laroche, *Revue Hittite et Asianique (RHA)* XIV/58 (1956), 28 f.; P. Houwink ten Cate, *RHA* XXV/81 (1967), 122 f.

[75] See most recently J. D. Hawkins, A. Morpurgo Davies and G. Neumann, 'Hittite Hieroglyphs and Luwian: new evidence for the connection', *Nachrichten der Akademie der Wissenschaften in Göttingen* (I. Phil.-Hist. Klasse, 1973) 145–97.

[76] P. Meriggi, *Manuale di eteo geroglifico*, II/1, Incunabula Graeca XIV (Rome, 1967), and II/2 Incunabula Graeca XV (Rome, 1975).

[77] Ibid., II/3.

[78] Ibid., II/1 nos. 34–40; also T. Özgüç, *Kültepe and its vicinity in the Iron Age* (Ankara, 1971), Pl. XLVII ff.

[79] For the syllabary, see the recent revision suggested by J. D. Hawkins, *Anatolian Studies* 25 (1975), 154–5.

[80] See e.g. A. Morpurgo Davies and J. D. Hawkins, *Annali Pisa* 8 (1978), 755 ff.; the origin of the following syllabograms is clear: *u* (Luw. *wawi-*, 'ox'); *la* (Luw.-Hitt. *lala-*, 'tongue'); *mi* (Luw.-Hitt. *mauwa-/meiu-*, 'four'); *nú* (Luw.* *nuwa-*, 'nine'); *pi* (Luw.-Hitt. *pi (ya)-*, 'give'); *sa*[5](Luw.-Hitt. *ša-/šiya-*, 'seal'); *tà* (Luw.-Hitt. *da-*, 'take'); *za* (Luw. *za-*, 'this'); *tara/i* (Luw.-Hitt.* *tri-*, 'three').

before 1500 BC. While the external sign forms of Luwian Hieroglyphic are drawn from a similar repertoire to Egyptian Hieroglyphic and the Cretan scripts (human figures, parts of the body, animals, pots, tools, buildings, etc.), similar forms in the respective corpuses can in no case be shown to have comparable values; yet internal characteristics show general similarities with Linear B, namely:

   (i) The use of (pictorial) logograms.

   (ii) the syllabary composed of vowel signs and consonant+vowel signs—but Luwian Hieroglyphic has only a three-vowel system, as against Linear B's five-vowel (a/i/u–a/e/i/o/u).

   (iii) the decimal numeration, especially I (units) and — (tens).

These similarities cannot be pressed too closely, and there are too many missing or unknown links, notably the antecedents of Linear B and the Luwian stage of Anatolian Hieroglyphic. Nevertheless it seems likely that the Anatolian script was devised under some Aegean stimulus stemming ultimately from Egypt.

THE RISE OF THE ALPHABET

Having considered the rise of logographic writing and the development of syllabaries in the third millennium BC, followed by the general dissemination of the mixed logographic–syllabic scripts from *c*.2500–1500 BC, we should finally turn to examine the rise of Alphabetic writing during the second half of the second millennium BC.

Proto-Sinaitic

A large group of Egyptian Hieroglyphic inscriptions dating from the Third to the Twentieth Dynasties (*c*.2700–1000 BC) has been discovered at Serabit el Khadem in Sinai[81] in the area of the Egyptian turquoise mines and local temple of Hathor.[82] Besides these, over thirty inscriptions in another script, 'proto-Sinaitic', often little more than graffiti, have been recovered on round-topped stone and rock-cut stelae and on statues.[83] The script is linear and

[81] Porter and Moss, *Topographical Bibliography* VII, § xvi, 345–66.

[82] K. Lake *et al.*, 'The Serabit Expedition of 1930'. I 'Introduction', II 'The Mines of Sinai', III 'The Temples of Hathor', *Harvard Theological Review* 25 (1932), 95–129.

[83] K. Lake, R. P. Blake, and R. F. Butin, 'The Serabit Inscriptions', ibid. 21 (1928), 1–67; R. F. Butin, 'The Protosinaitic Inscriptions', ibid., 25 (1932), 130–203; R. F. S. Starr and R. F. Butin, *Excavations and the Protosinaitic inscriptions at Serabit el Khadem*, Studies and Documents VI (London, 1936).

incised, usually poorly preserved and ill-written. It seems to contain some twenty to thirty signs, which in appearance suggest vaguely a connection with Egyptian Hieroglyphic. The inscriptions are not precisely datable and estimates vary from early to mid-second millennium BC.

Plausible hypotheses suggest that these are the work of labourers in the mines, that the script was alphabetic and that the language written was Semitic. Proto-Sinaitic has been hailed as the 'missing link' between Egyptian Hieroglyphic and the Alphabet, and attempts at reading have been based on this postulated intermediate character; thus the pictorial signs have been associated with Semitic words (partially those which make up the later letter names of the Alphabet) from which their values have been derived on the acrophonic principle. This hypothetical approach produced two generally accepted readings (*l-b'lt*, 'to the Lady', and *tnt*, 'gift', as dedicatory inscriptions on statues).[84] A more extended decipherment on the same lines, while not implausible, remains dangerously unconfirmed because of the doubts on the actual readings of the signs and their identifications, as well as the whole theory of acrophonic derivation.[85] The interpretations of the inscriptions are still largely guesswork, and until external confirmation is forthcoming (and it may be unobtainable), no finality can be attributed to the claimed decipherment.

Ugaritic

The next staging-post in the quest for Alphabetic origins is undoubtedly Ugarit, from the ruins of which inscriptions in no less than five different scripts have been recovered,[86] mostly dating to the late second millennium BC. Objects bearing Egyptian Hieroglyphic inscriptions of the Middle and New Kingdoms have appeared in limited numbers.[87] Much more numerous are

[84] For a summary of the progress and the bibliography, see F. M. Cross, 'The Origin and Early Evolution of the Alphabet', *Eretz-Israel* 8 (1967), 8*–24* especially 8 f.; M. Sznycer, 'Les inscriptions protosinaïtiques', in J. Léclant (ed.), *Le Déchiffrement des écritures et des langues* (Paris, 1975), 85–93.

[85] W. F. Albright, *The Proto-Sinaitic Inscriptions and their Decipherment*, Harvard Theological Studies XXII (Cambridge, Mass., 1966). The decipherment is accepted by, e.g. Cross, loc. cit., and doubted by, e.g. Sznycer, loc. cit. See further below, page 162 and note 104.

[86] Rivalling Ugarit in multiplicity of scripts if not quantity of documents is Aphek, where recently fragments of Cuneiform Akkadian, Hittite Hieroglyphs, and Egyptian Hieroglyphs have come to light (M. Kokhavi, *Qadmoniot* 10 (1977), 66 f.—in Hebrew). I owe this reference to Dr N. Na'aman, who has also given me news of the recent discovery of a letter from Ugarit. See also below, p. 165, Additional Items.

[87] Porter and Moss, *Topographical Bibliography* VII, 393–5; C. Schaeffer, *Ugaritica* III (Paris, 1956), Chap. II.

the tablets in Akkadian Cuneiform,[88] documents belonging to the period of Hittite domination of the city, many of which are sealed with seals inscribed in Hittite Hieroglyphs.[89] A number of Cypro-Minoan inscriptions have also been found.[90]

The fifth script is the remarkable Ugaritic 'Cuneiform Alphabet', written also on clay tablets found in large numbers[91] and dating to the period c.1400–1200 BC.[92] The language written is mostly Ugaritic,[93] a West Semitic language, though it is important to note that the script was also used to write Hurrian.[94] Ugaritic was used, in contrast to the international and diplomatic Akkadian, for local documentation (letters, legal and administrative texts), but above all for literary, mythological, and ritual texts. Scattered examples of the Ugaritic script found on various sites in Syria and Palestine attest to its wide dissemination.[95]

The script comprises thirty signs 'cuneiform' in external appearance (i.e. composed of wedge-shaped strokes in clay (see Fig. 51a, b).[96] Attempts to derive the sign forms themselves from Mesopotamian Cuneiform originals do not commend themselves,[97] and the script should be considered a free model. As to the internal character, the script is usually termed an Alphabet, though a consideration of the historical development of writing suggests that this is formally incorrect and that it represents an important transitional stage between syllabary and Alphabet.[98] The local scribes who devised it were likely to have been as familiar with the Akkadian syllabary (syllabograms of the type $Ca-aC:CaC$, etc. in a three vowel series) and its use of *scriptio plena* ($Ca+a$, etc.), as with the Egyptian uni-, bi-, and triconsonantal syllabograms which do not characterize the vowels. It seems probable that they were also familiar with an 'Alphabet' originating elsewhere. Small tablets, probably

[88] Published principally in the series *Le Palais royal d'Ugarit (PRU)*; *Pru* III (1955); IV (1956); VI (1970); also *Ugaritica* V (Paris, 1968), Chap. I.

[89] *Ugaritica* III, Chap., I.

[90] See above, note 57.

[91] Published principally by A. Herdner, *Corpus des tablettes en cunéiformes alphabétiques découvertes à Ras Shamra-Ugarit de.1929 à 1939*, Mission de Ras Shamra X (Paris, 1963); also by C. Virolleaud, *PRU* II (1957); V (1965); also in *Ugaritica* V, Chap. III.

[92] *CAH* II/2³, Chap. XXI (*b*) and bibliography on 932 ff.

[93] C. H. Gordon, *Ugaritic Textbook*, *An.Or.*38 (Rome, 1965).

[94] E. Laroche, in *Ugaritica* V, Chap. II, § iii.

[95] A. R. Millard, *Kadmos* 15 (1976), 138, note 20.

[96] Gordon, *Ugaritic Textbook*, Chap. III.

[97] Driver, *Semitic Writing*³, 148 ff.

[98] For this view of the character of the early Alphabet, see below, p. 163 and note 106.

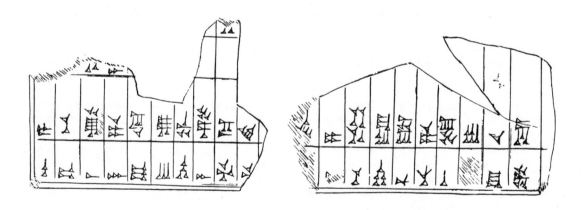

	R⁰				V⁰			
		a	a		20	..	..
		b	be			(p)	(p)u
		g	ga			ṣ	ṣa
		ḫ	ḫa			q	qu
5		d	di			r	ra
		h	ú		25	š	ša
		w	wa			ġ	ḫa
		x	zi			t	tu
		ḥ	ku			i	i
10		ṭ	ṭi			u	u
		......			30	ś	zu

FIG. 51 a,b. The Ugaritic ABC's.

school texts, known as the 'Ugaritic ABC's' have been found.[99] These have the thirty Ugaritic signs written out in the order of the traditional Hebrew Alphabet of twenty-two, with five extra letters (ḫ, š, ḏ, ẓ, ġ) which subsequently became obsolete, and the addition of three others at the end (i, u (vowels) and ś). Even more interesting is a 'bilingual' ABC, in which the signs listed in the same order are given Akkadian phonetic equivalents (a=a, b=be, g,=ga, etc.); see Fig. 51b. The addition of the two extra vowel signs i and u at the end, a specifically Ugaritic adaptation, is convincingly offered as evidence that the order of the main Alphabet was imported from elsewhere.

If this was indeed the case, the Ugaritic scribes made two important changes to the imported idea. First they altered the external form of the script into Cuneiform suitable for writing on clay, though the sign forms can no more plausibly be shown to be dependent on linear than on Cuneiform antecedents.[100] Secondly, they provided the import with three vowel signs,[101] probably taking Akkadian Cuneiform as a model. This they achieved by reserving the first sign ' for a and improvising the additional i and u signs at the end. These vowel signs were then used initially as in Akkadian a-, i-, u-, and also on occasion internally; in the latter case they have been termed *matres lectionis* by comparison with the later Alphabetic use of the letters w and y to denote u and i, but it seems more likely that this usage was modelled on Akkadian *scriptio plena*.

Canaan

The Ugaritic scribes, in devising a script for writing on clay, adopted the course most likely to transmit their work to posterity.[102] If, as seems probable, they took over an Alphabet already formed elsewhere, the corpus of early Alphabetic writing which this presupposes has almost entirely disappeared in the manner of Egyptian papyri which once circulated in the Levant. All that survives from the second half of the second millennium BC is a very limited number of short graffiti on metal objects (arrowheads, a spatula, a ring and a dagger) and upon sherds.[103] These tend to be difficult to date precisely,

[99] Virolleaud, *PRU* II , 199–203 (Les abécédaires). For a comparable Canaanite ABC, see below, p. 165, Additional Items.

[100] See above, note 97.

[101] Gordon, *Ugaritic Textbook*, Chap. IV, § 4.4–8.

[102] cf. Gelb, *A Study of Writing*, 166 ff.

[103] For a recent survey of these graffiti, see A. R. Millard, 'The Canaanite Linear Alphabet and its passage to the Greeks', *Kadmos* 15 (1976), 130–44, esp. the bibliography, 143 ff.

though most have come from regular excavations and are thus placed in archaeological contexts, *c*.1600–1000 BC. They are also difficult to read with any certainty since even when the signs are plausibly identifiable with later known forms, interpretation may still prove elusive, as is also the case with later short inscriptions in Semitic Alphabets. In any case, a combination of these jejune remnants and the evidence that an ordered Alphabet was available *c*.1400 BC to be adapted and remodelled at Ugarit permit the inference that by the mid-second millennium BC a linear script written on papyrus or other perishable material was in use in the Levant.

In an attempt to gain some impression of the nature of this largely lost script, we can only return to a consideration of its links with its presumed southern and northern congeners, proto-Sinaitic and Ugaritic. We have seen that attempts at reading proto-Sinaitic were based on the hypothesis that the script assembled a signary of signs generally similar in appearance to Egyptian Hieroglyphic and attributed values to them acrophonically from the Semitic words for the objects depicted. This theory is further used as an explanation of the origin of the Alphabet, which would thus be regarded as an original construct formed in an area of contact with Egyptian Hieroglyphic, taking from it only an adaptation of sign forms (as Ugaritic and later Old Persian improvised signaries freely modelled on Mesopotamian Cuneiform) but totally original in its internal system of phonetic values. However this view of proto-Sinaitic remains largely unconfirmed conjecture, and the concurrent theory of the acrophonic construction of the Alphabet has attracted telling criticism.[104] A different approach has been recently attempted, whereby the Alphabet is directly derived from the group-writings of Middle Egyptian (see above, p. 147) by comparison with the Hieratic sign forms (see Fig. 46).[105] Everything claimed about the circulation of Hieratic papyri in Canaan from *c*.1700 BC onwards is doubtless true, and the hypothesis as such is eminently reasonable, but the detailed attempt to establish this by comparison of both sign forms and values necessarily appears somewhat forced. While some such route of derivation may be accepted as very plausible, it seems likely that we lack at present the links necessary to establish the respective ancestry of each Alphabetic sign.

The theory of the acrophonic derivation of the early Alphabet naturally embraces the view that in its earliest form the Alphabet already possessed a fully 'alphabetic' (albeit purely consonantal) character, i.e. that to each sign

[104] Gelb, *A Study of Writing*, 140 ff.
[105] W. Helck, 'Zur Herkunft der sog. 'phönizischen' Schrift', *Ugarit-Forschungen* 4 (1972), 41–5.

could be attributed the consonantal value that in a later stage it undoubtedly possessed. The improbability of such a method of construction, which was parodied in Kipling's 'How the Alphabet was made', has been adequately demonstrated.[106] Even if the Alphabet was not as suggested derived immediately from Egyptian group writing values in their Hieratic forms, it certainly arose in a milieu of strong Egyptian influence. Most characteristic of the Egyptian syllabic writing was its omission to determine the vowels of the syllabograms whether uni-, bi- or triconsonantal. The assumption that the early 'Alphabet' also consisted of a syllabary of consonant+vowel signs, which like the Egyptian script omits to determine the inherent vowels, is much more convincing in terms of the history of script development, and readily explains why it did not include specific vowel signs. The use of weak consonantal signs to write long vowels is exactly parallel to, if not modelled on, the Egyptian group-writing's use of weak consonantal syllabograms, itself thought to be modelled on Cuneiform's *scriptio plena*. For the linear Alphabet,[107] this usage is only attested in the first millennium, but that it was known in second millennium 'Alphabets' is demonstrated by its occurrence in Ugaritic where the three vowel signs, probably devised following the Cuneiform model for initial use, might also on occasion be used internally in just this manner.[108] This Ugaritic invention foreshadowed by some seven centuries the Greek adaptation of signs in their borrowed Semitic Alphabet for genuine vowels. It was probably not until the Greek achievement that the old Semitic Alphabet could be clearly defined by comparison as a vowelless, purely consonantal script. The way was then open for the later Massoretic device of a system of genuine vocalization by diacritical points.

Byblos

Our alphabetic quest ends at the city of Byblos, a site so involved in the history of writing that the Greeks transmogrified its original name, Gubla, to *Byblos*, 'papyrus'. While in the Late Bronze Age we have seen the Alphabet to be represented only by short graffiti of dubious interpretation, it is at Byblos that connected Alphabetic writing is first attested in a series of stone inscriptions dating back probably to the eleventh century BC.

Earlier Byblos had belonged very much to the Egyptian cultural sphere, in that in the early second millennium BC its kings were already composing

---

[106] Gelb, *A Study of Writing*, 147 ff.

[107] Ibid. 166 ff.; also Millard, *Kadmos* 15 (1976), 139 f. and note 21.

[108] See above, note 101.

monumental inscriptions in Egyptian Hieroglyphic,[109] and in general Hiero-glyphic inscribed objects are common here.[110]

Byblos has also produced relics of a Bronze Age script of its own, which is known from a very few inscriptions on stone and bronze plates and spatulae, variously dated early or late in the second millennium BC.[111] From its sign forms' general imitation of Egyptian Hieroglyphic, it has been termed 'pseudo-Hieroglyphic', and some 114 signs have been identified. A decipherment has been claimed which regards it as a syllabary designed to write a Semitic language, a sufficiently plausible supposition. However, no decipherment so narrowly based can claim to be more than an unconfirmed hypothesis and the method employed looks fallible.[112] It is thus quite unac-ceptable to hypothesize further on the possible connections of this poorly attested script with the origins of the Alphabet.[113]

The monumental stone Alphabetic inscriptions of Byblos[114] on the other hand occupy a pride of place in the history of writing. They are the earliest known examples of the adaptation of the linear Canaanite Alphabet, a script presumed invented for writing in ink on papyrus, for this commemorative and durable purpose, and to this achievement we owe our earliest preserved passages of prose alphabetically written. We thus stand near the beginning of a line of writing descending down to modern times, where the present inquiry will leave the story. The earliest inscriptions are those of the King Ahiram, probably eleventh century BC, one from the lid of his sarcophagus and the other from the wall of his tomb shaft. The latter inaugurates the great Alphabetic tradition on a somewhat sinister note, for it may be interpreted as warning:[115] 'Beware! Behold (there is) disaster for you down here.'

[109] H. Klengel, *Geschichte Syriens* II (Berlin, 1969), 430 ff.

[110] Porter and Moss, *Topographical Bibliography*, VII, 386–92.

[111] M. Dunand, *Byblia Grammata* (Beirut, 1945), Chap. IV, 'Les inscriptions pseudo-hiéroglyphiques'.

[112] For a recent critique, with previous bibliography see M. Sznycer, 'Les inscriptions pseudo-hiéroglyphiques de Byblos', in J. Léclant (ed.), *Le Déchiffrement des écritures et des langues*, 75–84.

[113] But cf. F. M. Cross, *Eretz-Israel* 8 (1967), 12*f., note 30.

[114] H. Donner and W. Röllig, *Kanaanaische und Aramaische Inschriften* (2nd edn., Wiesbaden, 1962), Nos. 1–9, with bibliographies.

[115] Ibid., No. 2.

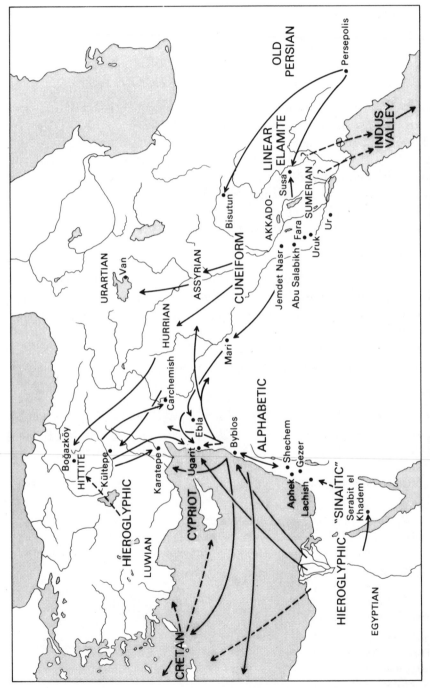

FIG. 52. The Centres and Routes of Transmission of Early Scripts.

SELECTED BIBLIOGRAPHY

COHEN, M., *La Grande Invention de l'écriture et son évolution*, I–III (Paris, 1953).

DIRINGER, D., *The Alphabet* (3rd edn. London, 1968).

——, *Writing* (London, 1968).

DRIVER, G. R., *Semitic Writing* (The Schweich Lectures, British Academy, 1944; newly revised edn., London, 1976).

FRIEDRICH, J., *Geschichte der Schrift* (Heidelberg, 1966).

GELB, I. J., *A Study of Writing* (2nd edn., Chicago, 1963).

——, 'Writing, forms of' (*Encyclopaedia Britannica*, 15th. edn., 1974).

DECIPHERMENT

DOBLHOFER, E., *Voices in Stone* (trans. from the German, London, 1961).

FRIEDRICH, J., *Extinct Languages* (trans. from the German, New York, 1957).

GELB, I. J., 'Records, writing and decipherment', *Visible Language* VIII/4 (1974), 293–318.

GORDON, C., *Forgotten Scripts* (London, 1968).

POPE, M., *The Story of Decipherment* (London, 1975).

Symposia

'The Undeciphered Languages', *JRAS* 1975/2, 94–209.

LÉCLANT, J. (ed.), *Le Déchiffrement des écritures et des langues* (Colloque du XXIXe Congrès International des Orientalistes; Paris, 1975).

Additional Items of Bibliography

Linear B

L. Godart and A. Sacconi, *Les Tablettes en linéaire B de Thebes* (Rome, 1978).

J. T. Hooker, *The Origin of the Linear B Script* (Salamanca, 1979).

F. Vandenabeele and J.-P. Olivier, *Les Idéogrammes archéologiques de linéaire B* (Paris, 1979).

Inscriptions from Aphek

A. F. Rainey, *Tel Aviv* 2 (1975), 125–29; 3 (1976), 137–40.

I. Singer, *Tel Aviv* 4 (1977) 178–90.

R. Giveon, *Tel Aviv* 5 (1979), 188–91.

A Canaanite ABC

M. Kochavi, *Tel Aviv* 4 (1977) 1–13.

A. Demsky, ibid. 14–27.

J. Naveh, *IEJ* 28 (1978), 31–5.

1. *Australian woman of the Wik Monkan tribe of Cape York, Queensland, with vegetable foods of the peak season and the utensils used in gathering them.*

2. *Bushman hunter distributing meat to members of the other band sharing the same waterhole.*

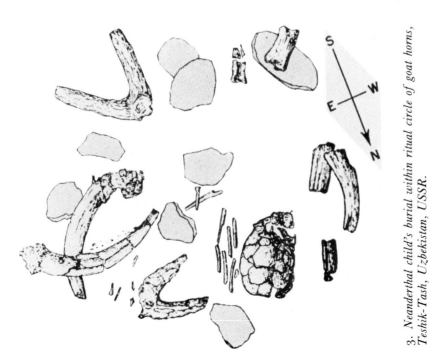

3. *Neanderthal child's burial within ritual circle of goat horns, Teshik-Tash, Uzbekistan, USSR.*

4. Right: *Ceremonial Upper Palaeolithic burial, Sangir, central Russia. Note the large number of personal ornaments.*

5. *Upper Palaeolithic house floor defined by stone boulders and mammoth tusks under a thick loess deposit, Dolní Věstonice, Czechoslovakia.*

7. *Clay model of the Cypriot Early Bronze Age showing two pairs of oxen yoked to ards or light Mediterranean scratch-ploughs.*

6. Left: *Forest clearance for agriculture: (a) Man attacking tree with stone-bladed adze, New Guinea, 1964; (b) Fire in use for clearance in the course of swidden agriculture in nineteenth-century Finland.*

9. General view of Çatal Hüyük in Turkey, looking west.

8. Left: *The pre-pottery Neolithic A Stone Tower at Jericho.*

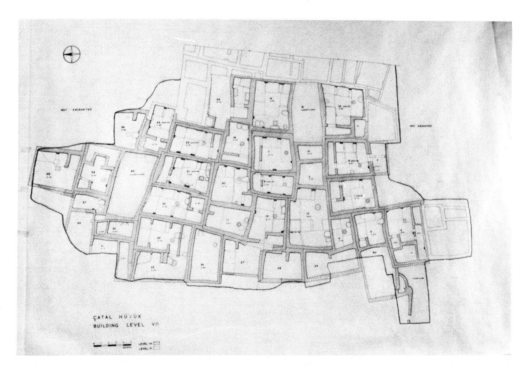

10. Above: *Plan of Çatal Hüyük level VII showing cellular construction.*

11. Right: *Corner of a shrine in Çatal Hüyük level VI with ram's head and bucranium.*

12. *Shrine in Çatal Hüyük level VI with cutout silhouette of a boar's head.*

13. *Wall-painting of a textile design in the shrine of level VII at Çatal Hüyük.*

14. *Wall-painting imitating cutout felt (?) in the shrine of level VIII at Çatal Hüyük.*

15. *Wall-painting in level VIII at Çatal Hüyük.*

16. *Wall-painting of textile design with grooved lines at Çatal Hüyük.*

17. *Flint dagger (flint imported from Syria), Çatal Hüyük, level VI.*

18. *Obsidian spearheads and flakes (E V 7 cache) from Çatal Hüyük.*

19. *Two fragments of a carbonized textile from level VI at Çatal Hüyük.*

20. *Excavations at Tell es-Sawwan in Iraq.*

21. *Excavations at Tell es-Sawwan in Iraq.*

22. *Pot of the Early Halaf period painted with bucrania and serpent from Tell Arpachiyah, Iraq.*

23. *Early Halaf period pot painted with figures and pithos, from Tell Arpachiyah, Iraq.*

24. *Inside of an early Halaf period pot painted with women holding a textile, from Tell Arpachiyah, Iraq.*

25. *Interior base of an early Halaf period pot painted with a shrine from Tell Arpachiyah, Iraq.*

26. *Recovery of a Karanovo house plan with remains of split-plank flooring (rear right); an oven (centre rear); stone tools; and antler sickles, their flint teeth* in situ, *lying within the house area. House dimensions: 5·15 m by 6·95 m. Located in level X of the Kazanlik mound, central Bulgaria.*

27. *Aerial view of the excavations at Biskupin, Poland.*

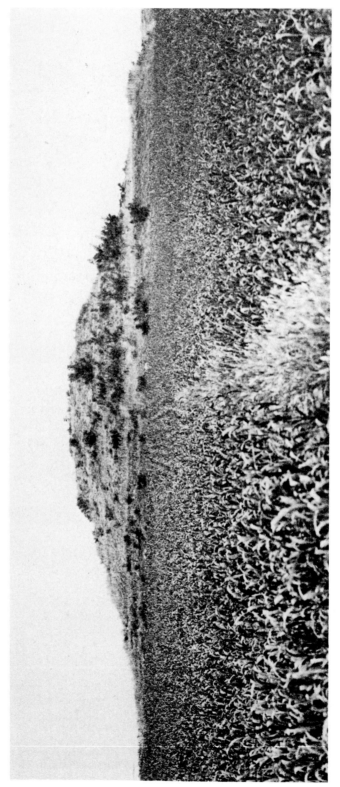

28. *A foundation on the east side of the precinct at Han-tan, seen from the south.*

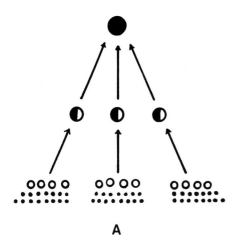

A

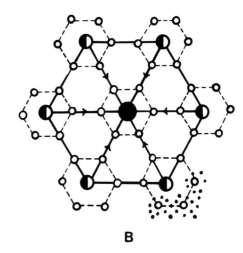

B

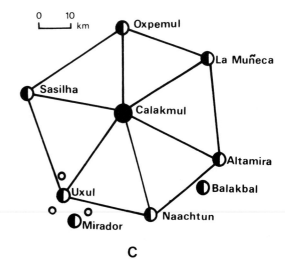

C

●   Metropolis (Regional Capital)

◐   Secondary Centre
      (semi-autonomous dynasty)

○   Dependencies (villages,
●   hamlets, farmsteads)

29. *The relationship between the ranking and spacing of sites.*

     (a) Ranking: three-tier pyramid model to show the political relationship between rural sites, city states, and a metropolis (or superpower). Arrows indicate the direction of tribute-payment, from lesser to greater centres.

     (b) Ranking as reflected by spacing of sites: an idealized diagram of territorial organization and the distribution of sites in a landscape.

     (c) An archaeological example: the distribution of settlement around the major lowland Maya centre of Calakmul.

30. *Platform foundation of a public building at San Jose Mogote, Oaxaca, in use about 1350 bc.*

31. *Group of four clay figurines arranged to form a scene, buried beneath the floor of a shed or lean-to shelter attached to the house of a part-time flint knapper at San Jose Mogote, Oaxaca. Nearby was the burial of a middle-aged women with unusual quantities of jade.*

32. *The oldest dated hieroglyphic inscription in Mesoamerica. Monument 3 at San Jose Mogote (c.600 bc) in course of excavation.*

33. *A system of irrigation canals and terraced fields of about the fifth century bc at Hierve El Agua, Oaxaca. The canals have turned to stone through the deposition of travertine contained in the water.*

34. *Carving of a man from Brno, Czechoslovakia, mammoth ivory, h. 20·5 cm.*

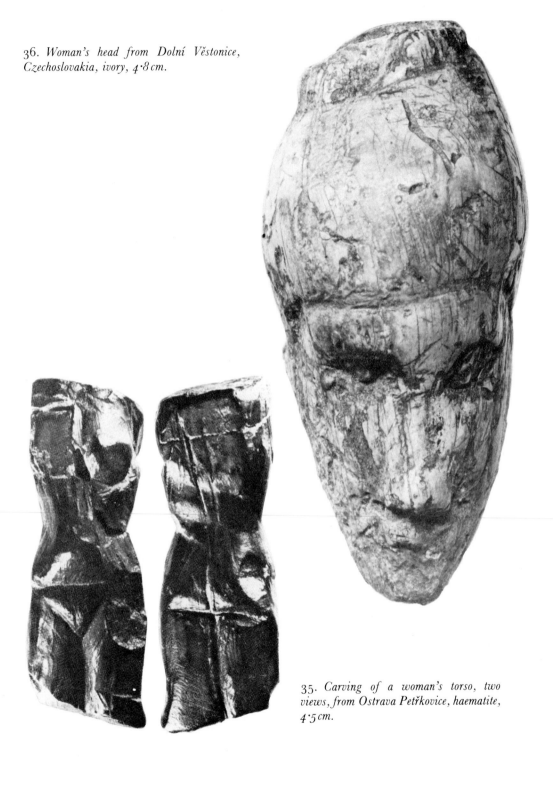

36. *Woman's head from Dolní Věstonice, Czechoslovakia, ivory, 4·8 cm.*

35. *Carving of a woman's torso, two views, from Ostrava Petřkovice, haematite, 4·5 cm.*

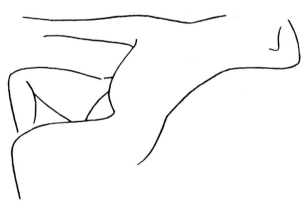

37. *Relief carving of reclining woman, cave of La Magdaleine, Tarn, France; l. 1·70 m.*

38. *Carvings of a horse, a panther, and a cave lion from the Vogelherd cave, Lontal, Württemberg, Germany, bone and ivory, l. of lion 9·2 cm.*

39. *Paintings of bulls, Lascaux, Dordogne, France; l. of largest 5·50 m.*

41b. Two seals of Indus Valley type.

41a. Linear Elamite inscription from Susa, with parallel Akkadian cuneiform text.

40. Silver vase from Telloh in Iraq with representation of storm-bird, h. 35 cm.

42. *The Narmer Slate Palette.*